Child Growth and Development

S E C O N D   E D I T I O N

by Elizabeth B. Hurlock

WATCH your child grow. *Child Growth and Development* will help you see your child clearly in *every* aspect of his or her development—physical, mental, and social. In this informal, easy-to-understand book, Dr. Hurlock presents findings of latest research in child development that enable you to analyze your child's growth and to deal with the problems involved—from preparing for the baby until the child's first days in school.

Part I, "How Life Begins," deals with preparations for the baby and the nature of newborn infants. "The Child's Growth" shows relationships between growth and learning. It gives advice on feeding, clothing, proper physical care, speech habits, and emotional development. "The Child's Problems and Habits" discusses good and undesirable habits, discipline, measurement of intelligence, and play. The last section, "The Child as a Person," deals with your

, his room and clothes, personality. It explains rmine his readiness for

d with illustrations that levels of development lems in each of these excellent sections on y traits—cheerfulness, e of humor, courage, thy, calmness, self-con- ertiveness in the pre- t discussions show you r child for the adjust- help him develop the e this adjustment.

than a handbook on it gives such practical l, bathe, and schedule ther—to show you the of a child from birth help you meet and ns that occur in the hild.

ck, an outstanding ychology, is in the gy at the University is author of three lolescent psychology thly page on child *Health.* She is the girls.

AMERICAN HOME AND FAMILY SERIES

CONSULTING EDITOR, Helen Judy Bond

Barclay-Champion: Teen Guide to Homemaking
Carson: How You Look and Dress
Carson-Ramee: How You Plan and Prepare Meals
Hurlock: Child Growth and Development
Landis: Your Marriage and Family Living
Morton: The Home and Its Furnishings
Shank-Fitch-Chapman: Guide to Modern Meals
Sturm-Grieser: Guide to Modern Clothing

(*Other Books in Process*)

ELIZABETH B. HURLOCK

Graduate School of Education, University of Pennsylvania

Child

Growth and Development

SECOND EDITION

Webster Division
McGraw-Hill Book Company

St. Louis
New York
San Francisco
Dallas
Toronto
London

CHILD GROWTH AND DEVELOPMENT

XIV

To my daughter
DARYL ELIZABETH

Preface

In order to bring *Child Growth and Development* up to date
and in response to suggestions from teachers who have
used the book in the classroom, a new edition has been prepared. This Second Edition differs from the First in the following respects:

1. It includes a new section of 36 pages on baby-sitting.
2. It incorporates new theories and practices with regard
   to infant and child care.
3. It includes new information in the fields of medicine
   and psychology.
4. It takes into consideration the fact that young people
   of today must be prepared to meet the demands of
   parenthood alone, relying less and less on advice and
   guidance from parents or other older people.
5. It brings up to date information on foods, clothing, and
   equipment.
6. It includes many new illustrations.
7. It has additional questions and activities at the ends of
   the chapters.
8. It has a completely new bibliography and list of visual
   aids at the end of the book.

Today, nearly every high school student is likely to be a

parent within the next few years. Part of every student's education, therefore—whether boy or girl—should include some guidance related to the care and training of children.

Now it is recognized that parents must *learn* how to bring up children, just as they learn how to read, write, cook, or play tennis. Gone are the days when people believed that the ability to produce offspring automatically brought with it the knowledge of how to care for and train children. True, a person might learn how to bring up children by using the trial-and-error method on their own child or children. But, learning "on the job" is never as satisfactory as preparation for the job before actually undertaking it. In such an important undertaking as rearing a human being, learning "on the job" might even prove tragic.

Child Growth and Development does not aim to give a detailed account of all aspects of child care and development. It merely aims to give a foundation knowledge of how children develop and of the most widely accepted practices in America at the present time in the care and training of infants and young children.

It is hoped that every student of children will have an opportunity to observe children in different situations—in a nursery, in the home, the school, the Sunday school, and on the playground. Observations, however, become more meaningful when they are guided. The Suggested Activities at the ends of the chapters and the films listed by chapters at the end of the book are intended to help in this guidance through discussion or as "guided observations" for the student.

ELIZABETH B. HURLOCK

Acknowledgment is made to Mary Furlong Moore for her review of the Introduction, "How to Be a Good Baby Sitter."

Editor's Introduction

When the First Edition of *Child Growth and Development* was published, it was recognized as the most complete high school textbook on the subject of child care. The Second Edition not only continues to deserve this same reputation but to merit added recognition by the inclusion of latest findings, methods, scientific discoveries, and the addition of a section on baby-sitting.

The mental hygiene aspects in the book, as well as information on physical growth, feeding, clothing, play therapy, discipline, and habits are presented simply and clearly. As a result of studying this text, the student should not only understand better his younger brothers and sisters, nieces, nephews, and children in the neighborhood, but also have a better background in preparation for parenthood.

One of the great values of Dr. Hurlock's text for high school courses is that it gives to the student authoritative information on infants and toddlers in such a way as to aid the student in understanding himself better—what society requires, how he developed the way he did, how he might change himself to become a more effective individual.

Because baby-sitting has become one of the major activities of the teen-ager—with 20,000,000 children in the country who are too young to be safely left alone—and in response to young people's requests for information on how to be a better baby sitter, Dr. Hurlock has added a section to the book on this very important subject to most teen-agers. The author has recognized her responsibility in writing this section and the need for giving factual, practical information in it. This new section on baby-sitting attempts to make practical application of the information in the text itself as a background for reference.

Dr. Hurlock has tried to show through her discussions of anticipating and preparing for the baby, caring for the child through the early years of life, and the responsibilities of baby-sitting, the importance of each individual life in our society.

HELEN JUDY BOND

Contents

Introduction: How to Be a Good Baby Sitter xiii

Part One: HOW LIFE BEGINS

1. Preparing for the Baby 3
2. The Newborn Baby 24
3. Facts about Children 34

Part Two: THE CHILD'S GROWTH

4. How a Child Grows 47
5. Feeding and Clothing the Child 63
6. Physical Care of the Child 94
7. Learning Body Control 117
8. Learning to Talk 137
9. The Child and His Emotions 152

Part Three: THE CHILD'S PROBLEMS AND HABITS

10. Mealtime and Bedtime Problems 171
11. The Child in the Family 193
12. Common Behavior Problems 206
13. Discipline, Good and Bad 221
14. Tests for Toddlers 238
15. Play and Playthings 255

Part Four: THE CHILD AS A PERSON

16. The Child's Companions   275
17. A Place of His Own   293
18. The Child and His Clothes   306
19. Personality Building   321
20. Getting Ready for School   338

Bibliography for Students   355
Bibliography for Teachers   359
Bibliography for Tests in Chapter 14   365
List of Visual Aids   366
Index   377

INTRODUCTION

How to Be a Good Baby Sitter

Baby-sitting is an occupation as old as mankind. But some aspects of it are new to our society within the last several years. Today's sitters, for instance, are more likely to be adolescents than adults. They are more likely to be outsiders who are hired by the hour than relatives or neighbors who take care of children because of their love for the child, as a friendly gesture, or for some reason other than that of making money.

The present demand for young people as baby sitters has developed because of the following changes which have taken place in American life and habits within the last several years: There are fewer people engaged in domestic work today and those who are do not "live in" as in the past. They also demand higher wages. Smaller homes prevent in-laws from living with their children and acting as sitters when the parents are gone. There is a tendency for young married couples to move to the suburbs or to another section of the country where they are too far away from relatives and old friends to call on them for help.

There is no evidence that the present demand for baby sitters will diminish in the near future. Each Census report shows that the birth rate is on the rise, which means that there will be more and more babies to be taken care of in the future than there are today. Nor is there any indication that the changes which have created the demand for young people as baby sitters will not remain.

For these reasons it is very likely that nearly every young person—whether girl or boy—will at some time in his adolescent years do baby-sitting as a part-time job and that he will need to know what is involved.

The Benefits of Baby-sitting

Like most teen-agers, you probably have need for more money to meet the demands of school and social life than your parents are in a position to supply. You cannot take many kinds of jobs because of the child labor laws in your state. Baby-sitting, however, is part-time work, within reach of all, that gives you a chance to earn some of your own money without interfering too much with your school work.

Being able to earn money is by no means the only benefit you derive from baby-sitting. There are many other benefits that are more important to you and far more lasting in their influence on you:

1. You learn to assume responsibility and to be independent in having to make decisions on your own, without an adult nearby to advise you.
2. You learn to cooperate with others.
3. You learn how to meet emergencies.
4. You learn to adjust to new people, new places, and new situations.

Taking care of children benefits you in many ways other than merely being a means to earn money. For a list of the many ways you can benefit by baby-sitting, see page xiv.

5. You gain a broader perspective of life by being able to see closely how other people live.

6. You learn what it means to work.

7. You learn about children as they actually are, and you learn to enjoy young children, which is good preparation for parenthood. Unless a young person comes from a large family, she may never have any experience in caring for children before she marries except through baby-sitting.

8. You become resourceful in spending time by yourself. In most cases as a baby sitter you must spend some time alone while a child is asleep.
9. You learn something about managing.
10. You learn the satisfaction of contributing where it is needed and of being appreciated, loved, and respected for it.

Benefits to Parents and Child of Having a Baby Sitter

The work of the sitter has advantages not only for the teen-ager who baby-sits but for the parents whose child is being taken care of and for the child himself.

For the Parent. Having a baby sitter part of the time is a "must" for modern parents. Some time off helps to relax them and make them better parents. No woman can be expected to be on duty twenty-four hours a day, day in and day out. She needs a change from the day's activities occasionally. Similarly, a man needs some recreation away from place of work and home. Without a sitter, the couple cannot go out together to share their recreation as they need to do occasionally. In every home, too, there are emergencies which require at least temporary help from outside. Sickness of a member of the family or of some distant relative or any situation that requires extra time and attention from the mother may make the baby sitter an invaluable help in getting through an emergency successfully.

For the Child. Even the child gains by having a sitter occasionally. The baby learns early to adjust to other people and to their ways of doing things. This is helpful to the child when the time comes for him to adjust to others outside of the family. He may also learn new games from the sitter, hear new stories, or get different points of view on life than those given him by his parents.

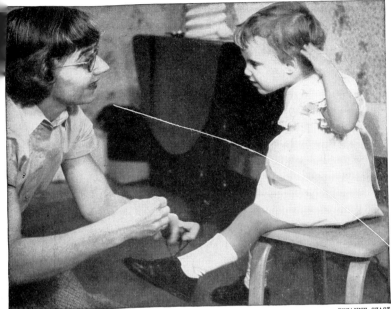

SUZANNE SZASZ

The most important qualification you can have for sitting is a real love of children. If you like them, they know it and you will get along with less difficulty. For other qualifications, see page xvii.

sary qualities. Having the necessary know-how to handle children and knowing how to keep them safe and happy are further qualifications. A baby sitter should be able to adjust to the people for whom she is working as well as to the child under her care. If she shows good judgment and behaves sensibly, she will inspire confidence in the parents who entrust their child to her.

No matter how much experience a young person has had in playing with children or being around them, she is not qualified to be a sitter unless she knows what to do in case of an emergency. Emergencies may be rare, but one emergency can be tragic—especially if not handled quickly and

The parents and the child benefit too when you baby-sit. No mother should stay on the job day in and day out, without some recreation or some sharing of outside activities with her husband.

MERRIM FROM M

Qualifications for Baby-sitting

Assuming the responsibility for the care of another son's child is a serious matter. Children are not piece furniture or china that can be replaced should anyt happen to them. Instead, they are the most precious th in the lives of their parents. Imagine yourself in the role parent and try to see how you would feel if you entrus *your* child to a sitter who was unworthy of the trust. H would you feel if anything happened to your child throu the ignorance or carelessness of a sitter?

Those Who Qualify. A genuine fondness for children the first qualification for being a good baby sitter. Unde standing children, being patient and kind are other nece well. It is a good idea for anyone who baby-sits to learn all she can ahead of time about what to do in case of fire, accident, illness, cutting off of heat and electricity, etc., as well as to get information from the parents on such emergencies as it pertains to their home. Some information on first aid is given in your school courses. The local Red Cross chapter generally gives courses in first aid. The first aid booklets put out by the American Red Cross are another source for suggestions on handling emergencies.

Those Who Do Not Qualify. Young people who do not have stable personalities and who are unable to take responsibility are not qualified to be baby sitters. A person who does not realize the seriousness of the work or a person who has no knowledge or experience in caring for children should not try baby-sitting until she has become aware of the responsibility involved and learned more about the work. Many young people who are not qualified to baby-sit and do not realize the responsibility they are assuming may be able to get jobs when the demand for sitters is greater than the supply available. Under such circumstances, it would be better for all concerned if they did not baby-sit, even when parents in desperation beg them to do so to help them out.

How to Become Qualified. Anyone who has been a sitter should want to learn how to be a better one. Anyone who has not been a sitter because of lack of experience or knowledge but who sincerely wants to be a sitter can prepare herself in several ways:

1. By reading books and pamphlets about children.*
2. By teaching a Sunday-school class, doing volunteer work in day nurseries or playground groups, or taking a course on child care.

* See "Bibliography for Students" on page 355.

3. By helping with younger children at home, or by helping care for a child under the supervision of the child's mother.

How to Get a Job Baby-sitting

The demand for sitters is so great today that any boy or girl who wants to get a job can easily do so. There are many ways in which baby sitters get jobs:

1. Through friends or neighbors who know you to be a responsible person. Some parents like to have a baby sitter who is already acquainted with their child. Often, too, the baby sitter's parents feel more secure when they know the family for whom their daughter or son is working. Sometimes, though, friends and neighbors, or people you and your family know personally, may take advantage of you if you are not careful to see that your arrangements are as businesslike as they would be with a stranger. Naturally, the treatment you receive from anyone—whether friend or stranger—depends a great deal on the kind of people they are and on how well you are able to handle yourself in receiving fair treatment without being overbearing or unpleasant about it.

2. By being recommended by a friend of yours to someone they know who wants a baby sitter. If you let it be known among your friends and your family's friends that you are interested in baby-sitting, people will keep you in mind and help you to find a job.

3. By typing an announcement with your qualifications, references, rates, etc. and distributing it in the neighborhood or placing it on a bulletin board in your apartment house.

4. By putting an ad in the community newspaper or answering an ad placed there by parents.

5. Through school, church, and youth organizations that have baby-sitting bureaus or services. Some of these bureaus will place you without charge; others may charge you a percentage of your earnings for getting you a job. If you don't know of any such bureaus, ask a teacher, your clergyman, or friends about those available in your community. The advantage of getting a baby-sitting job through a bureau or agency is that the work is regulated by certain standards of working conditions and pay, which sometimes is not true when a sitter obtains work from friends or neighbors. When you obtain a job through a bureau, the employer is told by them what she may expect from you, and you are told what you may be expected to do. Many parents prefer to deal through a bureau because they can keep the arrangements on a businesslike basis. Also they know that a bureau can supply a substitute sitter should the sitter originally employed be unable to come at the last minute.

Applying for a Job

When you apply for a job with a bureau, do so in person rather than over the phone. Even when contacting parents directly for the first time, it is a good idea to meet them in person rather than phoning. This gives people a chance to see you and size you up. It also gives you an opportunity to tell them what experience you have had, the locality in which you would like to work, the age level of children you prefer, the amount of time you have available, when you will be free to work, etc.

The bureau will record all of this information and will not call you unless they have something that is to your liking. In turn, the bureau will inform you of the duties, the usual pay, and the types of families they have on their lists.

CAMPBELL HAYS FROM MONKMEYER

Applying in person is better than calling by phone when you are considering working for someone the first time. In your conversation with the mother, you will want to get as much information as possible about the child, the home, and the duties, as well as to become acquainted with the child.

When you get a job through a bureau, you are expected to report back to them after you have finished the job. You may report any objectionable features or anything that wasn't satisfactory according to the information you received about the job before you took it. If you liked the job and the employer liked you, the chances are that you will be called to that home again. Satisfactory work is the best way to assure a demand for your services.

Once you have made contacts with one or two families through a bureau, you can make your own arrangements with them for future work.

Accepting a Job

Before you accept a job, you should settle a number of details with your employer. It is much better to be on an understanding basis before you start than not to know where you are or what your employer has in mind. If, after discussing some of these details, the job doesn't meet your requirements or expectations, you can decline it.

What Your Rate of Pay Is. Of great importance in this matter of settling things beforehand is that of letting people know what your hourly rate is and what you expect to be paid for. You should have the same rate for all families, and you should not charge more for a family with more than one child. The rate you quote will probably depend upon the current rate in the community or what you think is fair. Some sitters have prepared sheets containing their qualifications, expectations, and charges so there will be no chance for misunderstandings. Then you should have an understanding about such questions as these:

1. Will you charge for your time from the minute you arrive until you leave the house, or from the time the parents leave until they arrive home? (Most sitters charge from the time they arrive until the time the parents come home.)
2. Will you charge more for after-midnight hours? (Some sitters charge time and one-half for time after midnight; but others charge their regular rate.)
3. Will you charge for transportation? (You should not expect to receive pay for the time you spend going or

coming, but if your transportation expenses are unusual —such as for cab or train fare—you might feel justified in asking your employer to pay them.)

4. Will you charge for the fraction of an hour, in case the time you work is not an even number of hours? (It is best to charge for the exact time—that is, charge for the fraction of the hour according to your hourly rate.)

Other Questions to Settle. Some other questions not pertaining to money that should be discussed ahead of time— especially when you are sitting for a family the first time— are these:

1. What is the age of the child and what is the child like? (You should know as much about the child as possible before you baby-sit so you can get acquainted easily and take care of him properly.)

2. Will you be expected to do extra work, such as washing dishes or doing household tasks? (Ordinarily when you baby-sit you are not obligated to wash any dishes except those which you find it necessary to use for yourself and for the child you are feeding.)

3. Will food be made available in case you become hungry, or should you bring something with you? (Most families have food in the refrigerator for you, but some might not.)

4. What arrangements will be made for you to get home? (While you may be able to get to the home easily by yourself, you should not go home alone if it is late when you leave. Either the parents should promise to take you home, or you should know ahead of time that your parents or a friend can call for you. If you find that there is no way for you to get home, you may decide that it is better not to take the job.)

Getting Ready to Go to Work

At least a day before you go to work, you should consider what you will wear and what you may want to take along with you. Here are some suggestions:

1. You should try to wear clothes that are comfortable and that will not damage or soil easily. Whatever you wear should be neat and clean. In cool weather it is a good idea to take along a sweater or jacket in case the house becomes chilly late in the evening.
2. You should find out about transportation and how long to allow yourself to get there.
3. You might want to take along a notebook to jot down important items the mother tells you. (See page xxvii for the kind of information you should have on hand.)
4. You may want to take along a sandwich or some food you particularly like.
5. You may need to take along something to keep you occupied while the child is sleeping. Some of the things you can take along easily are stationery for writing letters; a crossword puzzle; magazines or a book; some knitting, sewing, or other handwork; or some of your homework. Be sure in each case that you take all the things you need in connection with any activity—that is, pencils, pens, paper, eraser, etc.
6. You might want to take something for the child. You don't *have* to do this because ordinarily the family will have toys, books, dolls, games, etc. and will know what the child likes. But it may please the child, help him to like you, and make it easier to get acquainted if you bring along some small new toy for him to play with or a book from the library or from home that you can read to him.

No matter how many toys or books a child may have, he is impressed when you bring him something new to play with or to read to him. Getting him interested in something new that you have brought for him is one way to get acquainted with him and to hold his interest when his parents leave and right after they have gone.

What You Need to Know from Parents

It is well to arrive for a baby-sitting job at least a few minutes early. If it is the first time you have worked for the people, you should arrive at least a half-hour early. During this half-hour, the mother will want to give you instructions about your duties; you will want to become acquainted with the child; you will want to familiarize yourself with the house—the layout of the rooms, placement of the light switches, where various articles are kept, etc. You may also have some questions you would like to ask the parents before they leave.

Most parents will tell you what you need to know about the house, the child, and what you are to do. Some of this information may be jotted down in a notebook so it will be handy in case you forget and for future reference when you baby-sit at that home again. You should be told

1. Where the parents may be reached and at what time they are likely to return. If the parents are visiting friends, you will want to have the name, address, and phone number of the people they are visiting. If they are going elsewhere, you should have a phone number where they can be reached or they should promise to call you during the evening. The phone number you have for them should be placed right beside the phone so you will not have to hunt for it if you need it in a hurry. If you are baby-sitting during the day, you might want the phone number of the father's place of business as well as the number where the mother may be reached.
2. The phone numbers for the doctor, police, hospital, and a nearby neighbor or relative who could be con-tacted in case of an emergency.

CAMPBELL HAYS FROM MONKMEYER

If you have never worked for a family before, it is a good idea to arrive a half-hour early so the mother can give you instructions on what to do, show you the layout of the house, tell you where things are kept, and help you to become acquainted with the child.

3. Where the flashlight is and where all first-aid supplies—such as adhesive bandages, iodine, cotton, etc.—are kept.
4. Where the baby's clothes are kept.
5. If and when the baby is to be fed, where the bottle or food is kept, and what needs to be done to it to prepare it for the child. Be sure you know how to use the range also.
6. How much he should play and when. What toys he likes, and where they are.
7. Where the diapers are, how often to diaper the baby, and how to diaper him. (See pages 81–87.) You may

know how, but the mother may want it done differently.

8. The time when the child is to go to bed and any details about his bedtime and sleeping habits.

9. How they would like to have the telephone answered, and what to tell people who call. A pad by the phone will make it possible for you to take messages quickly and correctly.

10. Where to find scissors, safety pins, needles and thread, and other miscellaneous items that you may need.

11. Where the blankets are kept and how the heating system works if it is cool or cold weather.

You and Your Attitude

Baby-sitting is not too difficult a way to earn money, but it shouldn't be considered a lark or a social visit. You are on the job to work and are being paid for it. Even when the baby is asleep, you are being paid to protect him and to be alert and awake to his needs.

While most parents wish you would "feel at home" while you are working, they hope you will not take advantage of the privilege. If you want to show consideration, you will

1. Be careful of all the possessions in the home. Handle any dishes and glassware you use with care. Don't put your feet on the furniture or set glasses on tables without putting something under them. See that your hands are clean when you read the family's books and magazines, and don't tear pages out of a magazine. Try to keep the house in as good order as it was when you arrived, and be sure to turn off the lights when you leave a room.

2. Find out ahead of time whether or not the family cares if you use the television or radio. If they don't, make sure you know how to operate it. They may suggest

You should find out ahead of time whether or not the family has any objection to your using the television set after the child has gone to sleep.

If you must make a phone call during the evening, keep it short. Long, chatty conversations hold up the line and keep you from being on the job.

that you modulate the volume somewhat after the baby has gone to sleep, and if they have close neighbors, they may not want you to play it after a certain hour. On the other hand, they may, for some reason, not want you to play it at all.

3. Ask the parents before they leave if it is all right for you to make a phone call if you need to. When you do call, make the conversation as short as possible. By all means don't make long, chatty calls to friends. When you do, you hold up the line and you don't have your mind on your job.

4. Find out first whether or not the parents object to your having a girl friend come over to sit with you and visit. Some people don't mind; others do.

Things to Avoid

There are certain things that definitely should be avoided by everyone who baby-sits—anywhere at any time. Doing any of these things may result in an unpleasant, if not a tragic, situation, either for you, the child, or the family. Needless to say, these mistakes may cost you your job and your reputation as a sitter.

1. Don't leave a child alone—even for a minute. Under no circumstances should you leave the house unless you can take the child with you. If the phone rings, be sure you have put the child in a safe place while you answer. It is better to miss a call than to have an injured child.

2. Don't go to sleep. Part of your preparation for the job is to get a good night's rest the night before. If you are the type that "just can't keep your eyes open" after ten o'clock, take a nap in the afternoon when you know you will be up late. When you go to sleep, you are just not "on the job."

CAMPBELL HAYS FROM MONKMEYER

If you have to go into another room to get something—even for a minute
—take the baby with you rather than leaving him alone.

3. Don't entertain your date while you are baby-sitting.
   Watching the child should be your prime interest while
   you are working, and the minute your date walks in,
   this is no longer true. It is sometimes permissible to
   have a friend of your own sex come in, but not someone
   of the opposite sex. By no means, of course, should you
   have a group in for a party.

4. Don't "snoop" around the house. Opening doors of

closets and drawers of chests and desks is "snooping," unless you have to look for something that you need. Reading people's mail is also "snooping."

5. Don't talk about the child, the family, or the home to outsiders. Anything you learn or overhear of a private nature should be forgotten or kept to yourself.

6. Don't open the front or the back door unless you are *sure* who it is. If someone rings the bell or knocks, pay no attention, unless you have been told by the parents that someone is coming. At night it is better not to open the door for anyone. This is for your own protection as well as that of the child and the family.

7. Don't baby-sit when you have a cold or feel you might be "coming down with something." Even if the parents don't object, you should cancel the date.

8. Don't baby-sit for a child who has a cold or is ill. Children can transmit colds to adults just as easily as adults can give colds to children. So protect yourself.

On the Job

Regardless of the family you are working for or the age of the child or children you are caring for, there are two things of paramount importance: 1) keeping them safe and 2) keeping them happy.

Keeping Him Safe. So many things can happen to a baby or a young child that it is necessary to be on guard constantly. Before doing anything for or with a child, stop to think about the matter of safety. For example, when you give a child a toy to play with, examine it carefully to make sure that there are no loose pieces that he might put into his mouth or any sharp edges on which he might cut himself.

You should be sure he is in a safe place at all times. It is better not to leave him alone at any time. If you have to step into another room to get something, take him with you.

Toddlers need more watching than do babies. It takes only a second for them to have an accident, so keep your eye on them.

CAMPBELL HAYS FROM MONKMEYER

Toddlers and young children need more watching than do babies because they can run around. It takes only a second for them to have an accident, so keep your eye on them.

A sitter must be even more cautious than the mother because she doesn't know the child and his habits, and the child is likely to take advantage when his mother is away. It is better to be overcautious than sorry.

Now what should you do if you think the child is ill or if he has an accident? First, you should discuss such emergencies with the parents before they leave and have a clear understanding as to what to do. But for help on the two emergencies most likely to occur—sickness or an accident— here are some ideas:

In the case of a baby: If he becomes fretful and hot, call the mother and inform her of this. She may suggest what to

You do not have to entertain children all the time to keep them happy. Young children may be perfectly happy a good deal of the time playing by themselves, although they may like to have you nearby.

CAMPBELL HAYS FROM MONKMEYER

do or come home to see what is the matter. Under no circumstances should you try to give the baby medication or quiet him by other means. If he continues to cry, you should get in touch with the mother, a neighbor, or the doctor.

In the case of a young child who has been injured: Call the doctor right away. Then call the mother. The doctor may be able to give you instructions over the phone if he can't come to the home immediately. But you shouldn't try to take care of a situation alone that might be serious. Don't be afraid of being an alarmist or of seeming incapable in calling when you *think* something is wrong. It is much better to have your concern turn out to be a false alarm than it is to try to take care of the situation yourself or to take the chance of the child's not receiving proper care immediately by a knowing person.

Keeping Him Happy. Keeping a child happy is often as difficult as keeping him safe. Your first problem may be fretfulness of the child in protest against his mother's leaving. That is why your first meeting with the child is so important and why it is a good idea to get to the house early enough to become acquainted before the parents leave. You should be careful not to overwhelm the child on your first meeting but to approach him quietly or let him approach you. Then you might leave him alone while you talk to the mother so that he can become used to your presence. Now get him engaged in some pleasurable activity so that when the mother leaves he will not protest.

You do not have to entertain a child all the time to keep him happy. If he is busy playing with something by himself, don't bother him. If he becomes fretful, you might let him help you when you put food on the table, prepare his bed, or straighten his room. If you chat with him while you do these things, he will enjoy it and probably will be happy.

One of the surest ways of making a baby or child *unhappy* is to upset his routine by doing things differently than he is accustomed to doing them. Babies notice differences in the way they are picked up, fed, or dressed. You can't be expected to do things exactly like his mother but you should try to do them as nearly like she does as possible. She will tell you how. Toddlers and older children can tell you or show you how their mother does something, and you should let them tell you and follow their way rather than trying to show them a new way—yours.

You may have some knowledge about child care, either from having read about or taken care of children, but as a sitter you are a substitute mother *not* the mother. Therefore, you should not try to press your methods on the child. By all means avoid trying to reform him. If you have some ideas about changes, you might tactfully mention them to his mother, but if you try to foist them on the child, you will only confuse and upset him.

Showing the child that you are interested in him, that you enjoy being with him and doing things for him, and that you are having fun will help to make him happy while he is with you. Even a baby senses the difference between interest and boredom, love and indifference. He will react unfavorably if he thinks you do not care for him, just as an older child will. When children sense you do not like them, they feel "lost" because they not only feel more lonesome for their parents but they feel that they are with an unfriendly person. This makes them dislike the sitter and makes taking care of them more difficult. So if you show them that you like them, you will be less likely to have trouble.

Taking Care of a Baby

The general routine of a baby's life is quite different from that of an older child because of the baby's helplessness. Most parents do not leave a baby under two months old with a sitter, unless the sitter is an experienced adult. Unless you have had a great deal of experience with very young babies, you will be wise not to accept a job when the baby is under two months of age.

After two months a baby's eating and sleeping habits have become fairly well established so that it is possible to know approximately when he should be fed, when he should sleep, and when he will have to be changed.

Most sitting for young babies is done at night after the baby has had his daily bath and his early evening bottle.

The most important things for you to know about, then, in caring for a baby are these: how to lift and hold the baby; when and how to diaper him; how and what to feed him; when and how to dress him for bed and put him to sleep; what to do if he cries. You should not be expected to bathe

HOW TO PICK UP AND HOLD A BABY

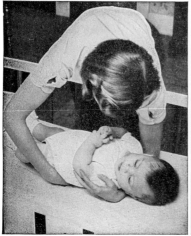

CAMPBELL HAYS FROM MONKMEYER

To pick up a young baby, slip one arm under his neck so that his head rests in the crook of your arm. When you hold him, place your other hand and arm under the lower part of his body so as to form a cradle.

After six months a baby's neck and head do not need so much support, so you can hold him by having him sit on one arm. Keep the other arm high around his neck with your hand flat on his back.

CAMPBELL HAYS FROM MONKMEYER

the baby, even though the parents ask you to do so. Bathing a baby is far too risky a task for a teen-ager to undertake. The baby should have had his daily bath before you arrive. However, it is a good idea for you to know how to bathe a baby. (See pages 100–106 for directions.)

The mother will tell you something about all of these activities, but you should also have some information beforehand or know what to ask about in case she fails to mention something you need to know.

How to Lift and Hold the Baby. A baby should be handled gently but held firmly. You pick up a baby by slipping your arm under him so that his neck and head rest in the crook of your arm. Your other hand and arm go under the lower part of his body so as to form a cradle. Of great importance is the matter of supporting the head of the very young baby. After six months a baby won't need so much support for his neck and head. So you can pick him up by placing one hand on each side of his body just below the armpits, and you can hold and carry him by having him sit on one arm. To be perfectly safe, keep one of your arms high around his neck with your hand flat on his back.

When and How to Diaper the Baby. The mother will probably tell you when to diaper the baby as well as how to do it. Generally a baby is diapered twice during the evening—just before feeding time and before going to sleep. You shouldn't try to change his diapers every time they are damp because they will be damp most of the time. You should never wake a baby to change him, and if he is crying for the bottle at feeding time, don't try to change him before you feed him.

Directions for folding a diaper and diapering a baby are given on pages 81–87. But you should also check with the mother to find out how she does it.

When you diaper a baby, place him on a large enough

When you give the baby his bottle, sit in a comfortable chair and hold the baby in one of your arms. Be sure to hold the bottle high enough so the milk will flow through the nipple.

CAMPBELL HAYS FROM MONKMEYER

surface—preferably a bed—so he can't roll off. He is likely to squirm and fuss when you try to diaper him. You can make it easier by being calm, by talking or singing to him, or by diverting him with a favorite toy.

How and What to Feed the Baby. For a young baby, the feeding will consist of giving him a bottle later in the evening. The mother will tell you when he should be fed, but the baby may let you know when he is hungry by crying even before that time. You will know where the bottle is and how to warm it. (See illustration on page 71 and directions on page 72.)

To give the baby his bottle, you should sit in a comfortable chair and hold the baby in one of your arms. Be sure to hold the bottle high enough so the milk will flow through the nipple. If he slows down or stops sucking before he has taken all the milk, it may mean that he feels "full." This can be corrected by bubbling, or "burping," him. Directions and illustrations on bubbling a baby are given on pages 72–74.

When the baby has had enough, he will turn his head or pull his mouth away from the nipple. A baby should always be bubbled, or "burped," when he is through with his milk. While you are caring for a baby, always keep a clean dry cloth or paper tissues in your pocket to wipe off his mouth because he spills and spits often.

Getting the Baby Ready for Bed. The mother will probably lay out the clothes that the baby will wear to sleep in, or she may change the baby's clothes before she leaves so he is all ready for bed. Preparing him for bed should be done on a bed or some place where he cannot roll off.

If you have to put the nightclothes on the baby, try to hold the neck openings wide enough when you put garments over his head so the garment does not touch his face, since this frightens a baby. You should put a garment on one arm at a time, being sure to support the baby's neck and head with one hand as you slip the garment down.

When you think he is ready for it, you can cover him as directed by the mother and take care of the ventilation and lighting according to her instructions. Be sure his bedcovers are tightly tucked in at the bottom and sides of the crib so he cannot pull them over his head or get tangled up in them.

He may not go to sleep right away—sometimes playing with a stuffed toy or just talking to himself. But if you leave him alone, he will probably fall off to sleep.

If he cries when put to bed, try leaving him alone to see if he stops crying. Avoid showing too much concern by running in to comfort him every few minutes. If, in time, he doesn't stop crying, you will have to pick him up and hold him until he has quieted down. The chances are he will go to sleep in your arms or go to sleep when you put him down again.

After the baby has gone to sleep, you should check every hour or so to see that he is covered and in every other way all right. Be sure to do this quietly, though, so as not to waken him.

What to Do If the Baby Cries. Having the baby cry in the night may be your biggest problem to handle. He may cry because he is hungry, thirsty, soiled, wet, or uncomfortable. He may be uncomfortable because he is too warm, too cold, or from having been in one position too long. He might also be crying because he has a pain or colic. You should go to him at once when he cries and try to determine what the trouble is. If you find that his diapers are dry, he may be crying because he is hungry. If he refuses his bottle and shows no interest in water, try bubbling, or "burping," him to see if he has some gas that he did not get up after his feeding. If all of these things fail, pick him up and hold him in your arms. Rocking him, talking or singing to him, or walking the floor with him may stop his crying. Many times just having the warmth of your body next to his is all that he needs. When he has not cried for some time, he will probably go to sleep when you put him back to bed. If you are unable to quiet a baby in a half-hour, call the mother or some other adult.

Taking Care of a Toddler

There are more duties entailed in taking care of a toddler —a one-to-two-year-old—than taking care of a baby.

Entertaining the Toddler. While he is awake, he will want to play. He will want you nearby, but you don't have to do things with him. Just being there to watch, take what he gives you, or do what he says is usually enough. Interfere as little as possible with his play, since, at this age, children generally amuse themselves. Sometimes, though, he may want you to tell him simple stories, sing little songs, or play easy games with him. If he decides to wander, you will have

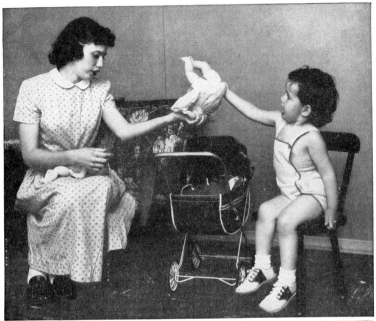

CAMPBELL HAYS FROM MONKMEYER

Toddlers may want you nearby while they are playing to watch them, take what they give you, or do what they say.

to follow because you cannot afford to take your eye off of him—even for a minute.

Feeding the Toddler. You may have to prepare a simple supper for him, which the mother will tell you about, and you will have to help him to feed himself or feed him if he is unable to do it himself. A toddler is likely to detect the difference in the way his food is prepared. As a result, he may insist that you feed him, or he may dawdle over his eating. A hungry child is likely to be fretful and hard to manage. Therefore, he should he humored at mealtime because it is important that he get enough to eat.

Getting the Toddler Ready for Bed. You will see that he cleans his teeth and goes to the toilet before going to bed.

When taking care of toddlers and young children, you should see that they brush their teeth and go to the toilet before going to bed.

CAMPBELL HAYS FROM MONKMEYER

Most toddlers have a short period of quiet play before bedtime. During this time you can tell him stories, show him pictures in a book, or play records for him. If you help him put his toys "to bed" he will be in a better mood to go himself. After he has said his prayers, tuck him in, and talk to him a little while until he quiets down and is ready for sleep.

You may have problems getting a toddler to bed—particularly if there is an older child in the family. He will find excuses to call you into the room or not go to sleep until the older child does. Give him special attention instead of scolding him. Remember he is only a child, and he may be lonely for his mother.

The child's attitude toward you may create bedtime problems too. If he likes you, he may not want to go to bed. If he doesn't like you, he may become rebellious and refuse to go to bed, tear his bed apart, run around the room, or cry for his mother. If he absolutely refuses to go to bed, stay in his room with him or let him come into the living room with you until you have quieted him or persuaded him to go to bed. He may be afraid or he may feel lonely.

Taking Care of an Older Child

A school-age child is likely to rebel more when a stranger comes to substitute for his mother than a younger child does. After the child goes to school, he begins to feel that he is "too big" for a sitter and regards her somewhat as an intruder. Boys especially at this age are likely to resent a girl sitter. A boy sitter who can play games with them is often much more to their liking.

An older child should be able to do most things for himself, so far as eating, bathing, and getting ready for bed are concerned. Therefore, your duties will be concentrated more on supervising the child than on doing things for him.

How to Treat the Older Child. To break down any resentment the older child may have toward a baby sitter, try to talk to him in your own way about things that interest him. Discuss his hobbies or interests and offer to play games with him or to show him how to play new games.

Preparing Food for the Older Child. You will probably be expected to prepare the evening meal, but the child will be only too glad to help you with the work. Unlike the toddler, he is less likely to rebel against eating food prepared in a slightly different manner than his mother prepares it. In fact, he may even enjoy the difference. Even a child that can feed himself, however, may get tired before he has finished the meal and want you to feed him the rest. He may eat more than you think he should, but the mother should have told you how much he is to have. No matter how much or how little he eats, don't try to force him to eat more or less.

Getting the Older Child to Bed. You may have bedtime problems with the older child too. The two-to-six-year-old may take advantage of his parents' absence by refusing to go to bed. One way to handle this is to set a time ahead at which he is to go to bed. When you come to this time, be firm about it. Don't give in and let him stay up as he will try to do. He may even get up afterward on one pretext or another because he is lonesome. Giving him some attention or staying in his room until he falls asleep may reassure him.

Disciplining the Older Child. Your problems with an older child will probably center around discipline. He is eager to assert his independence, and he will test you out to see how much he can "get away with." He will be especially trying if you antagonize him or threaten to "tattle" to his mother. If you can keep the child busy and happy, you should not have any trouble with him. With tact and firmness you can convince him that you are fair and reasonable and that you mean what you say, even if you are not old enough to be his mother.

Getting Along with the Older Child. There are two things you can do that will help you in handling the older child.

The first is to look as attractive as possible. Both boys and girls are impressed by the appearance of a sitter and will do more for one that favorably impresses them.

The second thing that will help you handle children of this age is to be a good sport. You can wear clothes that will not be damaged by any games you want to play and yet look attractive and neat. They may want you to sit down on the floor and play with them or play with them outdoors. If you can play their games with some amount of skill and can show them how to improve their game or play others, it will help you to get along with them.

Taking Care of More Than One Child

One advantage of sitting for a family with two or more children is that you don't have to give any one child as much attention as you do with an only child because the children

When you are taking care of several children, you will have to figure out a way to keep the older children occupied or out of mischief when it is necessary to give your entire attention to the baby.

play with each other. However, you will have a new problem —that of quarreling.

When Children Quarrel. When there is a quarrel, you will have to be the peacemaker without playing favorites. You will have to be careful that the children don't hurt each other, and you will have to decide how to settle the difficulty fairly without arousing the antagonism of any one of them.

Giving Each Child Attention. When any one of the children—because he is older or because he is younger—receives what seems like a special privilege, give the others some kind of special attention so they don't resent it.

If there is an infant in the family that needs your entire attention at times, you will have to work out some way to keep the older children from misbehaving while you give necessary time to the baby. You might tell them about some special plans you have to play with them after the baby has gone to sleep, or you might have them help you, or pretend to help you, while you feed or dress the baby. Older children can sometimes help you with an infant, but never, never, leave a baby alone with a young child.

Disciplining Children. You may be tempted to spank a child when he makes your duties difficult by leading the others into rebellion against you, but this is one thing that should be avoided. Spanking doesn't do much good (see pages 231–232), and it certainly will make the child rebellious and even more difficult to handle. Even though you know the mother uses spanking as a form of punishment, under no conditions should you, as a stranger, spank or slap a child you are taking care of.

◆ ◆ ◆ ◆ ◆ ◆ ◆ ◆ ◆

Undoubtedly when you baby-sit you will not be likely to have all or anywhere near all of the problems that have been presented here. Most of the problems that are likely to occur with some infants and children at some time have been discussed so as to help you if you do meet them.

If you remain calm, try to do your best, and give a child your love and attention when you baby-sit, you will find the problems fewer and those you have less difficult to handle.

Each time you baby-sit successfully you gain confidence in yourself in being able to understand and care for children better—a very great asset to have in adjusting to younger brothers and sisters, children of friends and neighbors, and your own children later on when you are a parent.

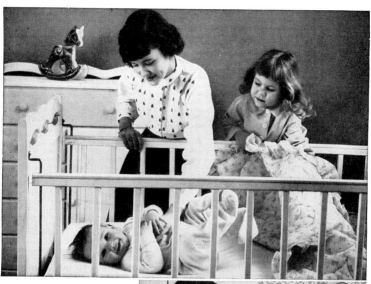

Letting older children
help you with a baby
is one way of keeping
them satisfied.

PART ONE:

How Life Begins

CHAPTER 1

Preparing for the Baby

The mother has nine months in which to prepare for the arrival of her baby. Most mothers emphasize their own physical care and the obtaining of a layette for the baby, but they may overlook the necessity for making personal and family adjustments before the baby is born. This "psychological preparation" is often more important than the physical preparation.

Ideally, all preparation for the new baby—physical, material, and psychological—should begin as soon as the doctor informs the woman that she is to have a baby. This gives her plenty of time to get ready or to be ready ahead of time should the baby arrive early. It avoids last-minute preparation for a baby, which causes fatigue and confusion.

The drawing on the opposite page, entitled *Maternité,* is the work of Mary Cassatt. As a young American art student Miss Cassatt went to France in 1875 and spent most of her life there studying the techniques of the Impressionists. In the portrayal of mothers and children she is unsurpassed. (Courtesy The Art Institute of Chicago.)

Psychological Preparation of the Mother

In spite of the joy that most expectant mothers experience when they are certain that they are going to have a baby, sometimes there are also feelings of worry and fear along with the joy. The reason for this can be traced to a belief in the past that childbirth is not only a painful experience but also a dangerous one. The more a woman thinks and talks about this, the more worried she will be.

The best psychological preparation for a mother-to-be consists in convincing her that all will be well, provided she follows her doctor's instructions carefully. Complications or death in childbirth is rare today, except in cases where there has been no medical care or where medical advice has been ignored. Pregnancy is a normal, healthy condition and should be regarded as such. If the woman can achieve and maintain this point of view, her psychological preparation will be excellent.

Like all adjustments, a slow, gradual realization of the responsibilities and sacrifices of motherhood will go far to help a young mother-to-be prepare herself psychologically for the arrival of her baby. Every day she should say to herself, "How would I manage my work and recreation today if I had a baby?" Then she should work out mentally a plan of action that would be practical with a baby in the home.

Psychological preparation should not be limited to the first baby, as many believe. The mother-to-be must get herself mentally ready to accept the new baby into her life, while at the same time avoiding any disruption of the relationship that exists between herself and her husband and other children. Furthermore, she must realize that a new baby will add new work and new responsibilities to her daily life. An

As soon as the doctor examines the mother and is sure that she is going to have a baby, preparations for the child in the home should begin.

COURTESY GENERAL FOODS CORPORATION

already busy day will be even busier after her new baby arrives.

Making Preparation with the Doctor

As soon as a woman suspects she is pregnant, she should go to her family doctor. If his diagnosis shows that her suspicions are correct, he will tell her if he handles pregnancy cases and, if not, he will recommend one who does. Should she be in a strange community and not yet have a doctor, she can call one of the hospitals and ask the director to recommend a doctor.

When the doctor's examination and tests prove that she is pregnant, the woman should discuss with him practical matters, such as where he wants the baby to be born, at home or in a hospital, how long he will want her to plan to be in the hospital, what type of room—private, semi-private, or ward—she feels she can afford, and what his fee will be. She should also inform him if she carries hospitalization insurance.

The doctor, in turn, will advise her about diet, exercise, care of teeth during pregnancy, the taking of vitamin and calcium pills, and how much she may do. He will inform her of what she may expect in regard to gaining weight, possible morning sickness, finicky appetite, and fatigue. Many doctors give their patients printed instructions and pamphlets describing the pattern of pregnancy and additional information about prenatal care. The doctor will set regular times for periodic checkups during pregnancy and suggest that she get in touch with him by telephone or at his office, should she need his advice between the regular visits.

Most problems preceding childbirth or at childbirth can be met successfully today if the woman puts herself in the care of a competent doctor as soon as she *suspects* that she is pregnant. More important still is that she follow his instructions to the letter, even though they are different from those given to her mother, her friends, or in newspapers, magazines, and books.

Physical Preparation of the Mother

The surest way to guarantee a healthy baby and a relatively easy childbirth for the mother is through careful prenatal care of the mother. The developing infant is completely dependent upon the mother for nourishment and protection during the months before birth. Therefore, it is essential that the environment in which the baby develops be as favorable as possible. Even with the best medical care, the responsibility for maintaining a favorable environment rests entirely in the hands of the mother.

The nourishment the baby receives before his birth comes from the absorption of nutritive products from the mother's blood stream. Her blood, in turn, is affected by her general health condition and her diet. That is why good health and a carefully planned diet are so important during the pregnancy period. In the past, the quantity of food eaten by the mother was emphasized as important. Today we know that it is the *quality* of the food in the diet that counts. In other words, it is not how much a mother eats that is important but what kind of food.

The daily diet most widely approved today for expectant mothers should include the following foods:

One quart of milk
One cooked and one raw leaf or stem vegetable, such as spinach, cabbage, celery, asparagus, or lettuce
Fresh fruits (at least two oranges)
One serving of lean meat, fish, or fowl
One egg
One serving of whole-grain or enriched cereal
Three slices of buttered whole-wheat or enriched bread
One teaspoon of fish-liver oil

If this diet is not adequate to satisfy the appetite, more vegetables and fruits can be added. Rich foods that are heavily seasoned, pastries, sweets, fried foods, and fatty meats should be avoided.

A craving for certain foods or unusual combinations of foods is fairly common, especially during the early part of pregnancy. This craving may be for foods that are sour, such as sour pickles or tart apples; for salty foods, such as salted peanuts or pretzels; or for sweets, such as candy and cake. These cravings usually develop when the diet is not properly balanced. If the expectant mother allows herself to be guided by these cravings, she may eat too few of the foods essential to her baby's well-being. Should the cravings be strong or persistent, the doctor should be consulted.

Deciding on the Hospital

What hospital the woman will go to for childbirth will depend largely upon the doctor she selects. Should he be on the staff of several hospitals, he will ask her which hospital she prefers. Being in a hospital near her home is preferable, provided the facilities there are as good as in a more distant hospital. The type of room she wants should also be decided on her first or second visit to the doctor so he may make a reservation.

Because babies rarely come on the exact day when they are expected, it is best to have the doctor make the hospital reservation. As pregnancy progresses, he can change the reservation, should he have reason to believe that the baby will come sooner or later than anticipated. This procedure will guarantee that there will be a place available for the mother-to-be, regardless of when her baby arrives.

Some hospitals today offer opportunities for the baby to be in the mother's room instead of being placed in the hospital nursery. It is wise for the expectant mother to ask her doctor about the "rooming-in plan," what hospitals in the community offer it, and what his opinion is about it for *her*. Where the rooming-in plan is being used, it is available for patients in private, semiprivate, or ward rooms.

There are advantages and disadvantages to the rooming-in plan which should be considered before a final decision is made. It gives the young mother an opportunity to watch the nurse bathe and dress the baby and, as her strength improves, for the mother to participate in the baby's care under the supervision of the nurse. Because the baby is within reach, the mother can nurse it when it cries instead of waiting for a nurse to bring the baby from the hospital nursery at set times. This not only encourages the flow of the mother's milk but it also eliminates the tension and fatigue a baby experiences when it cries in vain for food. And, finally, the rooming-in plan makes it possible for the father to share in the care of the baby when he visits the hospital instead of viewing it through the glass window of the hospital nursery.

On the other hand, having her baby right beside her may keep the mother from getting the rest she needs to regain her strength after childbirth. Should she be anxious about the baby's every move and become excited or frightened when it cries and she is alone in the room with it, it may delay her recovery. When childbirth has been accompanied by complications or when the baby is prematurely born, most doctors favor having the baby in the hospital nursery until the mother is well enough to have it near her.

A month or even better, two months, before the baby is scheduled to arrive, it is wise to make tentative preparations for going to the hospital. A list of what will be needed there can be made out and any articles not in daily use can be put in a suitcase. This list should include several nightgowns, a bed jacket, a housecoat, clothes for the return home from the hospital, clothes and blankets to bring the baby home in, toilet articles, writing paper, pen, stamps, and a book. With the list available, the suitcase can be packed very quickly, should a hurried dash to the hospital be necessary.

How Much Does a Baby Cost?

The cost of having a baby varies enormously from one community to another and from one family to another in the same community. One mother may have a suite of rooms in a hospital with private nurses in constant attendance, while another mother in the same hospital may be in a ward with the care of floor nurses.

When the two mothers leave the hospital, the baby of the first mother may go to a suite of rooms specially equipped for him with expensive nursery furniture and the most modern electrical devices for preparation of his food, the sterilization of his formula, and the control of sunlight and ventilation. The baby of the second mother, by contrast, may find his crib a makeshift box or basket, placed in the corner of the only room the family possesses, with his food prepared on an old range and without proper facilities for sterilization or care.

The *minimum* cost of having a baby in a city today, if the baby is born in a hospital ward or in a semiprivate room, would include the following essential items:

Hospitalization	$ 75
Doctor's fee	75
Equipment	150
Total	$300

Even if a baby is born at home, there are expenses for equipment, doctor's fee, and nurse. In case of a complication during birth, the cost might be more than if the baby were delivered in a hospital.

Of course these figures are only approximate. It might be possible to have a baby in some communities for less; in others, it might be more. The cost might vary according to what the doctor charges and whether or not the family has a hospitalization plan. It may also depend upon who takes care of the mother after her return from the hospital—that is, whether it is a relative or friend who does not charge or a nurse who is hired. The cost for equipment might be less if some is available in the family or if the father makes some of it.

In any event, it is a good policy to have a small sum available in cash when planning to have a baby. The psychologi-

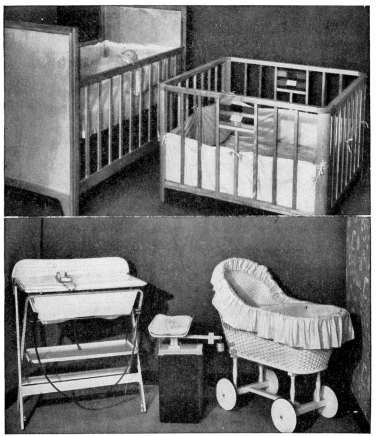

COURTESY LANE BRYANT

The five items of essential equipment are a crib, a playpen, a bathinette, scales, and a bassinet. For economy, a large tub may be substituted for the bathinette and a basket may be used instead of a bassinet.

cal effect of this "nest egg" is great enough to justify some sacrifice.

Equipment for the New Baby

One mistake that young parents often make is to acquire more equipment for the first baby than is absolutely necessary. They fail to recognize that a baby remains small for a very short time and hence outgrows infant equipment very soon. Another important fact, often overlooked, is that they will be receiving some equipment as gifts and offered the use of certain equipment on loan from relatives or friends.

Below are lists of items[1] generally regarded as essential for the newborn baby and additional lists of items that would prove useful, although not essential, if the family budget is adequate to provide them.

Minimum Nursery Needs (Essential)

Unfinished basket with handles
Crib
Chest of drawers

Bathinette or large tub
Playpen
Scales for weighing baby

Daily Necessities for Baby (Essential)

6 nursing bottles, nipples, and
   caps (if baby is bottle-fed)
2 small bottles and nipples
   for water and fruit juice
Pure castile bath soap
Baby oil

Antiseptic baby lotion
Baby powder
Assorted safety pins and holder
Sterilized cotton
Q-tips (sterilized swabs)

Minimum Layette (Essential)

BASIC ITEMS

3 dozen diapers (if diaper
   service is not used)
4 shirts
3 nightgowns

3 wrappers
3 absorbent pads
3 waterproof sheets
3 receiving blankets

CRIB NEEDS

4 crib sheets
2 cotton crib blankets

1 wool crib blanket

[1] Lists prepared by editors of *My Baby* magazine.

BATH NEEDS

3 wash cloths   2 bath towels
3 knit towels

Additional Nursery Needs (Useful but not Essential)

High chair   Small table and chair

Additional Layette Needs (Useful but not Essential)

2 sacques   1 bunting or carriage set (for
2 dresses   a winter baby)
2 gertrudes (slips)   1 carriage blanket
2 sweaters   2 woolen wrapping blankets
2 pairs bootees   4 bibs

When Will the Baby Come?

The usual length of time it takes a baby to develop in its mother's body is ten lunar months, or 280 days, or approximately nine calendar months. The mother can calculate the time of arrival of her baby by counting back three calendar months from the first day of her last menstrual period and then adding seven days. For example, if the first day of the last menstrual period came on November 10, counting back three months would place the time at August 10. Then, adding seven days would give the probable date of the baby's arrival as August 17 of the next year.

Only occasionally does a baby arrive on the exact date calculated for him. It is generally harder to predict the date of arrival of a first-born baby than a second, third, or later child, and a first-born child more often arrives ahead of schedule than late. Fortunately, the baby's development is completed by the end of the seventh calendar month, so that, if a baby is born in seven instead of nine months, he has a good chance of living, provided he is put in an incubator or given special attention at home.

How Much Can a Mother-to-be Do?

How much a mother-to-be can and should do depends largely upon what she has been accustomed to do before pregnancy began, though moderation should be used. Following the normal or usual pattern of activity is advisable. Some doctors today are advocating exercises to relieve tension and to re-educate the muscles. This, combined with reassurance, eliminates fear of childbirth and makes it possible for the mother to give birth to her baby without the use of anesthetics.[2]

Having a baby is a drain on the system. The weight of the baby plus the additional body tissue that is necessary to house the baby in the mother's body result in fatigue. Many things that a woman could ordinarily do without feeling tired now prove to be very fatiguing. For this reason mothers-to-be need plenty of rest and sleep. A minimum of eight hours of sleep at night plus a nap or rest of at least one hour after lunch should be included in the daily routine.

Emotional strain, if prolonged, produces chemical changes in the mother's blood stream. This, in turn, affects the developing baby. How serious these chemical changes are has not yet been definitely decided. There is, however, fairly definite agreement among doctors that emotional tension should be avoided as much as possible.

Possible Problems during Pregnancy

Having a baby is a perfectly normal experience and should not cause alarm. In recent years there has been a marked decrease in infant mortality and in the deaths of mothers during and following childbirth. This decrease is primarily

[2] For further information, see G. D. Read, *Childbirth without Fear*, Harper & Brothers, New York, 1953.

the result of new medical discoveries and new ways of caring for the mother during pregnancy and at the time of childbirth.

With the present knowledge available in medical science, the process of bearing a child today may be said to be almost free from obstacles. The modern mother, in most cases, is almost guaranteed the arrival of a normal, healthy baby. There are, however, still some conditions that may produce problems, and it is well to be aware of what these are and when they might occur.

Any abnormal condition of the mother's body can interfere with the normal pattern of development during the early part of the prenatal period. Chronic alcoholism, serious malnutrition, or other serious deficiencies or diseases may affect the development of the baby. Such cases, however, are infrequent because women suffering from a serious physical ailment rarely become pregnant. But the good health of the mother is the best assurance that all will go well.

Should there be a miscarriage, it usually occurs during the first month or two of pregnancy. In a miscarriage the ovum becomes dislodged from the mother's uterine wall. It then passes away in the menstrual flow and the woman loses her child. Miscarriages generally occur at the time of the month when menstruation normally takes place and during the first or second month of pregnancy. Miscarriages are usually caused by a glandular imbalance which can now be detected and successfully treated. For this reason, miscarriages are rarer today than in the past.

The most common ailment of pregnant women during the first few months of pregnancy is "morning sickness," or nausea. Occasionally nausea is so severe that it is almost impossible for the mother-to-be to retain any food or to have any appetite. Such a condition may result in loss of weight and therefore should be taken up with the doctor as soon as it occurs. Today doctors can generally eliminate nausea, at least to some extent, so there should be no need for a woman to experience discomfort for any length of time.

Another time that there may be a problem is at birth itself. If the baby is behind schedule in emerging into the world or becomes too large to be born normally without danger to the mother, the doctor may have to deliver the baby with instruments. There is today far less chance of injury from instrument birth than there was in the past. Further, whenever a doctor has reason to believe that birth will be difficult or a danger for either the mother or the baby, he may bring the baby into the world by means of a Caesarean operation.[3]

Old Wives' Tales

No aspect of medical science is more hampered by traditions from the past than is that which deals with the pregnancy period. Young mothers-to-be are warned by well-meaning relatives and friends that if they do this or that it will have some harmful effect on the babies developing within their bodies. Many claims are made to the effect that what the mother does or sees during her pregnancy period will leave some sort of impression on her baby. For example, some people believe that if a mother overindulges in strawberries or drinks wine the baby will have strawberry marks or wine blotches on his skin.

Because there is no nervous connection between the mother and her baby, it is impossible for the mother's

[3] A surgical operation in which the walls of the abdomen and uterus are cut, so called because Julius Caesar was supposed to have been brought into the world this way.

thoughts to have any effect whatsoever on her baby. However, as has been pointed out already, alcoholism, malnutrition, infectious diseases, and glandular upsets may affect the baby. As the baby absorbs water, oxygen, and nutritive products from the mother's blood, an unhealthy condition of her blood will affect the baby in proportion to the severity of the condition that exists.

The important thing about old wives' tales is that many people accept them in an uncritical way and, far worse, act in accordance with these beliefs, even when they are in direct contradiction to modern medical practices. A mother-to-be, for example, may have been advised by her doctor to cut down her food intake to eliminate the possibility of her baby's becoming so large that it would cause trouble at the time of birth. However, if she had always been told that a mother-to-be must "eat for two," she might ignore the advice of her doctor, thus endangering not only her own life but that of her baby as well.

Preparing the Family for the Baby

The arrival of a new baby in the home necessitates an adjustment for every member of the family, no matter how small or large the group may be. Life will have to change in one way or another for everyone. Making changes is not always easy, and the most painless way to go about it is to anticipate the changes needed and make them gradually.

The material preparations, for the most part, will take relatively little time, but the mental adjustments and the changes in behavior may meet greater resistance. For that reason they should be made more slowly. Every member of the family should get used to the idea that there will be new responsibilities that must be shared by all. (See Chapter 11, "The Child in the Family.")

A class of prospective fathers learns about child care at the Maternity Center Association, New York City. Most fathers today have a real desire to share in the responsibility of caring for their children, even during the limited time they have at home.

Many people believe that only the first-born baby brings about changes in the household and that, therefore, no appreciable preparation is needed for the second, third, or later child. True, the layette that served the first baby is usually adequate to meet the needs of the second or even the third with a few replacements and a little renovation. However, mental adjustments and changes in the behavior of the whole family must be made for every new baby.

The advent of a new baby in a family should never come as a surprise to the other children. The first-born child, who has been accustomed to being the only child in the family, will have a far more difficult adjustment to make than will later-born children who have never been "only children."

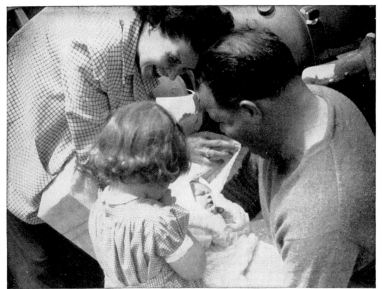

DURYEE FROM MONKMEYER

Young children find it even more difficult than the parents to make the adjustment to a new member of the family. Therefore, children should be prepared in advance for the coming of a new baby.

Therefore, he should know in advance about the expected baby so that he will have time to get used to the idea.

The best way to prepare a child for the arrival of a new baby is to see to it always that the child does not get too much time or attention from the mother or from any other member of the family. No matter how strong the temptation, parents, grandparents, and other relatives should learn to ignore the child at times so that he will not become accustomed to being the center of attention whenever others are present. His daily schedule should be planned so that he will have periods of solitude at certain times of the day.

In preparing the child for the new baby, he should be given small duties and responsibilities. Thus, he will learn to serve others and to help, instead of expecting others to wait on him. When the baby arrives, the child will be used to helping and will not be so likely to be jealous of the baby because he feels that the baby is usurping rights formerly reserved for him.

Finally, the child's preparation for the new baby should include training in consideration for the rights of others. He must learn to be quiet when others want to sleep or rest, to wait his turn instead of demanding immediate attention, and to share his belongings with others. This training will stand in good stead when the new baby arrives.

No matter how carefully the child is prepared for the new baby, there is little chance that his preparation will be adequate to meet every problem that may arise. Jealousy, if only in a mild form, is almost inevitable. Because of this, careful continuation of the preparation for the baby should be stressed even after the baby arrives.

If the adjustment period is begun early enough, the whole family will be ready to welcome the arrival of the baby. His presence in the home will then be a joyous occasion for all because there will be few problems to mar the pleasure of his arrival. Not all problems, of course, can be foreseen or prepared for, but if the major adjustment problems are anticipated and successfully met before the baby's birth, the less important ones can be ironed out as they arise.

Making Preparation for the Mother's Absence

Several months before the scheduled arrival of the baby the mother-to-be should give serious thought to the problem of caring for the home at the time of the baby's birth, as well as for several weeks afterward. Whether the baby is born in a hospital or in the home, someone other than the mother

If a couple do not have a relative who can help out, or if they cannot afford to have someone come in for the first weeks after the baby's arrival, they may obtain the services of a trained person in child care from one of several community agencies.

will have to assume the responsibility for the work the mother generally does.

Even when childbirth is normal, the mother should have a few days to regain her strength. When she returns from the hospital, some arrangement should be made for a member of the family, a friend, or a paid worker to help out with the heavy work of the home and the care of the other children. Many husbands take their annual vacations at this time so they can be available to help at home until their wives are ready to resume their usual home duties.

Ideally, a relative who has had experience in home management, such as a mother or mother-in-law, should take charge of the home at the time of a childbirth. If, however, the young couple have no relatives nearby, as frequently is the case when the husband's business takes him away from his childhood environment, the mother-to-be will be wise to ask one of her relatives or one of her husband's relatives to come and stay in the home.

In families that have no near relatives to come into the home while the mother is at the hospital, the mother-to-be should discuss this matter with her husband and her doctor in time to make suitable arrangements for outside help. In many communities, visiting and public health nurses are available to help in an emergency for a small fee or, if necessary, without pay.

It is a wise precaution for the mother to arrange in advance with the person who is to come in so there will be someone to take over in case she has to go to the hospital early. This is especially important when there are other children in the family. She should jot down any important information as to where important household equipment—such as extra blankets, medicine, etc.—is kept and leave telephone numbers of the doctor, relatives, friends, stores, etc. for use of the person who is to take charge. Knowing that someone is "standing by," ready to help out, gives the mother a feeling of assurance that all will be well.

Returning from the Hospital

Bringing the new baby home from the hospital should be a joyous occasion, but sometimes it is not. The father, a relative, a neighbor, or the person who has been employed to take charge of the household during the mother's absence should see to it that the home is in order, that the space provided for the new baby is in readiness for immediate use, and that all necessary baby equipment is out and ready for use.

Too often it is assumed that when the hospital releases the mother for return home she is perfectly well. True, she has recovered from childbirth, but, like convalescence from an illness, it takes time to regain strength lost during childbirth. The mother's return to the care of her home and family should be gradual rather than sudden, as it too often is.

For Discussion

1. What old wives' tales have you heard about the prenatal period?
2. What evidence would you use to disprove any statements you have heard about the mother's ability to mark her unborn child?
3. What evidence is there to prove that pregnancy is a normal period in a woman's life and not an illness?
4. How much of the care of a young baby should the father assume? How do young men of today feel about taking care of babies?

Suggested Activities

1. Visit the baby department of a store and ask to see the equipment recommended for a new baby. Find out its cost.
2. Get in touch with your local hospital and ask for the different charges for prenatal care and hospitalization at the time of childbirth.
3. Make an outline of the changes in the daily life of your family that would be necessary if there were to be a new baby.
4. Tell of an instance in which an older child was jealous of a new baby in the home. How did the child show his jealousy? How did the parents handle it?

CHAPTER 2

The Newborn Baby

Most people believe that life begins at birth. This is incorrect. Life begins at the time of conception, which is approximately nine months before birth. While this nine months may seem to be a short time in relation to the life span of the individual, it is vitally important in determining what the individual will be. Actually, by the time the baby is ready to be born, his development has already reached a relatively advanced stage.

Carriers of Heredity

Within the sex cell of every man and woman are twenty-four pairs of chromosomes. Each chromosome consists of a string of minute particles called "genes." The genes are the true carriers of heredity because they are the physical substances passed on from parent to child. As a sex cell ripens, it goes through a division process during which the twenty-four pairs of chromosomes split. The mature cell which is formed contains only twenty-four single chromosomes. If fertilization occurs, through the union of a male cell with a female cell, the new cell created contains forty-eight chromosomes, or twenty-four pairs—half from the father and half from the mother.

ELIZABETH HIBBS

The child inherits his traits, both physical and mental, in equal
amounts from his two parents and their family strains. His heredity is
determined even before birth, for he starts life as a completely new
cell, containing forty-eight chromosomes—half from his father and half
from his mother. These chromosomes are made up of the genes, which
are the carriers of heredity.

Boy or Girl?

From the beginning of history people have theorized and
experimented with the possibility of controlling the sex of
newborn babies. In many countries male offspring have been
considered more desirable than female. During certain periods of history, girl babies have been preferred. Further,
there have been millions of individual instances in which
prospective parents in all countries have, for one reason or
another, strongly desired either a son or a daughter.

There have also been numerous myths and tales connected

with the control of the child's sex. For example, it has been believed that if conception takes place just after menstruation a female child will be born; if a mother eats large amounts of sugar during pregnancy, she will have a girl; if she eats meat in large quantities, she will have a boy. Others have believed that the month of the year in which conception occurs determines the sex of the child.

Scientists have disproved all these theories and practices for controlling sex. We now know what determines the sex of the child, but up to the present time there is no known way to control sex. Sex is entirely a matter of chance, with the chances slightly more favorable to the male than to the female sex. Statistics show that the ratio of male to female is 105 to 100—that is, 105 males are born for every 100 females.

What determines sex is the presence or absence of Y, or an unmatched chromosome, in the male sex cell that fertilizes the female ovum, or egg. Before the male sex cell, or spermatozoon, is mature and ready to fertilize an ovum, it contains twenty-three pairs of X, or matched chromosomes, and one pair of unmatched, or X and Y chromosomes. When the spermatozoon divides into two, one part contains twenty-four matched, or X, chromosomes, and one part contains one Y and twenty-three X chromosomes. If a twenty-four-X-chromosome spermatozoon unites with an ovum, a female child is conceived. If the union is with a spermatozoon containing twenty-three X chromosomes and one Y chromosome, the result is a male offspring.

All spermatozoon divide in this way before they are mature and ready to fertilize an ovum, and each has an equal chance of combining with an ovum and fertilizing it. Therefore, there are almost equal numbers of boy and girl babies. There is no unmatched chromosome in the ovum; hence all ova are alike and have absolutely no control over determining sex.

FROM "ALL THE CHILDREN," NEW YORK BOARD OF EDUCATION

Although scientists have discovered that boys are the result of a certain combination of chromosomes and girls are the result of another, they have not learned of any way to control the sex of a baby or to ascertain before birth what the sex will be.

Will There Be Twins?

Normally, human mothers produce one baby at a time, but once in every ninety births twins are born. Scientific studies have shown that there are two distinctly different types of twins, *identical twins and nonidentical twins.* Identical twins come from a single ovum that splits into two parts shortly after fertilization, while nonidentical twins come from two ova released during the same menstrual cycle and fertilized by two different spermatozoa.

Because identical twins come from one fertilized ovum that has split into two parts during the course of development, such children have the same chromosomes and genes. Hence

Identical twins are produced when one ovum splits into two parts shortly after fertilization. Therefore, identical twins are always the same sex, are similar in appearance, and have the same mental and temperamental make-up.

it is logical to expect the babies developing from these two halves to be very similar in physical and mental make-up, and we find it true that identical twins are as alike in appearance as the proverbial "peas in a pod."

Because only one spermatozoon fertilizes one ovum to produce two children, identical twins are always of the same sex, and their mental and temperamental make-up is as similar as their physical appearance.

By contrast, nonidentical twins can be of the same or of

opposite sexes. It is purely a matter of chance whether or not the two spermatozoa that fertilize the two ova will carry the unmatched chromosome. Because the chromosomes are not the same in the two ova or in the two spermatozoa, nonidentical twins are more likely to be different in physical and mental make-up than to be alike. Actually, nonidentical twins are the result of two simultaneous pregnancies.

How Big Is a Newborn Baby?

The average American baby at birth measures approximately twenty inches in length and weighs from six to nine pounds. There are greater variations in weight than in length. Some babies, born prematurely, may weigh only three or four pounds; other babies, born normally, may weigh twelve to fourteen pounds. Proportionally, the baby's body is top-heavy. The head of a baby is about one-fourth of the entire body length, while an adult's head is one-seventh of his body length.

The newborn baby has practically no neck, his shoulders are narrow and sloping, and his abdomen is large and protruding, especially after feeding. The arms and legs, in proportion to the rest of the body, are short and scrawny, and the hands and feet are ridiculously small. In spite of the small size of a baby's feet and hands, his toes and fingers have well-developed nails even when the baby is born a month or two ahead of the scheduled time.

A baby's bones are made up mostly of cartilage or gristle and, consequently, are soft and flexible. The muscles are soft, small, and uncontrolled, with those of the legs less developed than those in the arms. His skin is soft, deep pink in color, and often blotchy. Frequently a baby is chubby, with soft, flabby fat covering most of his body. Quite often there is a heavy growth of fine-textured hair on his head, back, and

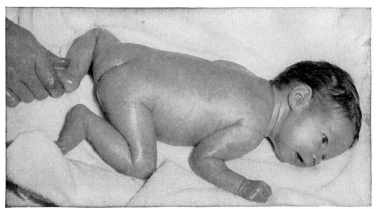

Proportionally, the newborn baby's body is top-heavy. The head is about one-quarter of the entire body; he has practically no neck; his shoulders are narrow and sloping; and his abdomen is large and protruding. The arms and legs are short and scrawny, and the hands and feet are very small.

arms. This is "prenatal hair" that quickly disappears soon after birth.

Behavior of the Newborn

Because his muscles are soft and his nervous system is uncontrolled, the newborn baby has no control over his movements. He cannot turn his body, sit up, reach for an object, or even coordinate his eyes. When he looks at you, one eye may turn in one direction and the other eye in the other direction. This, of course, gives the baby a queer expression but, of more serious consequence, it means that he cannot see clearly or distinctly. He is completely helpless and, when picked up, gives the impression that he may fall apart.

Most people believe that the only sounds the newborn baby can make are cries. A baby begins to cry as soon as he is born—sometimes during the actual process of birth. It is through the "birth cry" that the baby's lungs are inflated with air, thus enabling him to breathe for the first time. Every baby has his own characteristic cry. It may be harsh and piercing or low and moaning.

Well-meaning advice about allowing a baby "to cry it out" may at times be all right for an older baby, but it can be dangerous advice for a helpless newborn. Crying is the only way a baby has of letting us know that something is the matter with him. Therefore, it is serious to ignore this danger signal.

In addition to his cries, the infant can produce low, sighing sounds, such as "eh-eh" or "ah-ah." These sounds are sometimes referred to as "cooing" but, from the long-term point of view, these sounds are very important because they are the foundation from which speech eventually develops.

Sensitivities of the Newborn

It is very difficult to know what newborn babies are able to see, hear, smell, taste, or feel. However, from scientific research we know today something about the sensitivities of the newborn. At birth, smell and taste are well developed, as shown by the fact that an infant will cry when he is exposed to unpleasant odors or tastes. A baby's skin is sensitive to heat and, especially, to cold. A baby reacts promptly to touch and, after the first day or two of life, he reacts to pain.

Seeing and hearing, on the other hand, are poorly developed at birth. The baby's eye muscles are weak, so he cannot coordinate his two eyes well on any object. The result is that he sees things in a blurred, indistinct fashion. Whether or not he sees color is still undecided, but the chances are that the baby is color-blind for at least the first month of life. Most infants are totally deaf for a few hours after birth. This deafness is caused by the stoppage of the middle ear with fluid

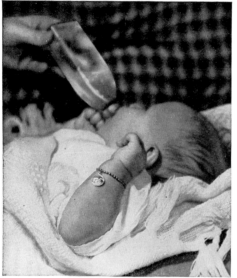

The newborn baby is truly helpless. He has no control over his movements; he cannot turn his body, sit up, or reach for an object. He cannot coordinate his eyes nor hear well. No wonder he must depend so completely on his parents.

COURTESY THE JAM HANDY ORGANIZATION, INC.

from the prenatal sac. As this fluid gradually drains out through the throat, hearing is improved.

Because of the relatively undeveloped sensitivities of the newborn, they are only partially conscious of the world in which they live. William James, the psychologist, pointed out many years ago that to the newborn, who can neither see well nor hear well, the world seems like "one great blooming, buzzing confusion." Most of the newborn baby's time is spent in sleep. He wakens only long enough to take nourishment and then falls off again into deep sleep.

For Discussion

1. What theories have you heard about controlling the sex of the child? How can you disprove these theories?

2. Give several reasons to explain why the phrase, "the helpless newborn infant," is correct.
3. How does scientific knowledge about heredity agree with the old saying about a "chip from the old block?"
4. What theories have you heard about twins?
5. What are the advantages and disadvantages of the constant contact of twins with each other, especially as they grow older?
6. If a baby cannot see clearly and distinctly during the early days of his life, what explanation is there for the fact that babies react differently to handling by different people?

Suggested Activities

1. Through your doctor, obtain permission to visit the maternity ward of a hospital. Observe the babies in their cribs and note how they differ physically one from another.
2. Listen to the cries of the newborn babies while you are observing them and see if you get any clues from the tones of their cries to help you understand why they are crying.
3. Observe their eyes, arms, and legs, noting how little control the baby has over them.
4. Make a list of theories you have heard about controlling sex in babies. Also make a list of theories you have heard about controlling heredity.
5. Observe the heads of newborn babies, noticing especially the shape of the head and the amount of hair. Try to find out, from the nurse in charge of the nursery, which are premature, Caesarean, and full-term. Is there any relationship between head shape, hair, and these factors of birth?
6. Visit a hospital nursery where prematurely born babies are kept in incubators. Contrast their appearance and behavior with that of full-term babies in the hospital nursery.

CHAPTER 3

Facts about Children

In spite of the fact that nearly everyone sees and meets thousands of children during a lifetime, few people really *understand* children. It is even questionable whether parents know very much about children in general. True, they learn about their own children from observing them in day-in and day-out living; but, since individual children differ so much, it would take the average person years of study to know the fundamental facts about all children.

Fortunately, the findings of scientists in their study of children give us a short cut to the understanding of children. From years of painstaking research in laboratories, schools, homes, and play yards, with thousands of children of all types at their disposal for study, scientists have learned what children are really like and, of even greater importance, what can be expected of children at different ages.

There are a few essential principles about children that will give you a basis for understanding most of the children you happen to meet. It is impossible, of course, to lay down any hard and fast rule that will apply equally well to all children. However, the principles found out as a result of scientific research will go a long way toward helping you to

COURTESY THE CENTAUR COMPANY

Very few people really understand children. Many mothers try to learn by the trial-and-error method. Is this fair to the child when science has already discovered so much about what children are really like and what can be expected of them at different ages?

handle most children successfully. This chapter is devoted to a discussion of these principles.

Children Are Children

For centuries it was believed that children were little men or little women—that is, that they were miniature adults. They were dressed and fed like adults and were expected to behave like adults. All you have to do to realize the faultiness of this belief is to look at a young child. If you try to visualize the child enlarged to adult size, you create an image that would be a freak of nature unlike any person you have ever seen.

It is equally illogical to assume that a child has the mental competence of an adult at a proportionally less degree because of his age. Mentally, the child is not a miniature adult

THE BETTMANN ARCHIVE

For centuries in the past, children were dressed like adults and were expected to act like miniature adults. Even today, many people expect grown-up behavior from children.

but a child. Every phase of his behavior reflects his childish mentality. He lacks foresight and judgment; he is impulsive; he is illogical in his reasoning; he has a parrotlike memory, with far less understanding of the meaning of what he remembers than most adults realize; and he is almost completely lacking in emotional control.

Why is it important to realize that children are children and not miniature adults? It is important because we should neither expect adult behavior from them nor judge them by adult standards. We must have different standards of behavior for children according to their ages, and reserve our adult standards for our judgments of adult behavior.

All Children Are Problem Children

There is no child who does not at some time become a problem for his parents, his teachers, or the members of the community in which he lives. A child becomes a problem because he wants to express his natural impulses in ways that are not accepted by society, about which he does not understand.

Many years ago, when life was simpler and families larger, the "problem child" was not so common as he is today. In a family group of six, eight, twelve, or more children, parents could not possibly see or hear all that went on. Unless the child did something especially naughty or troublesome, his acts would escape the attention of the busy mother.

But today, when the family is limited to two or three children, and the mother-child contact is closer, mothers see and hear things that, in the past, would have gone unnoticed. Often, what they see and hear does not please them. They interpret a child's actions as problem behavior and turn their attention to the correction of the young offender.

Furthermore, the tendency to regard children as miniature adults has resulted in judging children by adult standards. Naturally you could not expect children to show up well under such conditions. The only fair thing to do with children is to judge them by children's standards, which means standards for the child's own age.

All Children Are Different

From the moment of birth no two children look alike except identical twins. Because the physical make-up of children is different, it would be logical to suppose that their mental and temperamental make-ups would be different also. This is true partly because of a difference in heredity and partly because of a difference in environment. Even within the same family children are not alike physically, mentally, or temperamentally.

There are differences in boys and girls that are important to know about. Physically, boys and girls are different in appearance and in size. Boys at most ages are slightly larger

All children, even in the same family, are different. Brothers and sisters develop from different germ cells, and each germ cell carries within it different hereditary characteristics. Furthermore, the same environment has different effects on different people because our reactions to the same situation differ according to our make-up.

and heavier than girls of the same age. Girls, on the whole, have fewer illnesses than boys. There is a lower infant and child mortality rate among girls; girls have greater endurance; and girls fatigue less quickly, although boys have greater physical strength. Girls, as a rule, have greater muscular control and coordination and can acquire skills involving the small muscles more easily than boys can.

So far as general intelligence is concerned, there are no real sex differences. There are dull boys and bright boys, just as there are dull girls and bright girls. But girls seem to have better memories and better control of language than boys, while boys surpass girls in reasoning ability and mathematical skills. These differences are probably the result of different emphasis in schooling, but they are universal enough to be considered usual.

One can find sex differences in temperament also. Girls are required to exert more emotional control than boys. For the most part, they are more law-abiding and easier to control. Once again, these differences are probably environmental. From earliest childhood girls are kept more closely under parental supervision than are their brothers. Therefore, their behavior is more regulated by adult standards.

Importance of Individual Differences

Why do we emphasize the fact that children are different? Because we must not expect any set of rules to work with all children. What proves to be effective in controlling the behavior of one child may prove to be a total failure when applied to another child. The most you can hope to do is to know what to expect, in a general way, for children of different sex and age and then to study each child individually to see just how he differs from other children of his age.

Growth Follows a Pattern

Studies of large numbers of children, year after year from birth to late childhood, reveal that growth does not take place in a haphazard, chance fashion but rather that it follows an orderly, predictable pattern. In some children the pattern unfolds more quickly or more slowly than in others, but marked similarity is always apparent.

The reason for this orderly pattern of growth is that *maturation*, or the natural unfolding of traits inherent in the child, is somewhat set. The environment in which a child grows in-

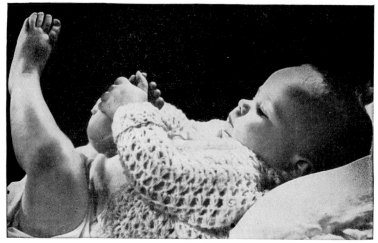

The baby shows an interest in his own body before he shows an interest in other people. This stage, like all other stages of growth, is part of a well-set pattern of development which takes place in all babies.

fluences only to a limited extent the speed with which this unfolding occurs. Naturally, favorable conditions in the environment make the maturation period easier, while unfavorable conditions may tend to make it more difficult.

The pattern of development is the natural foundation for all learning. You cannot expect a child to learn a given task until he is ready for it—that is, until the natural foundation is laid. In the case of walking, for example, a child cannot learn to take steps until he has developed enough so that he is able to support his body in an upright position.

How can we know when a child is ready to learn? The child's own interest in an activity is the best indication of his readiness to learn. Interest and ability go hand in hand. When a child begins to show an interest in some activity, such as

A child is not ready to learn a new activity until he shows an interest in it, for interest and ability go hand in hand. The child who is taught something before he is ready will establish unfavorable attitudes that will handicap his development and interfere with learning when he is ready for it.

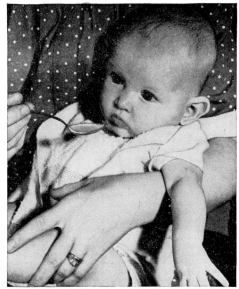

COURTESY H. J. HEINZ COMPANY

feeding or dressing himself, it means that his development has reached the level where it is possible for him to carry out that activity without too much strain or effort. This is the time to begin teaching him the activity.

Why Is a Pattern of Development Important?

The reason for emphasizing the seriousness of proper learning time is that children may suffer certain consequences from being forced or held back in the learning of any activity. Children who have been forced to do things before they were ready are either retarded unduly in their learning or establish unfavorable attitudes of fear, timidity, or even anger and disgust at their failure. Thus, further handicaps are developed to interfere with the child's ability to learn.

It is almost as bad to hold back a child as it is to try to

force him ahead. Many adults make this mistake unsuspectingly, either because they do not realize that the child can do the very things for himself that they insist upon doing for him or because they feel that the child is so slow and inefficient that they can do it better for him.

As the Twig Is Bent

Childhood is the foundation period of the individual's life. The early years are truly critical ones in the life span of an individual because it is during these years that the pattern of the child's future development—physical, mental, temperamental, and moral—is established. The old Chinese proverb, "Just as the twig is bent the tree's inclined," is so true in the case of a child's development that if you remember it you will never make the mistake of believing that a child will "outgrow" undesirable traits as he grows older.

As a matter of fact, undesirable traits, like desirable traits, become more firmly established with each succeeding month of the child's life. In time they become so firmly set that changing them is a very difficult task. For this reason a young child needs constant guidance and supervision to guarantee that the pattern being established shall be a desirable one—one that will prove useful to the child in the future as well as acceptable to the social group to which he belongs.

Every Child Needs Guidance

Allowing a young child to do much as he pleases, with minimum guidance and control, is mistaken kindness. No child has the worldly wisdom or experience necessary to know how he should direct his energies or how he should behave. He needs guidance and direction by those who have learned what society expects and what society will not tolerate. Only in this way can he learn how to control his natural impulses so that his behavior will conform to the standards set by the group to which he belongs.

Because the early years of life are the years when the pattern of behavior is set, they may be regarded as the "foundation years" of the individual's life. Like the foundation of a house, they must be firmly established in the right way if they are to stand the test of time. Weak foundations of buildings soon crumble and the buildings collapse when a real test of strength arises, such as a fire or a flood, which tend to undermine the foundations. Individuals who "crack up" in adolescence or maturity invariably have a life history that shows faulty training in the early years.

A Poor Start Is Serious

Poor foundations should be uncovered and rebuilt on a better basis as soon as their imperfections are apparent. No builder would be so foolish as to continue with the superstructure of a building when he knows that the foundation is of poor quality and might at any time crumble under the weight of the superstructure. The same common-sense point of view should be taken in regard to the building of a human character. As soon as an undesirable trait makes its appearance, it should be eradicated.

The importance of the early years of childhood as the foundation years of life is well illustrated in the many cases of poorly adjusted adult personalities. The petulant, spoiled woman who pouts or sheds tears when she cannot have her own way was a petulant, spoiled child who dominated her family by bursting into tears whenever she could not get what she wanted. The miserly man, as a boy, had the reputation among his friends of being a "sponge." The happy-go-lucky man, liked by everyone but unable to keep a job, is remembered by his friends as a carefree, happy-go-lucky boy who was liked by everyone in spite of his irresponsible ways.

These undesirable traits could have been changed, of course, had the individuals wanted to do so and had they been willing to exert the necessary effort to bring about the change. Each year, as traits become more and more firmly established through repetition, making the change becomes increasingly difficult. That is why it is so important to spot traits that may later prove to be a handicap to the individual and to give the child the necessary encouragement to substitute more desirable traits to replace the undesirable ones.

For Discussion

1. Give examples of situations, such as naughtiness or stealing, in which the young child's point of view about the matter differed greatly from the adult's. Suggest ways in which the adult might have been able to understand the child's point of view and explain why this is much fairer to the child.
2. Illustrate individual differences in children by showing how differently they react to the same situations, such as the receipt of a gift, the demonstration of affection, or reproach for naughtiness.
3. Give examples of behavior that is found almost universally in normal children and yet is commonly labeled "problem behavior" by adults.
4. Discuss tactful methods that might be used to impress upon parents the importance of well-planned guidance of their children's lives during the formative years of childhood.
5. What evidences have you to show that all children follow much the same pattern of development?
6. How would you go about helping a child to eliminate some form of behavior, such as selfishness, which you know will prove to be a handicap to him as he grows older?

Suggested Activities

1. Measure the different parts of your body—head, arms, legs, and trunk—and see what proportions they are of your total body length. Then do the same for a young child. See how this disproves the theory that children are "miniature adults," at least as far as their physical make-up is concerned.

2. The next time a young child in your home, on the playground, or on the street does something that is naughty or rude, talk to him kindly and sympathetically to see if you can find out what his reason was for behaving in that manner. You will doubtless be surprised to learn that, from his point of view, his behavior seemed perfectly justified and right.

3. Think back to your own childhood and see if some of the outstanding traits you now possess, such as selfishness or unselfishness, bravery or cowardice, generosity or stinginess, were present then. Perhaps your parents could help you to judge by telling you some of the things you did as a young child.

4. Observe the family groups—children, parents, and grandparents—of your acquaintances. Note that some children resemble one side of the family, some the other. You will be surprised at how different they are. Then observe groups of children of the same age who are not related and see how different they, too, are in their general appearance.

5. Select a young child's toy, such as a stuffed animal, and offer it to different children individually. Watch their reactions to see if their behavior is similar or different in the same situation.

6. Observe the furnishings of the home in relation to the size of young children and of adults. Note how the child has difficulty in manipulating doors, drawers, etc. Could this, in part, explain some of the so-called "problem behavior" of young children?

PART TWO:

James Chapin

The Child's Growth

CHAPTER 4

How a Child Grows

Physical and mental growth are interrelated. Slow physical growth is generally accompanied by slow mental development, and with rapid physical growth there is generally precocious mental development. Also, poor health during the growing period not only stunts physical growth but also affects unfavorably the child's mental growth and the development of his personality.

A good physical condition with a minimum of illness, on the other hand, enables the child to grow normally and with a better chance for a well-rounded personality. If, in addition, his environment is favorable, the healthy child has a good chance of growing up to be a well-adjusted adult.

The lithograph opposite, which is called *Little Girl with Doll,* was done by James Chapin. Although the artist is best known for his portraits, this picture could be almost any little girl. By making the drawing simple, the artist has caught the simplicity of a four-year-old with her favorite doll. (Courtesy Associated American Artists.)

Pattern of Growth

Physical growth follows a definite, predictable pattern that is marked by spurts and rest periods. At no time is growth even and regular, nor do all parts of the body grow simultaneously. When the child is growing in height, for example, his increase in weight is slight. At the time when his internal organs are experiencing a growth spurt, his external features remain relatively unchanged. This *pattern* of growth is much the same for all children, although there may be individual differences in the rate of development among different children.

The pattern of growth for boys is slightly different from that of girls. At every age, boys are slightly heavier and taller than girls until around twelve or thirteen years, when girls temporarily spurt ahead of boys. On the average, girls cut their teeth sooner than boys; and, at adolescence, girls mature sexually sooner than boys do.

Intelligence seems to affect the pattern of growth. Dull children are likely to be slower in their growth rate than children of average intelligence, while bright children are likely to spurt ahead of those who are average in intelligence.

Height and Weight

The first year of life is marked by phenomenal increases in both height and weight. During the baby's first year, he experiences a 50 percent increase in height so that at one year he has an average height of twenty-eight to thirty inches. After the first year, his growth in height slows down to an average gain of three to five inches annually. By the fifth or sixth year, the child's height should be more than twice what it was at birth, or forty-three to forty-five inches.

Increases in weight are even greater than those in height

HEIGHT AND WEIGHT GAINS
DURING FIRST YEAR

By the end of the first year, the baby should have increased 50 percent in height. The average height of babies at birth is nineteen to twenty inches. Therefore, by their first birthday most babies are from twenty-eight to thirty inches tall.

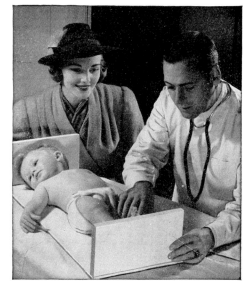

Increases in weight during the baby's first year are even greater than those in height. The birth weight is doubled at the end of four or five months, and by the time the baby is a year old his weight is about three times what it was at birth.

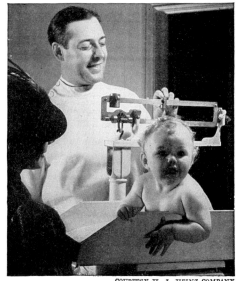

during the first six years of the child's life. By the time the average baby is four to five months old, his birth weight should have doubled; and, by the end of the first year, he should weigh three times what he weighed at birth. Between the first and sixth years the child normally increases in weight only four or five pounds a year. By his sixth birthday, therefore, he should be at least six times as heavy as he was at birth. Many children show even more pronounced gains than this average pattern.

Body Proportions

It is frequently said that the young child spends his time "growing legs." This implies that the most noticeable growth is in the trunk and legs, or the lower part of the body. Of course, the child grows all over but not in the same proportion.

The upper part of his head, or the "brain region," is much too big for the childish face with its small mouth and teeth. When a young child wears anything but a cap or a hat with a small, upturned brim, the overlarge head is even further exaggerated. This gives him a somewhat ridiculous appearance. The absence of neck during the first year of life makes his head appear to be sitting on his shoulders. Gradually his neck develops, and his head is in better proportion to the rest of his body.

The narrow shoulders and protruding abdomen of the little baby also change in time. The shoulders become broader, and the abdominal region becomes flatter. Throughout the early childhood years, however, a healthy child who eats well always has a rounded "tummy," which is especially pronounced after eating a hearty meal.

The small, spindly, crooked legs and thin arms of the

newborn baby grow longer, straighter, and chubbier during the first two years of life. Not until adolescence, however, will arms and legs seem long enough for the rest of the body or have any real shape. The tiny hands and feet of the infant grow bigger early in babyhood. The fingers and toes length-en, the palms broaden, and the feet get bigger both in length and width. Increases in the size of the feet neces-sitate a change in shoe size every three or four months. The young child's foot is flat, with no semblance of arch to it. Therefore, it looks even larger than it ac-tually is. Actually, it is still small for the size of the child's body and the weight that it must support.

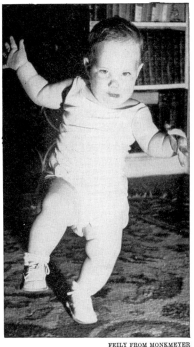

FEILY FROM MONKMEYER

Babies often appear clumsy. This is because the child's body is out of proportion and because his muscles do not work in coordination.

Significance of Body Proportions

The effects of the disproportions of the young child's body are very far-reaching. Top-heaviness makes it difficult for the young child to control his body. The result is that he topples over easily when he sits, stands, walks, or runs. What appears to be clumsiness is not traceable to poor muscular control alone but also to the fact that too much weight is in the upper part of the body.

Small hands, like small feet, contribute to clumsiness. A young child's hands are neither large enough nor strong enough to hold on to heavy objects. Add to this the fact that he has far less control over his muscles than an adult has, and you will readily understand why he drops and breaks things so frequently. When a child throws or catches a ball, his small hands and weak muscles handicap him. Not only is he unable to throw the ball straight, but he cannot hold the ball or catch it without dropping it.

Children's Bones

At birth the infant's bones are more like cartilage or gristle than like bones. Gradually, throughout childhood, they harden, provided the child's diet contains an adequate supply of mineral salts. This hardening, or "ossification," begins shortly after birth and ends just before puberty.

The soft texture of a young child's bones is very apparent in the "soft spots," or fontanelles, on the baby's skull. The largest and easiest fontanelle to observe is on the top of the head. These soft spots in the bones of the head allow for the rapid growth of the brain in the early months of life when the need for protection of the brain tissue underneath is not so great as it is later on as the child becomes more active. By the age of eighteen months, the child's fontanelles are closed, and by two years nearly all of them are well hardened. The closings of fontanelles occur somewhat sooner in girls than in boys.

There are two significant facts that should be borne in mind about the bones of young children. First, breaks in bones mend rapidly; second, soft bones are easily misshapen. Young children who are active have many falls,

No adult could possibly get himself into the position that a baby can, because a baby's bones are soft like cartilage or gristle. For this reason, his injuries mend rapidly. On the other hand, because his bones are soft, they can be easily misshapen if too much pressure is put upon them.

FREDERIC LEWIS

often from high places. They have less caution than older children or adults; they take many chances; and they often hurt themselves.

Notice the strange positions a young child can get into and you will realize how soft his bones really are. He can literally bend in two or roll himself into a ball.

The softness of the bones which produces this body elasticity also makes it possible for the bones to be misshapen readily if too much pressure is placed on them. A baby who is permitted to lie on his back for too long a time may de-

velop a flat head instead of a head that is slightly rounded in
the back. Shoes that are too short will throw the child's feet
out of shape. Sleeping on a pillow may produce a slight
curvature of the neck. Poor posture when sitting or standing
may cause slight curvatures of the spine that become set as
time progresses.

The Child's Teeth

The teeth are a part of the bone formation of the body
and, like bones, are soft at first. The early teeth, generally
called the "milk" or "baby" teeth, are twenty in number.
They are small in size, soft in texture, and have small, shal-
low roots; so, therefore, they frequently decay before they
are replaced by permanent teeth.

The first baby tooth starts to form during the third or
fourth month of pregnancy, but it usually does not erupt
until the baby is six months old. Here is a table showing the
approximate ages at which the baby teeth are cut.

Ages at Which the Baby Cuts His Teeth

ORDER OF APPEARANCE	AGE
Two middle lower incisors	6 to 8 months
Four upper incisors	8 to 12 months
Two lateral lower incisors	12 to 15 months
Four first molars	12 to 15 months
Four canines	18 to 20 months
Four second molars	24 to 30 months

It is frequently said that bright children cut their teeth
earlier than dull children. While there are some cases in
which this is true, there is not enough evidence to make sure
that it is generally true. The child's health and diet are important factors in determining how quickly the teeth will
appear. If the young child is healthy, has a well-balanced

Between the ages of six months and two years, the child is cutting his teeth. No way has yet been found to reduce the painfulness of this experience for the baby. During this period he is likely to have a fever, indigestion, and loss of appetite and to be listless and fretful.

diet, and is average or above average in intelligence, the chances are that he will cut his teeth sooner than if any one or more of these factors is neglected.

Sometimes teething is accompanied by fever, digestive upsets, loss of appetite, colds, or earaches. Even without any of these disturbances, the baby will not feel up to par but will be listless or fretful. He does not sleep as well as usual, his appetite is poor, and he shows less interest in his surroundings than usual. Once the gum has been pierced and the tooth can be seen, however, he begins to be normal and spirited.

The important thing to remember about teething is the effect it has on a baby's disposition. When he is not feeling well, he is fretful and irritable; nothing pleases him, and he shows his displeasure by rebelling against anything and everything. If he cannot have just what he wants, he cries.

Primary Sensory Experiences

The sense organs of the child are, in many respects, different from those of an adult. As a consequence, his sensory experiences are different. While his eyes are well developed, the muscles that attach the eyes to their sockets are weak. As a result, too much use of his eyes for close vision causes eyestrain and fatigue. Soon this fatigue becomes general.

Eyestrain shows its effects in listlessness and irritability. For this reason, young children should not be permitted or encouraged to concentrate for too long a time on any activity that requires close vision. Nor should they be permitted to do more than glance at small print, small pictures, or objects with small detail work.

The young child's hearing is very acute except when there is some hereditary ear defect or inflammation from a nasal cold. Sometimes what appears to be poor hearing is merely inattention. Inflammation of the ear from a cold may cause discomfort and poor hearing for a few days. Defective hearing should be checked with the doctor as soon as apparent and not neglected. A ruptured eardrum will not cause deafness if detected in time and properly treated.

Other Sensory Experiences

The child's skin has the same number of sense organs for touch, pain, and temperature as an adult's skin, but the child's skin is thinner. Therefore, the child feels pain, touch, and temperature stimuli more keenly than an adult does.

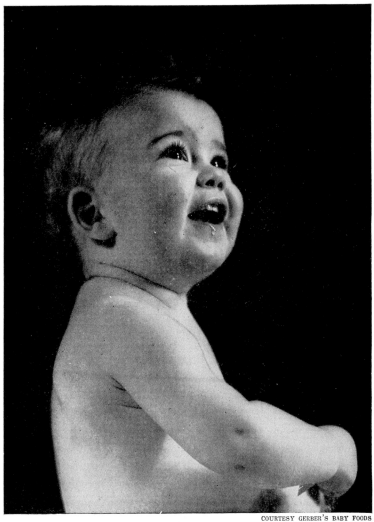

COURTESY GERBER'S BABY FOODS

A healthy child is happy and active; he has a good appetite and sleeps well. His skin is clear; his eyes sparkle. He has enough fat to cover his bones. His hair is glossy and grows fast. His fingernails and toenails are strong enough not to break. If a child has these qualities, you may be sure he is healthy.

The child's "taste buds" are not only found on the surface of the tongue, as they are in adulthood, but they also line the insides of the cheeks. This makes the child very sensitive to the taste of whatever he puts in his mouth.

Much of our taste also comes from smell, and the child can smell better than the adult can. The hairy network that lines the nasal cavities of an adult, keeping smell stimuli from penetrating to the sense cells at the base of the nose, is absent in the child's nose.

The significance of the child's keener sense of taste is that he dislikes many foods because the tastes are too strong for him. Food cooked to suit the taste of an adult often proves to be unpleasant to a child, and, as a result, the child refuses it.

Children's Diseases

Illness in childhood is more frequent than at any other time in life, even for healthy children. It is most unusual for a year to pass without having a child experience some sickness, even if it be only minor in nature. For the first four to six months of life the child has a period of immunity to disease. After that, most young children have their ups-and-downs.

Colds, earaches, upset stomachs, and such children's diseases as mumps, German measles, and chicken pox are fairly common among children. Some young children may become anemic. Many children may have slight skin infections, rashes, and sties. Most children have innumerable bruises, scratches, cuts, burns, and insect bites.

Illness in childhood need not be serious if the child is in a good physical condition when the illness occurs and if prompt treatment is given. Unfortunately, many adults believe that because they, as adults, get over a minor illness without going to bed and calling a doctor, the child will recover with equally little attention.

However, this is not always true. A minor illness in childhood may develop very rapidly into a serious illness with many complications unless prompt treatment is given. What appears at first to be merely a slight case of "sniffles," for example, may, in several days, turn into an earache so severe as to necessitate calling in an ear specialist to puncture the eardrum. Likewise, a slight temperature in the morning may run to alarming heights by midafternoon.

Psychological Effects of Illness

Illness necessitates a change in the young child's routine. He sleeps and wakens when he feels like it, whether in the middle of the day or night. His environment is restricted to his room. He must rest quietly in bed or be propped up in a chair. Consequently, his play must be restricted to whatever activities he can carry on without moving around.

As a precaution, other children are not permitted to play with him, and he must rely upon himself or the adults of the household for amusement. This break in his well-established routine soon becomes monotonous, and he is likely to become fretful and irritable. As he recovers, he is increasingly annoyed by the restraints imposed upon him.

The child's attitude changes as illness forces a change in his behavior. He demands more attention than usual; he finds that he can have his own way if he frets and cries because his mother is afraid that fretting and crying may make him worse; and he discovers that naughtiness is not punished as it is when he is well.

If he does not feel well, he is waited on and amused. In fact, his every whim is satisfied. All this adds up to one

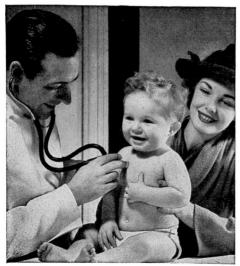

Babies should have fre-
quent checkups by the
doctor so as to discover
any hidden defects. Of
course, parents should
call the doctor as soon
as there is a sign of
something being wrong
with the baby, because
children can develop
serious illnesses quickly
from what seems to be
a minor complaint.

COURTESY H. J. HEINZ COMPANY

serious fact—namely, that he is being "spoiled." Even after a
short illness, it will take time for a young child to return to
normal and to assume a healthier attitude about himself and
his relation to the group.

Minor Defects

There are few young children who do not have one or more
minor defects at some time during the early years of life.
These are often regarded as too trivial to bother about and,
as a result, are neglected. Frequently, defects that seem
minor at first become serious if nothing is done to check or
cure them.

The most common of the minor defects that occur in early
childhood are (1) defective vision, which causes the child to
squint, complain of headaches, or be unable to see what other
people see; (2) defective hearing, which shows itself in the

child's turning his head to one side when he listens or in asking for a repetition of what has been said; (3) diseased tonsils, which lead to severe sore throats accompanied by high fever; (4) enlarged adenoids, which make it difficult for the child to breathe with his mouth closed or to pronounce his words without a nasal sound; (5) skin eruptions, such as pimples, hives, or boils; and (6) sties or other eye infections.

Some defects are difficult to diagnose and, consequently, are often overlooked. Among these are (1) anemia, which is accompanied by pallor of the skin and a more or less constant listlessness with a tendency to complain of being "tired"; (2) allergies to different foods or inhalants, which lead to the sudden appearance of hives, nausea, heavy breathing, sneezing, swelling of the eyes, and running of the nose; (3) excessive skinniness in spite of a good appetite; and (4) a tendency to obesity, even when the diet is moderate and relatively free from fattening foods.

For Discussion

1. When a young child is consistently quieter than the other children of his age and seems to take little interest in their play, how would you proceed to discover if this condition is the result of poor health or of environmental restraints?
2. Suggest practical ways of dealing with the self-consciousness that accompanies being overweight or underweight, taller or shorter than other children of the same age.
3. What arguments can you give for and against having children's diseases in childhood rather than at a later age?
4. How can one deal with the common parental attitude that the child will outgrow minor defects?
5. When a child is small for his age, should he be encouraged to play with children of his own age or with children of his own size, even though they may be younger than he? Give reasons for your answer.

6. What methods can be used to eliminate the discomforts and disturbances that accompany teething? How effective are they and how do they affect the baby's behavior?

Suggested Activities

1. Select three or four children of different ages—one, two, three, and five years old, for example—and make the following measurements: (a) width of step; (b) length of step; (c) chart of teeth; (d) head circumference; (e) strength of grip (measured by squeezing a rubber ball or an orange). Then compare the results obtained for the children of the different ages.

2. Observe a child when he is ill or not feeling well and when he is healthy. Make a list of characteristic symptoms for the healthy and for the unhealthy states.

3. Make a list of home remedies you have heard of for such common childish ailments as colds, croup, hives, sties, tummy-ache, etc.

4. From your parents and grandparents collect information about common childhood diseases in their day. Then compare this with the common childhood diseases of today.

5. Collect information on present medical methods of controlling childhood diseases—such as measles, chicken pox, scarlet fever, etc.—that most children of past generations had.

6. Observe a baby and a preschool child. From their appearance and behavior, try to rate their general health conditions. Then compare your ratings with their parents' and teachers' reports about them.

CHAPTER 5

Feeding and Clothing the Child

Two important phases of child care relate to feeding and dressing. Radical changes in both of these have occurred during the past twenty-five years. This has resulted in a conflict of views between parents of the older generation and parents of the new. Many a grandmother of today is heard to say, "When you were a baby, I did this or that, and you grew up to be a healthy person."

This conflict of views has raised doubts in the minds of many parents as to whether the new methods may not be just newfangled ideas. Because of these doubts, the reasons for the new methods will be presented in the hopes of justifying their superiority over older methods.

Feeding a Newborn Baby

Within twelve hours after delivery, the newborn baby is put to the mother's breast. The nourishment he gets at first is not milk but "colostrum," a yellowish secretion from the breasts. It takes from three to five days before milk begins to flow from the mother's breasts. Until then the newborn baby receives scanty nourishment and loses anywhere from several ounces to a pound of weight. On the baby's first day,

The advantages of breast-feeding over bottle-feeding are so many that every mother should try to nurse her baby. The mother's milk agrees better with the baby than does a formula and contains ingredients that are beneficial to the health of the baby. In breast-feeding, the baby also develops, through exercise, the muscles of the lower part of the face.

PETER BASCH

he should be nursed for approximately five to ten minutes at four different intervals. From that time on, he should be nursed about every four hours. A bottle may be substituted for the 2 A.M. feeding so the mother can rest at night.

The advantages of breast-feeding are so great that all new-born babies should be nursed if the mother's condition will allow it. However, whether a baby is breast-fed or bottle-fed, the mother should have a relaxed and loving attitude.

Breast-feeding is advantageous to the mother because the stimulation of her breasts through sucking helps to speed up

CHARLES PHELPS CUSHING

One way to find out whether or not the baby is getting adequate nourishment from the breast is to put him on the scale just before and just after he is nursed.

the normal return of the uterus to its former size and condition. It also removes the fluids formed by the glands in the breasts. If the baby is not nursed, the breasts become painful until the secretions are pumped out by a breast pump. Breast-feeding eliminates the time- and energy-consuming job of sterilizing bottles and making a formula. Finally, breast-feeding eliminates any possibility of contamination.

From the infant's point of view, the value of breast-feeding is first and foremost the fact that the mother's milk not only agrees better with the healthy infant than does a formula but it also contains certain ingredients beneficial to health and growth that are never completely duplicated in a formula. Digestive disturbances and constipation are rare for the breast-fed baby but rather common when bottle-feeding is used. The vigorous sucking needed to draw the milk through the nipple of the mother's breast gives exercise to the muscles of the tongue, cheeks, lips, and pharynx which, in turn, stimulate the development of the bones of the jaws, mouth, and nose. This helps greatly in the development of the lower part of the baby's face.

Bottle-feeding

There are many cases in which it is impossible, for one reason or another, for the mother to nurse her baby. If she works outside the home, for example, it is not practical for her to try to nurse the baby at the times of the day when she can be at home. The best plan for such a mother to follow is to put the baby on the bottle at least a week before she is ready to resume her work. This will give her time to see whether the formula used in the bottle-feeding agrees with the baby and, if not, she should change it until it does. A mother who remains at home may have to abandon nursing her baby because of an illness or because her milk gives out as a result of fatigue from overwork or emotional tension. Many mothers today who are unable to nurse their babies worry about it. But there is no reason to believe that a baby cannot be healthy and normal if he is bottle-fed, provided the mother gives the baby the affection that should accompany feeding.

Is Bottle-feeding Necessary?

Before supplementing breast-feeding with a formula, or before substituting the bottle for the breast, two approaches to the problem should be used to determine whether or not the baby is getting enough nourishment from the breast. The first approach is to see how much milk the baby takes at each feeding, and the second is to see how much weight he gains from day to day or from week to week. It is easy enough to find out how much milk the baby gets when he is on the bottle but difficult when he is being breast-fed. The length of time a baby sucks in feeding from the breast is no indication whatsoever of the amount of milk he has swallowed. One quick and easy way to know how much milk the baby is getting from the breast is to put him on the baby scale just before he is nursed and again immediately afterward—always with exactly the same clothing on at both weighings.

Roughly, the amount of milk required by a young baby at each feeding at different ages is as follows:

AGE	AMOUNT
1 week	1 to 1½ ounces
2 weeks	2 to 3 ounces
1 month	3 to 5 ounces
2 months	4 to 6 ounces
3 months	4 to 6 ounces
4 to 6 months	5 to 7 ounces

These amounts, of course, are only rough estimates since no two babies have exactly the same requirements. However, when the scales show, for example, that a one-month-old baby is getting only two ounces of milk from both breasts, it is obvious that he is not getting enough and that a supplementary feeding from a bottle must be given. When the milk from both breasts is consistently an ounce or less, even after every possible effort is made to increase the supply, then breast-feedings should be abandoned entirely, for the baby is not getting enough nourishment from the mother's milk to make it worth while to continue nursing him.

The second criterion to use in determining whether or not

bottle-feeding should supplement or take the place of breast-feeding is the baby's gain in weight and his behavior between nursing periods. The weekly gain in weight for babies under two months of age should be, roughly, from four to six ounces; and babies from two to four months old should gain six to eight ounces weekly. When the baby's gain is less than this, it is time to consider seriously whether breast-feeding is adequate. If he wakens and cries for a half-hour or more before his next feeding period, he is not receiving adequate nourishment.

The Baby's Formula

No one formula is necessarily satisfactory for all babies, nor do all doctors agree on a "standard" formula which they prescribe with slight variations for different babies. Some doctors prefer fresh milk for the baby's formula, some prescribe a formula based on evaporated milk, and others use powdered milk, especially when the parents are traveling or living in an area where it is difficult to get evaporated milk or safe fresh milk. If a baby has difficulties with a formula made with fresh, evaporated, or powdered milk, lactic acid or sour milk may be prescribed in place of other milks.

All formulas for young babies contain some sweetening. While ordinary granulated sugar is most commonly used, sometimes doctors prescribe brown sugar, corn syrup, dextrin and maltose preparations, or lactose. Which form of sweetening to be used should be determined by the doctor to meet the individual needs of the baby.

As most babies thrive on simple formulas, many doctors today prescribe complicated formulas only when a baby is not able to adjust to the simpler formulas. The usual formula for a baby consists of milk, water, and sugar. The amounts of water and sugar are gradually decreased as the baby grows older and is able to take milk alone. This is generally when he is six or seven months old.

A simple formula that meets the needs of most young babies is made as follows:

Evaporated milk............4 ounces
Water ....8 ounces
Sugar ....1 tablespoon (level)

or

Whole milk................8 ounces
Water ....4 ounces
Sugar ....1 tablespoon (level)[1]

This amount may be divided into six bottles of about two ounces each or eight bottles with about one and a half ounces, depending upon how frequently the doctor recommends feeding the baby. When the baby is no longer satisfied with these small feedings, the amounts in this formula may be doubled and later tripled. A baby usually needs for each twenty-four hours from two to three ounces of this formula for every pound of his weight.

Any change in the baby's formula should be made only after consulting the doctor. You should never attempt to change the formula yourself. By doing so, your baby may not get enough nourishment or you may upset his digestion.

Preparation of the Formula

In preparing the baby's formula, the following method may be used: Carefully wash bottles and nipples in warm water and soap; then thoroughly rinse them in hot water. Also thoroughly wash and rinse mixing pitcher, glass measuring pitcher, measuring spoon, funnel, and rubber caps for the bottles. Use special brushes for washing bottles and nipples

[1] This formula has been recommended in *Infant Care,* Children's Bureau, Washington, D.C., 1955.

BOTTLING THE FORMULA

1) The formula should be poured into the bottle through a funnel and a sieve—both of which have been sterilized along with the other equipment by boiling for several minutes.

2) After the formula has been poured into the bottles, they should be covered by a rubber cap and allowed to stand for half an hour until cool. Then they should be placed in the refrigerator until time for use.

COURTESY DAVOL RUBBER COMPANY

Shortly before feeding time a bottle may be heated in an electric bottle warmer or in a pan of hot water. The flame should be turned off before the bottle is placed in the water. The rubber cap should be replaced by the nipple before the bottle is heated. If the milk feels pleasantly warm when shaken on the mother's wrist, it is just right for the baby.

to help remove all particles of milk that may have caked on them. Then sterilize them by boiling for several minutes. Remove them from the boiling water, and place them on towels that have been sterilized by boiling after each using. The tops of the milk can or bottle should be washed with hot water before opening.

First, measure the boiling water carefully with the measuring pitcher and pour it into the mixing pitcher. Into this boiling water then pour, in order, the sugar and the milk. After the ingredients have been stirred together, the formula is ready for bottling. If the baby is on a four-hour feeding schedule, six bottles should be prepared. Divide the formula equally by pouring it into the six bottles through the funnel and sieve. Put a rubber stopper or bottle cap on each bottle and allow the bottles to stand for about half an hour until they are cool. After that, place them in the refrigerator until time for use. The full day's supply can be made at one time and, if done systematically, requires about thirty minutes.

After sterilizing the nipples, put them in a sterilized glass jar and cover until feeding time. It is wise to have several extra nipples just in case you run short. After many boilings the holes in nipples sometimes become smaller, and, when the baby tries to suck, he cannot draw the milk through the holes. Instead of taking time to enlarge the holes when preparing the formula, change the nipple and fix the holes after the feeding period. The best way to enlarge the holes in a nipple is to sterilize a needle with a lighted match and, while the needle is still hot, insert it in the holes, moving it slightly from side to side. If the holes become too large, the nipples should be thrown away, as large holes permit the baby to get too much milk too quickly, thus choking him or causing "bubbles."

Shortly before feeding time, heat the bottle in an electric bottle warmer or in a pan of hot water. The fire should not be turned on while the bottle is in the water, and the water should not be too hot. Before the bottle is heated, remove the rubber cap and put the nipple on the bottle. It is important to test the milk's temperature before giving it to the baby. The safest way to ensure right temperature is to shake several drops of milk on your own wrist. If the milk is pleasantly warm to you, it will be right for the baby.

Bubbling

Whether babies get their milk through the nipple of a bottle or from the mother's breast, they tend to swallow air. This frequently occurs also when they cry. Swallowed air makes a baby uncomfortable. The swallowed air takes up room in his stomach, and hence, after eating, he becomes un-

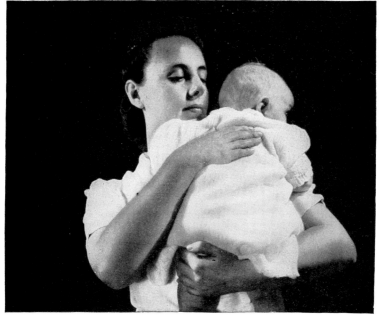

COURTESY DAVOL RUBBER COMPANY

The best way to bubble a baby is to place a towel or clean diaper over the shoulder. Hold the baby in an upright position against the shoulder, with his face toward your back and his head over your shoulder, and gently pat his back until he "burps."

comfortably "full." Unless something is done to remove the air, the discomfort continues, and digestive pains occur. Sometimes the milk comes up again, and the baby becomes hungry long before his next feeding period.

The best way to bubble a baby is to place a towel or clean diaper over the shoulder, just in case some milk should come up with the swallowed air. Then hold the baby in an upright position against the protected shoulder, with his face toward your back and his head over your shoulder, and gently pat his

back until he "burps." It may take only a few minutes to bring
up the air, or it may take ten or fifteen minutes. It is never
safe to put a baby under three months of age down to sleep
until at least a faint burp is heard. After the baby is three
months old, he will cooperate in the "bubbling," and by the
time he is five or six months old, he will have learned how to
burp by himself so that the bubbling can be discontinued.

If a baby slows down in his eating soon after he begins to
eat, it is a good idea to bubble him then. The slowing down
may be the result of an uncomfortably full feeling that comes
from swallowing air in his zeal to get nourishment quickly.
Some mothers find it helpful to bubble the baby before the
feeding period begins, in the middle of the period, and again
at the end.

Foods in Addition to Milk

In the days of our grandmothers, it was a common practice
to feed babies exclusively on breast milk or a formula until
after the "second summer." For many babies, this meant that
the diet for the first year of life was exclusively milk. While it
is true that milk is generally regarded as the perfect food because it contains all the necessary chemicals for growth and
physical well-being, doctors of today are agreed that before
the second year the baby's diet should include foods other
than milk.

Today, by the time the baby is two weeks old, it is custom-
ary to give him orange juice. At first, a small amount, diluted
with water, is put into a bottle and heated just as the formula
is. Gradually, less water is used and more orange juice. When
the baby is a month old, he should have at least one teaspoon
of orange juice daily. Each month after that, the daily intake
is increased by one or more teaspoons until the baby gets the
juice of one good-sized orange daily.

It is frequently necessary to add some starch to the baby's formula even before he is given his cereal if his formula does not have enough sustaining quality to carry him from one feeding to the next. Barley flour is generally used in the formula because it is an easily digested form of starch. It should not be given to a baby, however, without consulting the doctor first for his advice as to how much to add to the formula.

Beef juice, made by searing a piece of top sirloin on both sides and extracting the juice with a meat press, may be added to the daily diet of a baby when he is two to three months old. At first, only one teaspoonful is given, but this amount may gradually be increased. At the same time, vegetable juices, made from straining steamed vegetables—such as peas, carrots, beets, or tomatoes—or unseasoned tomato juice, may be introduced in small quantities.

Very thin cereal, diluted with milk, may also be given in small quantities. Many doctors also recommend feeding a three-month-old baby a spoonful or two of soft-cooked egg or part of the yolk of a hard-cooked egg put through a sieve and mixed with milk. This is given on alternate days instead of beef juice. At this age, all foods other than milk should be fed to the baby with a spoon to accustom him to eating by other methods than sucking. Likewise, the vegetables should gradually be made of a thicker consistency.

By the time a baby is four months old, his midday feeding should include one vegetable, put through a sieve and, if necessary, diluted with water or milk; beef juice or egg; and milk. One or two teaspoons of the solid foods are all that he should have until he is five months old. Likewise, a spoonful or two of cereal may be given with the morning meal and a small amount of boiled custard or rennet custard may be given with the evening feeding. Gradually the amounts of solid foods may be increased and the consistency thickened.

During the second half of the baby's first year, new foods should be added gradually every week to his diet. By the time he is a year old, he should be eating nearly all kinds of fruit, stewed or mashed; nearly all vegetables, except corn, in sieved form; lean meats and poultry; soups, custards, and cereals; as well as bread, toast, crackers, and simple cookies.

When the baby is six months old, his diet resembles that of an older child except for the consistency of the food he is given. His morning meal will include orange juice, cereal, and milk. At midday he will have meat in soup form, a sieved vegetable, zwieback or dried toast, custard, rennet, or gelatin, and milk. For supper he will have an egg, or custard made with egg, or cottage cheese, stewed fruit, zwieback, and milk.

During the second half of his first year new foods should be added gradually every week. Nearly every kind of fruit may be given, if stewed, as well as mashed fresh bananas and baked apples. Nearly all common vegetables, except corn, should be introduced in sieved form. Likewise, all lean meats, chicken, turkey, and fish may be included in the diet. Soups, custards, and all cereals, as well as bread, toast, crackers, simple cakes, and cookies, should be a part of the baby's diet as he approaches his first birthday.

Prepared Baby Foods

Most of the foods needed for a baby are now available in ready-to-heat form at the grocery stores. Baby cereals, which require no cooking but only the addition of hot milk or water, sieved vegetables and meats, stewed fruits, and soups suitable for a baby are all readily obtainable in small cans or jars. The preparation of a baby's food today is so simple that there is no excuse, even on the part of a busy mother, for not introducing variety into her baby's diet or for not giving him new foods as soon as he has learned to eat and like the foods he already has had.

Weaning

Weaning a breast-fed or bottle-fed baby generally begins when the baby is eight or nine months old. The development and needs of each baby vary so greatly that no exact time can be given for all babies. Before beginning the weaning, it is best to consult the doctor so as to avoid problems that result from weaning too early or too late.

Weaning is a difficult adjustment for babies whose diets are limited almost exclusively to milk. But, if babies have had their milk supplemented with foods and liquids from spoons and cups, weaning is relatively easy. However, weaning must be done gradually if it is to be successful.

At each meal, part of the milk should be taken from the

cup and part from the nipple. In the beginning of the meal, when the baby is hungry, he should be given his milk from the nipple. Otherwise, he is likely to suck in air as he drinks. Later, when his hunger is partially satisfied, he can drink from the cup. If weaning is not delayed beyond the ninth month, it should not require more than a month, and generally less, to eliminate the sucking form of eating completely. As soon as the baby is drinking all of his milk from a cup, the weaning period is over.

Vitamins

In spite of the widespread belief that milk, whether it be from the mother or from a cow, is the perfect food, it is lacking in vitamins C and D and possibly in vitamin A also. Therefore, vitamins from fish-liver oils must be added to the baby's diet not less than two weeks after birth. From the fish-liver oil he gets vitamins D and A, and from his orange juice he gets vitamin C. At first, five to ten drops of the oil on a spoon can be given to the baby twice daily. This is done by gently opening the baby's mouth while he is in a reclining position and then slipping the oil over his tongue and into the back of his mouth. If chilled, the oil has little taste, and what taste it has seems to appeal to a baby.

As the baby grows older, he will need more vitamins. This means larger doses of fish-liver oil. Generally, one teaspoon twice daily is sufficient during the winter and half that amount during the summer when he gets plenty of sunlight. By the time the child is two or three years old, he can swallow a capsule easily. Many capsules containing all the necessary vitamins for a day's intake in concentrated form are available now. These may be substituted for the fish-liver oil as a child grows older and is likely to revolt against the "fishy taste" and "slippery feel" of the liquid oil.

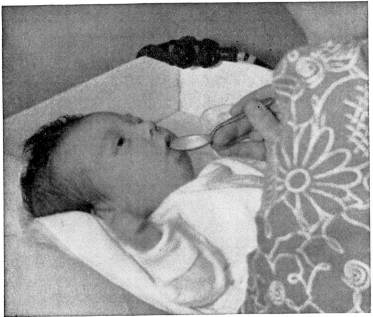

JOSEF BOHMER

Five to ten drops of fish-liver oil in liquid form should be included in the baby's diet to provide vitamins A and D, which are lacking in milk. It should be administered by opening the baby's mouth when he is in a reclining position and slipping the oil over his tongue and into the back of his mouth.

Of course the young child will get some of his necessary vitamins from his daily diet. Fish-liver oils and vitamin capsules should be regarded only as supplements to the diet and not as substitutes for vitamins in the food. Orange juice, grapefruit juice, or tomato juice; whole-grain cereals and dark breads; egg yolk; green leafy vegetables; and meat or fish should appear in the daily diet of every baby after the age of four to six months.

Foods for Young Children

After the baby's first year, his daily diet should include the following food items, which are needed for body-building, energy production, and body protection:

Milk	1 pint minimum to 1 quart maximum
Butter	3 teaspoons
Green or yellow vegetables	½ to 1 cup daily, preferably one vegetable at dinner and one at supper
Potato	1 small potato—baked, boiled, or mashed—or a small portion of noodles, macaroni, or spaghetti
Eggs	1 egg and part or all of an extra egg in a custard
Cooked fruit	½ to 1 cup daily
Orange juice, grapefruit juice, or tomato juice .	4 or more ounces daily
Cereal	1 cup of whole-grain cereal
Bread	1 to 3 slices of enriched or whole-wheat bread, toasted or untoasted
Meat, poultry, or fish .	For the two-year-old, one portion daily of 2 to 3 tablespoons is adequate. When the child is three years old, the portion can be increased to the equivalent of a small- or medium-sized adult helping; crisp bacon, in addition to the other meat, may be given with breakfast or supper.
Fish-liver oil or vitamin concentrate . . .	From October to May, 2 teaspoons of the oil should be given daily, while during the summer months, 1 spoonful is sufficient. When the child is able to swallow a capsule, 1 vitamin concentrate capsule daily is sufficient.

Vegetables for the two-year-old may be mashed or diced but not put through a sieve. Meats, likewise, may be minced or finely ground. By the end of the second year, vegetables may be prepared as they are for adults, and meats may be cut into small-bite sizes. When the child is approaching three, a raw vegetable—such as carrot strips, celery, tomatoes, grated cabbage, or cauliflower—may be substituted for the second cooked vegetable and given at dinnertime. Uncooked fruits—preferably apples, bananas, pears, grapes, oranges, and grapefruit—may be eaten once a day in addition to a cooked fruit. This may be given in the middle of the morning, in the middle of the afternoon, or as a dessert for dinner. Also, uncooked fruits may be combined with custards or gelatins for the dessert at dinnertime.

After the child is three years old, his meals may be prepared with those for the family, and he may eat what the family eats except for fried foods; foods with rich sauces and gravies; indigestible vegetables like corn, eggplant, cucumbers, and radishes; melons; dried or smoked fish or meat; nuts; pastries, hot bread, waffles or griddlecakes; tea or coffee; and rich candies. It is no longer necessary to chop up meats or vegetables, but they should be cooked with only a touch of salt and should never be fried or overcooked. Simple food, well prepared, makes the best diet for a young child.

Dressing a Baby

For a young baby, the most important single item of clothing is the diaper. There are many ways to diaper a baby, but the easiest kind of diaper to put on and the one that gives the wearer maximum comfort and protection is the modern, oblong diaper, twenty by forty inches. By folding it to fit the baby's size, it is possible to use the same

1) The modern oblong diaper, measuring 20 x 40 inches, will give the baby maximum comfort and protection. The most satisfactory method of folding it is to bring the right end of the diaper to within 12 inches of the left end.

2) Then fold the right end back on itself 6 inches. This makes a panel of three thicknesses.

A DIAPER

3) Next, bring the left end of the oblong over to the fold on the extreme right.

4) Now there are four thicknesses in the middle, which provides maximum protection. As the baby grows, the width of the diaper can be increased by narrowing the panel. (Photographs by courtesy Curity Diapers.)

diapers for the entire period of diaper-wearing. For traveling, for emergencies, or for everyday use, disposable diapers may be used.

There are many ways to fold a diaper but, for the oblong-shaped diaper, the most satisfactory folding is to bring the right end of the diaper to within twelve inches of the left end. Then fold the right end back on itself six inches. This makes a panel of three thicknesses of the diaper. Next bring the left end of the oblong over to the fold on the extreme right, thus putting an extra thickness in the middle where it will give maximum protection. As the baby grows larger, the center panel of the diaper becomes narrower.

The simplest technique for diapering a baby after his bath is to place the baby flat on his back on the bath table or in his crib. Place a clean towel or diaper under him to protect the surface on which he has been placed. With one hand gently lift up the baby's buttocks by holding his two feet in one hand and pulling him up. With the other hand, slip the folded diaper under the baby so that one end of the panel reaches up to the baby's waistline.

Then lower his legs and return him to a flat position. Next bring the other end of the diaper up between the baby's legs so that the two ends are ready for pinning.

The back and front pieces of the diaper should be pinned together thus: Place the front side of the diaper over the back side and pull the shirt over the lapping of the diaper. To avoid pricking the baby, slip one hand under the diaper lapping before the safety pin is inserted. After one side has been securely fastened, the other side can be done in the same manner.

Diapers should be changed before and after each feeding period and at times when the baby is obviously uncomfortable because his diapers have become wet or soiled. This is

DIAPERING A BABY

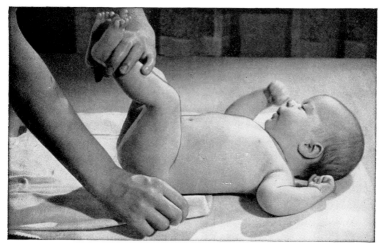

1) Place the baby flat on his back. With one hand lift the baby's buttocks by holding his two feet and pulling him up. With the other hand slip the folded diaper under the baby so that one end of the panel reaches up to his waistline.

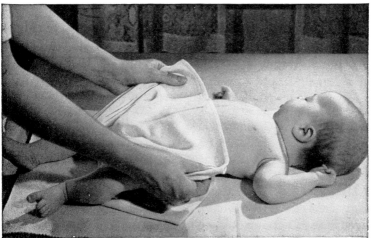

2) Then lower his legs and return him to a flat position. Next bring the other end of the diaper up between the baby's legs so that the two ends are ready for pinning. (Courtesy U.S. Office of Education.)

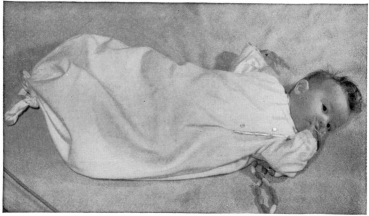

Aside from a diaper and a shirt, the baby needs little else except a sleeping garment during the first few months, for he sleeps most of the time. Such a garment may open down the back or the front and be fastened with tape or buttons.

generally sufficient. In changing diapers, it is important to sponge off the buttocks and genital organs of the baby with a clean washcloth that has been wrung out in warm water. If there is some chafing, apply baby oil, cream, or baby powder, as recommended by the doctor.

Waterproof panties to cover the diaper should be used for a young baby only when it is important to have his clothes remain dry, such as on occasions when he is dressed up. Generally, a folded diaper gives adequate protection, and even when it doesn't the crib is protected by pads that are easily laundered. Most waterproof panties today are made of nylon, which does not produce a steamy feeling as rubberized ones do, nor do they produce chafing. By the time the baby starts to sit up, and later to stand, waterproof panties may be used to avoid the unpleasant chill which comes from wet diapers which are not covered.

Clothing for a young baby should be very simple. In addition to his diaper and shirt, which may or may not have short sleeves, depending on the weather, the baby will spend most of his time in a sleeping garment of kimono style, which opens down the back and is fastened by means of tapes which are tied together. While the baby is lying on his back, his arms may be inserted quickly into the sleeves. He may then be rolled over on his stomach while the tapes are tied. Should he need a wrapper or sack, each of which opens down the front, this may be laid over his back before he is rolled onto his back. Then his arms can be inserted into the sleeves and the garment quickly fastened in the front by ribbon ties or buttons with loop fastenings.

For very cold weather, the young baby may be dressed in a bunting. This is an all-in-one garment, opening down the front and fastening with a zipper. Thus, the body is covered with a baglike covering that is ample in size to permit the baby to move his arms and legs. The hood attached to the bunting protects the baby's head, neck, and ears. For cool weather, a sweater and light wool cap are sufficient outer clothing. Socks or booties are not necessary, since the baby's legs are completely covered with his carriage blankets.

Dressing the Older Baby

After the baby is five or six months old, his infant-size clothes will no longer fit him. Since he is now active during most of his waking time, his clothes should be selected to enable him to have maximum freedom of movement. Diapers and shirts will still be worn; but for sleep, pajamas are better than a kimono-style sleeping garment, and for play, rompers are better than wrappers. These garments not only

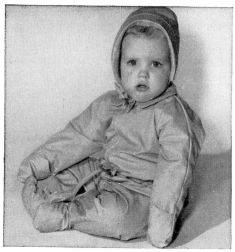

The child of six months or more should have a snow suit for cold-weather wear. The best garment is an all-in-one with a hood, mittens attached to the sleeves, and feet attached to the leggings.

COURTESY LANE BRYANT

permit greater freedom of movement, but they also offer greater protection in cool weather. As soon as the baby begins to stand up, he will need socks and soft, flexible baby shoes. If, however, he does his first walking in warm weather, it is better for him to go barefoot, since he can get a firmer grip when his feet are unhampered by socks and shoes.

For outdoor clothing during cold weather, the older baby needs a snow suit. Preferably, the suit should be an all-in-one garment with a hood, mittens attached to the sleeves, and feet attached to the leggings. The baby can quickly be slipped into this garment, which zips up the front, and be completely covered from head to foot. It is not even necessary for him to wear socks and booties, since most of his outdoor time will be spent in a carriage or in a playpen that has its own floor and hence keeps the baby off the cold ground or pavements.

Clothing for the Toddler

By the time the baby is beginning to walk, even if only when holding on to the sides of his playpen, "training panties" should replace diapers for daytime wear. These have an added thickness of material where protection is needed, although it is generally necessary to cover them with waterproof panties until the child is "trained." During the period of training, it is frequently wise to leave off the waterproof panties at times of the day when it is not serious if the baby becomes wet. Feeling the wet panties, especially as they become cold and clammy, gives the baby an added incentive to make it known when he wants to go to the toilet.

For play a toddler will need a shirt, with or without sleeves, depending on the weather. A play suit of cotton knit material with shorts and separate shirt is

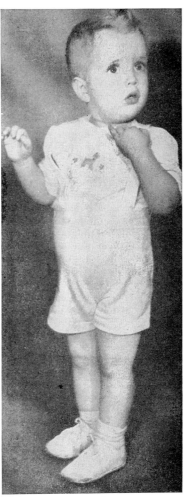

COURTESY LANE BRYANT

When he begins to walk, the baby will need play suits of cotton knit material. Shorts or overalls with separate shirts are ideal for boys.

During the summer months children should wear sun suits on hot days. These may be simple and made at home or elaborate for dressy occasions.

COURTESY GERBER'S BABY FOODS

ideal for boys. For girls, knitted shirts and shorts made of cotton gabardine with pleats to make them resemble a skirt give the active child plenty of freedom for movement. In cool weather, corduroy overalls, sweaters or jackets, and berets may be used; while in very cold weather, a snow suit will be needed. For young children, snow suits are often made in a one-piece style that the child can get into without help. By the time the child is four years old, a two-piece model with hood or a separate cap is preferable, as it gives more freedom for movement than is possible in the one-piece model.

During the summer months, both boys and girls should wear sun suits on hot days. These come in simple to elaborate styles and may be used for either play or dressy occasions. The upper part of the child's body is exposed to the sun's rays, except where the straps of the suit cover the skin, and no shirt is needed. Shoes with flexible soles and soft leather tops are worn until the child has mastered the skill of walking. Then he should wear the oxford model for winter and sandals for summer. Shoes should always be well fitted and should be worn at all times except when the child is in his pajamas. To avoid blisters, the child should always wear cotton anklets, even in warm weather.

The best sleeping garment for a young child is pajamas, made of thin material for summer and of heavy material for winter. These materials should require no ironing, as a child's pajamas require frequent washings. Children should also have bathrobes or housecoats to wear over their pajamas for dinner and for after-dinner play. The material selected for a bathrobe or housecoat will depend upon the season of the year and the warmth of the house.

Care of Clothing

For busy mothers, the washing of baby clothes and diapers is often too much of a burden. Diapers present the biggest problem. In many communities today there are diaper services which provide clean diapers daily for a nominal charge. Then, too, there are the disposable diapers which, in the long run, cost little more than regular diapers or the price of the diaper services.

As soon as a wet diaper is taken off the baby, it should be dropped into a diaper pail, which has been partially filled with water and covered with a lid. If a diaper is soiled with feces, it should be scraped off with toilet paper and the feces thrown into the toilet. Then the diaper may be placed in the pail.

Once daily the diapers can be washed. If there is an automatic washer and dryer, this is a simple operation. Otherwise, they should be washed in warm water with soapflakes or a detergent, then boiled in a large pail of water with a pinch of washing soda. After boiling, they should be rinsed in clear water, stretched out, and hung up to dry.

Babies and young children should not wear the same clothing twice. They are fresher, cleaner, and less likely to have skin irritations if they change to clean clothes once or twice a day. Since young children of today wear so few clothes and since much of their clothing requires no ironing, it is easy to keep them clean. Clothes may be washed every other day if the supply is sufficient.

Woolens and corduroys are easy to launder if done correctly, and after washing they look like new. To launder woolens, the water should be tepid, not hot. A good quality of white soapflakes should be thoroughly dissolved before the garment is placed in the water. The dirt may be squeezed out, but the wool should never be rubbed. For rinsing, a few drops of ammonia or a few dissolved soapflakes may be added to the water to keep the wool from getting hard.

After the woolen article has been carefully rinsed, it may be pulled into shape and hung on a clean towel over a clothesline or drying rack. The full weight of the garment should never be allowed to be suspended from one or two clothespins. Hanging woolen garments over the edge of the bathtub is a satisfactory way to dry them, since there is never a line in the center of the garment as there is when the garments are hung on a rack or a clothesline.

So many of the play garments for young children today are made of corduroy that it is important to know how to launder them correctly. They should be washed in tepid water in which a detergent or soapflakes have been dissolved. Like wool, corduroy should be squeezed but not rubbed. After the garment is clean, it is rinsed thoroughly in clear water to remove all dirt and soap. Then the tub or basin should be filled with clear, warm water and the garment placed in it to soak for a minute or two.

The garment should be removed from the water dripping wet and hung up immediately. It should never be squeezed or wrung out. Surplus water will drip from the garment very quickly, and the garment itself will dry in two or three hours if hung in the open or in six or eight hours if dried indoors. When it is partially dry, it may be pulled gently into shape without ironing so the nap will stand out.

For Discussion

1. Explain why it is important to introduce new foods early in the child's life.
2. Give arguments for and against the practicability of breast-feeding.
3. What reasons can you give in favor of the modern methods of feeding babies and young children? What arguments are there against the new methods?
4. What is a young child's attitude toward new clothes?
5. In a family where there are several young children, which would be a "better buy"—an automatic clothes dryer or a television set?

Suggested Activities

1. Go to a large grocery store and ask to see the different baby foods available today. Make a list of them, and then check it with the food requirements discussed in this chapter.
2. Prepare a typical noon meal for a one-year-old with prepared baby foods and a similar meal in which prepared baby foods are not used. Compare the amount of time spent on each.
3. Examine closely the clothing available in the stores to see which garments for babies and young children will simplify the laundry problem.
4. Get estimates on the cost of diaper services, disposable diapers, and the initial cost of a suitable number of regular diapers. Which is the most economical in terms of money and work?

CHAPTER 6

Physical Care of the Child

Because of the close relationship between physical and mental growth, and because good health promotes favorable behavior while poor health has the opposite effect, it is essential that the various aspects of physical care of the child be considered in detail. Sleep, bathing, exercise, sunshine, and all other care factors that contribute to the physical well-being of the child will be discussed in this chapter, with emphasis on the most widely approved modern methods.

Sleep Requirements

A newborn baby requires approximately 80 percent of the entire twenty-four hours of the day for sleep. As the months pass, he needs less and less sleep. By the age of one year, the baby sleeps approximately 50 percent of the time. This amount of time remains practically the same until the child is five or six years old, at which time it drops to 40 or 45 percent of the day. Unlike an adult, a baby sleeps in short periods of two to three hours, with waking periods between when he must get the necessary nourishment to hold him over until the next feeding period.

As the baby approaches his first birthday, his stomach grows in size, making it possible for him to take more food at each feeding. As a result, he sleeps for longer periods of time at one stretch. As physical growth begins to slow down, the baby will need less sleep. Therefore, he will be awake more during the day and will sleep through most of the night. Except for a morning nap of approximately one hour and an afternoon nap of two hours, the one-year-old will be awake from six or seven o'clock in the morning until his bedtime at 6 P.M. After the second year the morning nap may be given up and, except for a nap or rest period in the early afternoon, the young child may stay up all day.

Sleep Positions

The sleep position is important in establishing good sleep habits and in promoting restful sleep. Until the baby is three or four months old, he is unable to move his body from the position in which it is placed. Therefore, he should be rotated during sleep from his side to his back, from his back to his other side, and from his side to his stomach. The reason for this rotating of position during sleep is twofold. First, the baby's bones are so soft that they are easily misshapen if too much pressure is placed on them for too long a time; second, shifting of sleeping position eliminates fatigue and results in a deeper and more restful type of sleep. When the baby is able to roll from side to side or from back to stomach of his own accord, he will shift his sleeping position when he feels the inclination.

As a rule, each young child has his own favorite sleep position. One of the most relaxing positions is lying on the stomach. This position should be encouraged during the second or third month by placing the baby on his stomach more often than on his side or back. Lying on the stomach

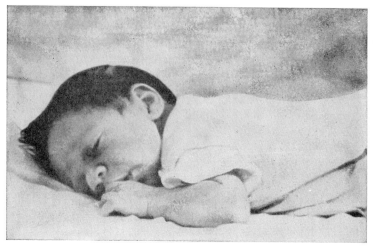

FROM THE FILM "KNOW YOUR BABY,"
NATIONAL FILM BOARD OF CANADA

One of the most relaxing sleep positions for the baby is lying on his stomach. It enables him to stretch out to his full length and use his lungs to their full capacity; it prevents undue pressure on the bones of his skull; and it encourages the baby to lift up his head and chest with the aid of his hands and arms, thus strengthening his muscles.

has certain advantages that other sleep positions do not possess. First, the baby can stretch out to his full length, enabling him to use his lungs to their full capacity. Second, pressure on the bones of the skull is prevented, thus minimizing the possibility of having a flat spot on the back of the head. Third, the baby is encouraged to lift up his head and chest with the aid of his hands and arms, thus strengthening his muscles. Finally, the baby is far less likely to kick off his bed covering when he sleeps on his stomach than when he sleeps in any other position. Once he becomes used to this position, it will be his favorite, and he will voluntarily select it when he is put to bed.

Safety in Sleep

To ensure safety while sleeping, a young baby may be put in a sleeping bag. This can be purchased in any store that has a baby's department, or it can be made easily at home. Sleeping bags are made of different materials and should be selected according to how cold the baby's room is. When the baby is put into his sleeping bag, he is thoroughly covered, and there is no need to fear that he will kick off his covers in the middle of the night or that he will get under the covers and smother. If it is very cold, the baby will need an additional blanket, tucked in firmly at the bottom of the crib and held in place at the top by large blanket safety pins or blanket clips.

The sleeping bag is generally used until a baby is eighteen months old. After that a "safety belt" may be substituted for the sleeping bag. The safety belt, which is attached to the mattress, has straps to go over the baby's shoulders. These straps, in turn, are attached to a belt around the baby's body. The safety belt gives the baby plenty of freedom to change his sleep position by rolling from side to side, but it does not permit him to pull himself above his covers or to snuggle so far under them that he might smother. This may be used until the child is two-and-a-half or three years old, but generally it may be abandoned before this time.

The Child's Bed

For the first two months, the baby's bed may be a bassinet or a large basket that has been lined and fitted with a mattress. The basket-type bed is conveniently moved about and particularly suitable for sleep out-of-doors when the weather is mild enough. After two months, however, the baby needs more room and a firmer mattress. Therefore, a crib should be

MARY BRANDEL HOPKINS

A basket type of bed is used for the baby during the first two months. These may be carried around with ease and are suitable for sleep out-of-doors.

available for use when the baby is large enough to turn his body.

The most important feature of the crib is its mattress. It should be well stuffed so that the baby's body will not sink into it. A hair mattress is most satisfactory. This should be protected with a rubber mattress pad and covered with a cotton mattress pad that can be changed frequently if wet. Sheets are not necessary when the baby is in a sleeping bag, but sheets made of diaper cloth, which requires no ironing, may be used if desired.

Many parents keep young children in a crib until they are so big that they almost fill up the entire sleeping space. When it is impossible for the child to shift his sleeping position, he is cramped and uncomfortable, and sleep is not as beneficial as it should be. Furthermore, the springs and mattresses of cribs are not intended to hold the weight of a four-, five-, or six-year-old child. A mattress will sag in the middle when too much weight is placed on it so that the child's body is in a curved position during sleep.

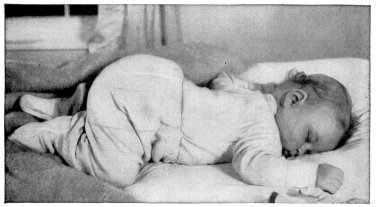

COURTESY HANES MERRICHILD SLEEPERS

If the baby does not wear a sleeping bag, he should wear flannelette pajamas with feet attached. These can be bought with two pairs of bottoms so that a change can be made if the pants become wet.

Therefore, the child should be put in a youth-sized, or small bed, or a regular bed when he is two or three years old, depending upon how large he is and how sturdy his crib. For the first several months, the bed should be placed so that one side will be against the wall. A sturdy chair can be placed on the other side, with its back against the upper part of the bed, so that the child will not fall out of bed in case he rolls over too far on either side.

Sleeping Garments

During mild weather the sleeping bag alone is sufficient protection, but during cold weather the baby should wear additional nightclothes. The six-month-old baby should have a kimono-style garment made of cotton flannelette that opens down the back like the typical hospital sleeping gown. When the baby has outgrown the infant size, he may begin to wear nightgowns that open down the front. Nightgowns made of seersucker are very satisfactory for wear during spring and summer when a sleeping bag is used.

If a sleeping bag is not used, the baby should have winter-weight pajamas with feet attached for winter wear. It is well to buy pajamas with two pairs of bottoms so that a change can be made if the pants become damp. For the baby, as well as for the young child, one-piece pajamas of thin material that can be washed easily and requires no ironing are the best sleeping garments for summer. The young child may wear one-piece pajamas without feet in the winter, but nightgowns for little girls are not desirable because they do not remain in place well enough to cover the child, especially on very cold nights.

The Child's Bath

The baby's first bath should be an oil bath, followed by a warm-water sponge-off. Sponge baths should be given until the navel is healed. Then a tub bath may be given daily at a time convenient for the mother. This is generally in the middle of the morning just before the ten o'clock feeding period. Before the baby is bathed, the bathroom should be pleasantly warm but not hot. All the equipment needed for the bath—soap, baby cream, baby oil, boric acid, cotton, washcloth, and towel—and clean clothing should be laid out in a convenient place before the water is prepared.

A bath table and tub combination, known as a "bathinette," is convenient but not essential for the young baby. A wash basin or large dishpan may be used as a tub, and a flat-topped table, covered with rubber sheeting and a bath towel, may be used for the place on which the baby will be laid for drying and dressing after his bath.

When the water is ready and has been tested so that it is pleasantly warm when your elbow is placed in it, or about

100 degrees, bring the baby from his crib, place him on the table, and completely undress him. Place a clean bath towel over him and wash around his eyes with absorbent cotton dipped in boric acid solution or boiled water. Then carefully clean out the lower parts of his nostrils and ears with twisted cotton or the corner of a washcloth. Following this, wash his face with a cloth wrung out in clear, warm water.

After these preliminaries have been completed, place the baby in the tub in a semireclining position, supported by your left arm if you are right-handed or your right arm if you are left-handed. With your right hand, use the washcloth to bathe the baby. Put pure castile baby soap on the wet cloth and rub it all over the baby's body, even into his hair if necessary. Then quickly wash off this soapy water with a fresh washcloth that has been dipped in clear water. If the baby's scalp seems dry and scaly, the shampoo should be given only when necessary.

As soon as the baby's body has been rinsed off, place him on the bath table and wrap him in the bath towel that covers the top of the table. A small wiping towel may then be used to dry him. While he is being dried, only one part of the body should be exposed at a time. When his entire body has been dried, he can be sprinkled with baby powder. If the skin is dry or chafed, baby oil may be massaged gently into his skin—especially in the creases under his chin, arms, at the bends of his elbows and knees, and around his genitals. This should be done only when necessary.

When the baby has been bathed and dried, dress him in clean diapers and clothes and put him back into his crib. Cover him lightly with a cotton blanket and begin to prepare his food. The food after the bath should be prepared quickly, as a bath stimulates a baby's appetite and he becomes fussy if he has to wait too long for something to eat.

(*Continued on page 106*)

HOW TO BATHE

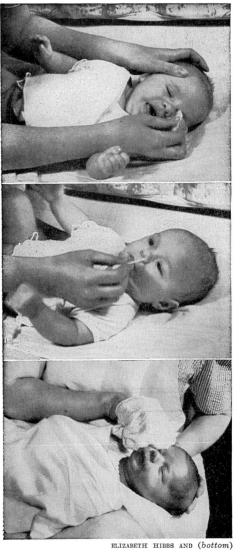

1) Before you bathe the baby, place him on a clean towel and wash around his eyes with absorbent cotton dipped in boric acid or boiled water.

2) Carefully clean out the lower part of the baby's nostrils and ears with twisted cotton or the corner of a washcloth. It is better not to use cotton rolled on the end of a toothpick or other hard object.

3) Before the baby is put into his tub, wash his face with a cloth wrung out in clear, warm water.

ELIZABETH HIBBS AND (*bottom*)
BUREAU OF EDUCATIONAL SERVICES

THE BABY

4) Next test the water to see that it is pleasantly warm but not hot. A safe way is to use a thermometer. The thermometer should register 100 degrees.

5) Place the baby in the tub in a semireclining position, supported by your left arm.

6) Put a small amount of pure castile soap on the washcloth and rub it all over the baby's body and into his hair if necessary.

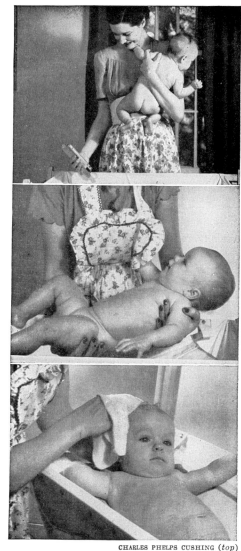

CHARLES PHELPS CUSHING (*top*)
AND ELIZABETH HIBBS

(See over)

HOW TO BATHE

7) Quickly wash off the soapy water with a fresh washcloth that has been dipped in clear water.

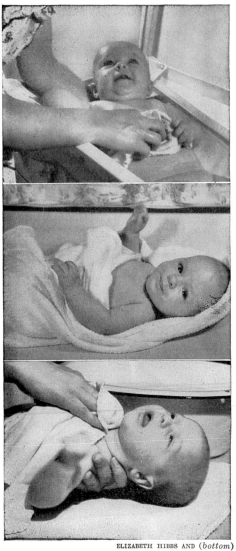

8) Place the baby on the bath table and wrap him in the bath towel that was used to cover the top of the table.

9) Use a small wiping towel to dry the baby, exposing only one part of the body at a time.

ELIZABETH HIBBS AND (*bottom*)
U. S. OFFICE OF EDUCATION

THE BABY (continued)

10) If the baby's skin is chafed, massage baby oil gently into the creases under his chin, arms, at the bends of his elbows and knees, and around his genitals. Then sprinkle baby powder over his body unless his skin is too dry.

11) Dress him in clean diapers and clothes.

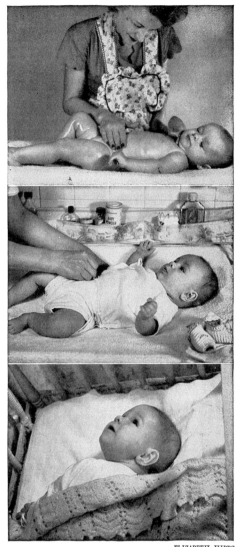

12) Put the baby in his crib, covered with a light blanket, while you are preparing his food.

ELIZABETH HIBBS

Sometime between the ages of six and eight months, when the baby can sit up with only a slight amount of support at his back, he is ready for a bath in the big tub. At first he will have to be held up while he is being bathed, but before he is a year old this will no longer be necessary. To be safe, run only two or three inches of water in the tub and never, under any circumstances, leave the baby alone while he is in the tub. This precaution should be carried out until the child is three or four years old.

Until the baby can sit up easily without support, he should continue to be dried and dressed on the flat-topped bath table. When he is a year old, however, he may be placed on the toilet seat for drying and dressing. When he can stand securely, he may be dried and dressed while standing up.

Care of the Teeth

A child should be taught very early in life the habit of keeping his teeth clean. When the baby is eighteen to twenty months old, his teeth should be cleaned for him two or three times a day, preferably after meals. By the time the child is four or five years old, he can be taught to brush his own teeth. The brushing should always be supervised by an adult, and the teeth should be inspected after the brushing to be sure that they are clean.

For cleaning the teeth, the child should use a small-sized toothbrush with bristles set in tufts. The head of the brush should be five or six tufts in length and two tufts in width. Any pleasantly mild tooth powder or paste may be used.

To encourage healthy gums, the baby's gums should be massaged gently twice daily with a mildly flavored tooth paste. This practice should be continued until the child is old enough to take over the task himself. This is a pleasant experience for children, and even very young babies make no protest when it is gum-massaging time.

After the massaging has been completed, the child may be given part of a glass of water to which some pleasant-tasting mouthwash has been added. This should be used to rinse out his mouth, but if he accidentally swallows it after swishing it around in his mouth, it will cause him no harm.

The Sun Bath

Babies need vitamin D, furnished by sunlight, for the development of bones, teeth, and muscles. Direct exposure to the rays of the sun should not begin until a baby is one month old. Then, if the weather is suitable, he may be exposed to the sun with only a diaper on or without any clothes at all. He should be placed first on his back and then on his stomach. When the baby is on his back, his eyes should be protected, either by the hood of his carriage or by a shade held over the basket in which he is lying.

The mother can determine whether the weather is suitable by holding her hand in the spot where the baby is to be placed for his sun bath. In moderate climates, sun baths can be given on sunny days from the middle of March to the middle of November. Except during the hot months of the summer, the middle of the day is the best time for a sun bath. During the hot months, the sun's rays are less strong in the early morning or late afternoon than they are in the middle of the day.

Ideally, sun baths should be given out-of-doors, in the garden or on the porch. For apartment-house dwellers, however, such spots may not be available. Therefore, a good substitute is to place the baby's basket under an open window when the sun's rays are coming in. The length of time

for the sun bath will vary according to the heat of the sun
and the baby's coloring. The first sun bath should be one
minute on the back and one on the front. If, after the sun-
bath is over, the skin shows no redness, the time can be increased by one minute for the back and one for the front
daily until the entire sun bath takes from thirty to forty
minutes. If the baby gets tanned, and if his skin is pleasantly
warm, all is well. When, however, his skin becomes red and
moist with perspiration, there is evidence that the sun is too
hot or that he has been permitted to remain exposed to its
rays too long. It is always wise to rub oil into the baby's skin
at the end of his sun bath.

Fresh Air

How soon the new baby will have his first out-of-doors
airing will depend partly on how well he is thriving and
partly on weather conditions. Babies who are born between
April and November can generally be taken out-of-doors
for the first time when they are three weeks old. Winter
babies get their first real airings indoors at this age. They
should be warmly wrapped in sweaters and caps, or buntings,
and covered with blankets, and placed in a crib or coach. The
windows of the nursery may then be opened wide to permit
the fresh air to come in. The baby's first airings should be on
clear, sunny days and never more than half an hour in
length. Gradually the time may be lengthened so that the
baby is sleeping four or five hours a day out-of-doors or, if
the weather is too cold, indoors with the windows open.

As soon as a baby begins to use his playpen, he should
spend most of his time out-of-doors in the playpen, either
on the porch or in the garden. In cold, windy weather, a
secluded spot on the porch should be selected; and in hot
weather, a shady spot should be found, except for the time

when the baby is having his sun bath. With some of his favorite toys to play with, the baby can have just as good a time outdoors as inside, and it is far better for him to be in the fresh air.

After a baby has learned to walk with relatively few falls, he has outgrown his playpen. Then is the time to fence off a small area of the garden for the child to play in or to put protecting gates at the entrances to the porch. No child of sixteen or eighteen months of age can safely be left alone out-of-doors unless some provision is made for his protection.

Exercise

In order for the child's muscles to develop, they must be used. Babies must have an opportunity to exercise their muscles for at least one half hour daily. Their exercise period may be given either in the morning or afternoon, depending upon the mother's convenience and the warmth of the room. For the exercise period, the baby should be completely naked, even without diapers. He should be placed on a flat surface, either in his crib or in the center of a large bed, and away from drafts. For safety, the bed should be protected with a rubber pad, covered with a cotton bed pad. As the baby approaches his third or fourth month, he should never be left alone for his exercise period, unless the sides of his crib are pulled up to prevent his rolling out of the crib. A playpen offers a safe place for the exercise period when the baby is able to roll.

Part of the half-hour period may be devoted to spontaneous kicking of the legs and waving of the arms. In order to take care of the muscles that the baby cannot exercise for himself, at least half of the time should be given over to exercises that require the assistance of an adult. The help

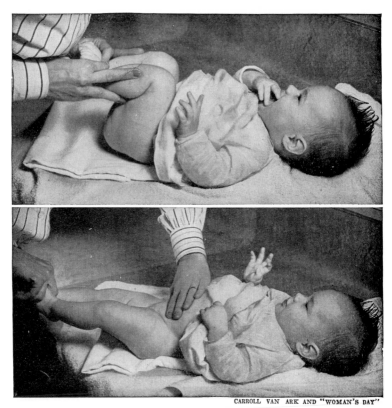

The baby should have at least a half hour a day for exercise to help strengthen the muscles and prevent constipation.

of an adult is needed particularly for exercises to help strengthen the back muscles. For these exercises, the baby should grasp firmly with his two hands the hands of an adult. Then, while the baby is holding on tightly, the adult should gently pull him to a sitting position and slowly permit him to return to a reclining position while he is still holding on. This exercise may be repeated from five to ten times, depending upon the baby's strength to do the exercise without becoming fatigued. A good exercise to strengthen the leg muscles and to help overcome a tendency to constipation consists in flexing the baby's legs, first together and then alternately. The adult should take hold of the baby's feet and gently push his legs up so that the upper part of the baby's legs touch his abdomen. After four or five flexings with both legs, a similar number of flexings may be given to the right and the left legs alternately. An exercise to facilitate rolling consists of placing the baby first on his back and, while grasping his hands firmly, pulling him first to the left side and then to the right. This exercise will help to strengthen the trunk muscles that are not used for the sitting-up exercise.

Most babies six to eight months old try to pull themselves to a sitting position by holding on to the bars of their cribs or playpens. As soon as they start to pull themselves to a sitting position, they should be permitted to exercise alone for at least a half hour every morning and again in the afternoon. As is true of younger babies, they should be as unhampered as possible by clothes at these times. In warm weather, no clothing is needed; but when it is chilly, the child should wear a shirt or a light sweater and diapers. Soon after mastering the ability to sit up, the child will try to stand up, and later he will try to walk. From this time on, it is no longer necessary for an adult to assist the child with his exercises. It is more likely that the child will need warnings to lie down or sit down for rest to avoid fatigue.

Immunization

Not all diseases of a serious nature are preventable, but sometimes they can be warded off. Even though a disease may not be warded off entirely, its severity can be lessened by making the child immune to the germs that cause the disease. The protection of the individual against disease is known as "immunization." Immunization consists of introducing into the blood stream some of the disease germs themselves or other germs that will kill the disease germs if they should enter the individual's body. Immunization can be carried out only by a doctor, but every person should know what diseases are preventable and at approximately what ages immunization against these diseases should take place.

1. Smallpox. Smallpox is still one of the most dreaded diseases, not only because it is frequently fatal, but also because it leaves pockmarks or scars on the patient's skin. However, smallpox is rare in America today because of the universal use of vaccination.

Babies are generally vaccinated for smallpox between the ages of three and twelve months. It is advisable to vaccinate them before they are six months old while they are unable to reach the spot where they have been vaccinated. Thus the possibility of infection by scratching is eliminated.

The vaccination reaction lasts at least two weeks. During the two or three days when the reaction is at its height there may be a slight fever, fretfulness, broken sleep, loss of appetite, and digestive disturbances. The height of the reaction begins from five to six days after the vaccination has been given.

Four or five days after vaccination, the spot on the skin where the serum has been injected becomes red and slightly elevated. Then a blister forms. When this occurs, the baby should be given sponge baths and not placed in the tub again until the scab falls off.

The blister usually reaches its peak of redness and size between the ninth and twelfth days after vaccination. Then a crust or scab forms that later falls off of its own accord, leaving only a small scar. The child should be revaccinated just before he enters school and whenever there is an epidemic of smallpox.

2. *Diphtheria.* Immunization against diphtheria is usually given during the second or third month of a baby's life. Some doctors use a combination of diphtheria and tetanus toxoids and whooping cough vaccine while other doctors prefer to inoculate for just one or two. When the combination is used, the vaccine is given at three separate times at intervals of about a month. This is followed by a booster dose a year later and then every two or three years. Should the doctor prefer to inoculate with diphtheria toxoid alone, two or three injections with a month's interval between are given.

Six months to a year after the diphtheria inoculations, the young child should be given a "Schick test" to determine his immunity. If the test is negative—that is, if there is no reaction to it—all is well. Generally, another Schick test is given just before the child enters school to make sure that his immunity is still present.

3. *Whooping Cough.* Because whooping cough is a very serious disease for babies and very young children, especially those who have a tendency to be asthmatic, many doctors today give whooping cough vaccine when the baby is two months old. This may be given separately or in combination with diphtheria toxoid, tetanus toxoid, or both. Three injections, a month apart, are needed to produce immunity. Later, should the child be exposed to whooping cough, the doctor may want to give the child a booster shot.

4. *Scarlet Fever.* In recent years, epidemics of scarlet fever have been few and the disease has been of a mild type. Furthermore, because immunization against this disease requires five injections, each of which is often accompanied by

a reaction on the child's part, immunization is recommended only when there is an epidemic of scarlet fever in the community or when there is a case in the family.

5. *Measles.* Measles in childhood is usually not fatal, but it may leave the child with an eye or ear disturbance or kidney trouble. Furthermore, unless great care is taken during the illness, pneumonia may develop. Therefore, it is considered wise to prevent measles from developing in a child under six years of age and to minimize the severity of the disease in an older child. Measles in a modified form will give a child just as much immunity from it for the remainder of his life as will a very severe case of the disease. If the child is given an injection of "gamma globulin," there is relatively little chance that he will develop the complications that make measles a serious disease.

6. *Poliomyelitis (Infantile Paralysis).* For many years infantile paralysis has been one of the most dreaded of children's diseases, with "polio" epidemics occurring every summer and fall. The Salk vaccine, made available in 1955, was the first vaccine to offer immunity to this disease. It is hoped that as preventive inoculations for infantile paralysis are given to more and more children throughout the country there will be fewer and fewer "polio" epidemics.

7. *Colds and Influenza.* Serums to prevent colds are rarely given to babies. However, if a child of five or six years old shows a marked tendency to have colds frequently and severely, his doctor may inoculate him to minimize his colds.

8. *Allergies.* When a child's skin becomes red and itchy, his eyes water, he sneezes without any apparent reason, and his nose becomes stuffy, the chances are that he is allergic to something he has just eaten or to something he has inhaled. The allergic condition may be so severe that it will produce vomiting or heavy asthmatic breathing, or both. This condi-

tion should be reported to the doctor, who will probably make skin tests to determine the cause of the allergy.

9. *Tetanus* (*Lockjaw*). Immunization against tetanus, or lockjaw, is important if the child lives in the country or is going to run barefoot during the summer months. Tetanus toxoid is given in two or three successive injections with an interval of one month between each or it is given in combination with diphtheria toxoid, whooping cough vaccine, or both. Booster shots should be given every year or two throughout childhood.

Is the Child Thriving?

To find out whether or not the physical care being given a baby or a young child is suitable, we can check on his development. The following specific criteria may be used to determine whether the child is developing as a child of his age should normally develop.

1. *Weight.* Throughout the early years of life there should be a gain in weight from month to month, even though at times it be only a slight increase.

2. *Appetite.* When a baby or child eats his meals with relish and gives indications of being hungry at mealtime, all is well. Even though he may eat what, to an adult, seems to be a very small amount of food, it is undoubtedly adequate for him.

3. *Digestion.* A healthy child normally has one or two bowel movements daily. Furthermore, he is free from gas, colic, and vomiting except when he eats under emotional tension or when he eats some new food that does not agree with him.

4. *Activity.* A child who is thriving is in constant motion, even when he is asleep. Each year, as he grows older, he becomes increasingly active.

5. *Joy of Living*. The child who is more or less constantly in good humor, who laughs and sings, and who always has a pleasant smile on his face is developing normally.

For Discussion

1. What theories have you heard about sleep positions for young babies? Which are scientifically correct and which might be regarded as "old wives' tales"?
2. How can you determine when it is safe to leave a baby alone on a bed, a chair, or in a bathtub?
3. Suggest ways in which babies and young children in a city can have plenty of fresh air and sunlight without interfering too much with the mother's duties.
4. Suggest practical ways of preventing a young child from contracting a cold or a contagious disease when an older child in the family is suffering from such a disease.
5. What is primarily responsible for poor nutrition—ignorance or lack of money?

Suggested Activities

1. Find out from a doctor or the local board of health what the immunization requirements of your community are.
2. Visit a baby department in a department store and ask the clerk to show you the different safety devices, such as sleep belts and gates for stairways, that are available today.
3. Observe several young children closely, using the criteria given in this chapter to determine whether or not they are thriving.
4. Study newspaper reports of the use of vaccine to prevent infantile paralysis. When a case of "polio" is reported, note whether the child had been inoculated and what type of infantile paralysis he was reported to have contracted.
5. Observe babies and children of different ages at sleep. Note different sleep postures, degree of restlessness, etc.

CHAPTER 7

Learning Body Control

At birth the baby is so helpless that he could not survive if he were not cared for constantly. He cannot move his body from the position in which he is placed; he cannot grasp for anything held within his reach; he cannot put food into his mouth; and he cannot even see anything, except as a hazy, indistinct blur. This state of helplessness remains until he can control his muscles.

Fortunately for all concerned, the child naturally lays a foundation for increased independence during the early years of life when his muscles gradually enlarge and harden and his nervous system rapidly develops to provide the necessary machinery for the control of these muscles.

Opportunity to Acquire Body Control

Many parents find it difficult to realize that, because a baby starts life as a helpless creature, he will not always remain so. They get into the habit of doing things for a baby and continue to do them as the child grows older, even when he is quite capable of doing things for himself.

Sometimes, too, when parents do give a young child a chance to do things, they become so discouraged by his slow-

Many parents are so afraid that the child will be hurt or get dirty
that they will not allow normal activity for him when he is ready for
it. Of course the child will fall, will become bruised, and will get
himself and his clothes dirty, but no child can learn body control and
remain "presentable" in appearance.

ness and clumsiness that they may decide it is easier to do it
themselves. You have probably seen mothers literally snatch
a task out of a child's hands because they are impatient to
have it done more quickly.

Naturally a young child cannot be expected to do as good
a job of any task he may undertake as an older child or an
adult. His dressing will be slipshod of course. For example,

he is likely to put his shoes on the wrong feet, wear his shirt inside out, or button up his coat incorrectly. In feeding himself he will do no better. As much food will land on the table, on the floor, or on his clothes as in his mouth. This prompts many an adult to "help" him by doing the task for him.

Other Obstacles to Learning

Another very common obstacle to the child's acquiring of skills is the adult's fear that the child will hurt himself when trying new skills. Because of this fear that the child will have an accident, the adult checks the child's adventuresome tendency and he may keep him from experimenting, from trying to learn, or from doing the things that would help him to learn how to control his body.

Even as babies, some children are kept in their playpens when alone or, if released, kept under the mother's watchful eye lest they hurt themselves. When out-of-doors some babies may be just as much restricted as at home. They may be kept in their coaches, securely strapped so they cannot climb out, even long after they are capable of walking. And when they are finally permitted to walk, they are compelled to hold their mother's hand so as to be sure that they will not run, trip, or fall.

The child's environment itself may offer ample opportunity for him to learn body control, but adult interference may prevent him from taking advantage of his chances. First-born children and children whose parents can afford to have someone constantly watching them and waiting on them are the usual victims of this interference. Children from large families or from families in which there is little extra help learn to help themselves sooner and more easily than others.

COURTESY MERCK AND COMPANY, INC.

The child should never be forced into learning an activity. He is ready to learn only when he shows sustained interest and progress after practice in the activity.

Readiness to Learn

"How," you may ask, "can we know when a child is ready?" Scientists use three criteria that are easy to apply to any given child in order to determine a child's state of readiness for an activity.

First, an *interest* in the activity. For example, when a child tries to sit up or stand up, when he begs for a tricycle, or when he makes a straight line to the jungle gym as soon as he reaches the playground, he is obviously showing an interest in doing these things, and there is reason to believe that he is ready to acquire the necessary skills to carry them out.

Second, a *sustained interest* rather than a transitory one. Does his interest lag quickly as soon as the opportunity to carry out the activity is given, or does it persist and seem to dominate his other activities?

Third, the *progress* that follows practice in the activity. Day-in and day-out practice of a fitful sort that shows no tangible evidence of improvement indicates that the child is not yet ready for the activity. For instance, when a young child toys with his spoon, his mother may take this as a signal that he is ready to learn to feed himself, and she may become irritated when she finds that day after day he continues to be a "sloppy feeder." Furthermore, she may find that she has to force him to keep at the task once he has started it. She has applied the first criteria but not the second and third ones.

Force versus Readiness

Forcing a child to do something before he is ready for it defeats its own purpose. Instead of speeding up the child's control over his body, it is more apt to retard it. Forcing a child too soon will give rise to an attitude of stubborn antagonism and revolt against learning to do the things when the child is ready and capable of learning.

Many self-feeding problems of young children, for example, can be traced directly to the fact that the child was forced not only to feed himself too soon but also was scolded or punished for being untidy in his eating habits. The same is true with regard to toilet habits, which will be discussed at the end of this chapter.

Pattern of Body Control

Fundamental control over the muscles of the different parts of the body does not come in a hit-or-miss fashion but rather in an orderly, predictable manner. This pattern shows that control occurs first in the upper part of the body and last in the lower, or leg, region. While not all children develop the same degree of control at the same time, the pattern, nevertheless, is so similar for all that we are forced to conclude that this development is caused primarily by maturation, or a natural unfolding of traits potentially present, and not by learning alone.

The purpose of knowing at approximately what ages different aspects of body control can be expected to appear is that it gives us a general picture of the state of readiness of the child to acquire useful skills connected with his everyday life. Put in another way, it means that we can proceed with a fair degree of certainty in teaching him and will not have to rely upon trial-and-error methods.

Head Control

By the time he is six months old, a baby should be able to control all the muscles of his head. At the third or fourth month, he can control his eye movements so that the two eyes will coordinate on the same object no matter in what direction that object may move. This enables him to see clearly and distinctly instead of in a hazy, blurred fashion. At the same age, a baby can control the muscles of his lips to enable him to smile when he wishes. When lying on his back, the average baby can hold up his head when he is five months old, and when seated on the lap of an adult and provided with support, he can hold up his head at six months.

Trunk Control

By the second month, the average baby can turn from side to back; by the fourth month, he can turn from back to side; and by the sixth month, he can turn completely around. As soon as the baby develops the ability to turn his body, the "days of safety" are over, and he should not be left alone on an unprotected surface—such as a bathinette, a bed, a table, or a chair—for even a moment.

Between the sixth and ninth month, the trunk muscles are usually strong enough to enable the baby to sit unsupported for several minutes. To keep from toppling over, he leans forward slightly, bows his legs so that the soles of his feet are turned toward each other, and frequently holds his arms outstretched at the side of his body.

Arm and Hand Control

Control of the arm and hand muscles comes later than trunk control. At eight to nine months, the average baby picks up an object with his thumb used in opposition to his fingers, not with a whole-hand grasp as he previously did. This gives him greater control over his hand than he formerly had.

When the baby is four to six months old, he can reach and grasp an object with few random movements, although he finds it harder to grasp a dangling than a stationary object. By the age of five months, the average baby should be able to accept one object that is handed to him; by seven months, two objects; and by ten months, three objects.

Is a Child Naturally Right-handed?

Studies of large groups of babies show that during the first three to four months of life all babies are *ambidextrous*— that is, they use both hands, with no preference for one or the other. By the middle of the first year, however, definite signs of hand preference appear.

Which hand will be the dominant hand is, in most cases, a matter of practice. Some children show a tendency to use their left hands. In such cases, if a child seems anxious to use his right hand and shows by his behavior that it is no strain for him, he should be encouraged to try to make the right hand the dominant one by being handed things in such a manner that it will be easier for him to use his right than his left hand.

If a child resists the change, however, it should not be attempted, and he should be allowed to use his left hand. Trying to change a child from the use of the left to the right hand, once the left hand has been definitely established

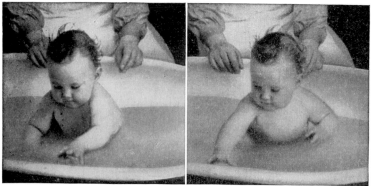

FROM THE ENCYCLOPAEDIA BRITANNICA FILM "LIFE.BEGINS"

Babies are not born either right- or left-handed, but learn by practice to use one or the other hand more frequently. During the first few months of life babies are ambidextrous. Note the way this child uses first his left hand, and then his right, to grab for an object.

as the dominant one, is risky business. Not only does it mean relearning for a child, which is always difficult and time-consuming, but it also means emotional tensions arising from feelings of insecurity on the child's part.

Leg Control

During the first year of life, the baby shows no evidence of being able to control his legs. He kicks in a random, meaningless fashion, but he does not use his legs to move his body. By the age of seven months, the average baby turns himself on his stomach and moves forward or backward by pulling with his arms and pushing with his legs. This is known as "crawling." It is a slow method of moving because the weight of the trunk rests on the floor.

By the age of nine months, the leg muscles of the baby have strengthened enough so that he can raise his trunk from the floor and *creep* on his hands and knees. One month later he will be able to stand if he has something to hold on to, and by the time he is a year old, he will be able to stand alone.

With the confidence that comes from being able to stand alone, the baby cautiously tries to walk. At first he will hold tightly to some support, but gradually, with practice, his skill and confidence increase to a point where he is willing to let go, first with one hand and then with both. The average baby reaches this point of development when he is fourteen months old.

At first the baby stands and walks with his legs spread apart, his knees stiff, his feet turned outward, and his arms outstretched or pulled tightly up to his body. Gradually he relaxes this "wooden-soldier" posture. By the middle of the second year, the average child walks like an adult, with a relaxed, easy stride.

Early Childhood Skills

Early childhood is the ideal time for acquiring many skills and for learning to do things that will lead to independence. Acquiring skills is fun for a child, and he rather enjoys the constant repetition needed for learning. He is fearless as compared with older children and is willing to try anything. Furthermore, he has no conflicting skills to interfere with the new ones, and this makes it easier for him to learn.

Only the cruder skills, however, should be learned during early childhood; they are the foundations for the finer skills. Until they are well mastered, it will be impossible for the child to learn the skills required for finer muscle coordination. It is a case of "learning to walk before learning to run."

Until the child can coordinate his body movements well enough to maintain his balance in walking, he should not be expected to perform the more difficult tasks of body balance that running necessitates. Similarly, no child can be expected

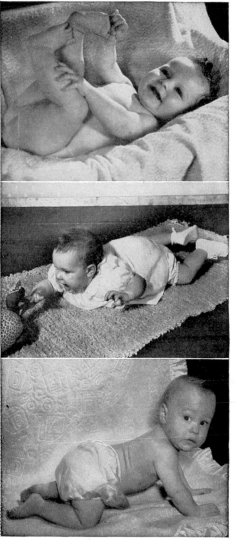

1) Before the baby is seven months old, he kicks his legs in the air.

2) After that, he can turn himself by pushing with his legs or crawling.

3) By nine months he can raise himself from the floor to creep.

COURTESY GERBER'S BABY FOODS, H. J. HEINZ COMPANY, AND BAKELITE CORPORATION

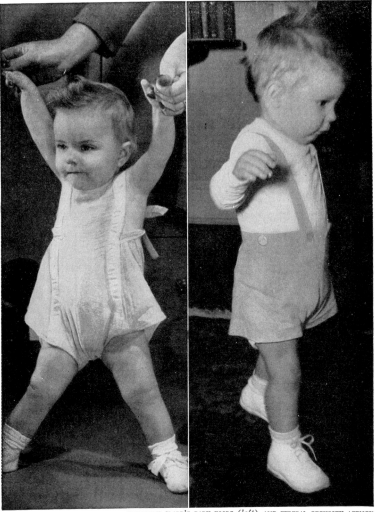

COURTESY CLAPP'S BABY FOODS (*left*) AND FEDERAL SECURITY AGENCY

4) At ten months he will be able to stand if he has something to hold on to. 5) And by a year he can stand alone.

to learn to write with a pencil until he has learned to control his arm and hand muscles through months of practice in scribbling, drawing, and painting with the use of crayons, paints, and pencils.

Other Childhood Skills

The skills connected with personal habits that a young child can master are primarily related to eating, bathing, dressing, and posture. Before he is six years old, a child should be able to feed himself with no help other than in the cutting of tough meat or cutting meat from bones. He should be able to bathe himself except for assistance in washing his back and shampooing his hair.

He should be able to dress himself completely and comb his hair, although he may need help in parting it. Little girls frequently need more aid in dressing themselves than boys do. Many garments for girls button down the back, and their hair styles necessitate more adult assistance.

Early childhood is the ideal age to develop posture skills. The sooner the child learns to stand and to sit correctly, the easier it will be for him to hold his body in the right position. In standing, most children have a tendency to slump, which causes the shoulders to droop and the abdomen to protrude. It is just as easy, when learning how to stand, to learn the correct way—that is, standing up straight—as it is to learn the wrong way—that is, drooping.

Likewise, it is as easy to sit up straight as it is to slump in or loll over chairs. Good posture is never a matter of chance. It should always be regarded as one of the grosser skills involving the larger muscle teams that must be acquired as a foundation for the finer and more graceful movements of the body.

Skills used in the young child's play should also be of the

LEARNING THE LARGER SKILLS

1) Among the *personal skills* the child of five or six learns to dress, bathe, and feed himself.

2) Among the *play skills* he learns how to run, jump, climb, skip, cut, paste, hammer, and paint.

3) Among the *home skills* he learns how to set the table, wipe the dishes, empty wastebaskets, dust, or help to make cakes and cookies.

COURTESY LIBRARY OF CONGRESS, YOUNG PEOPLE'S RECORDS, INC.,
AND BRISTOL-MYERS

cruder sort. Leg skills should include running, jumping, climbing, skipping, hopping, skating, riding tricycles, free spontaneous dancing to music, swimming, and diving. Skilled movements of the hands that should be developed in early childhood are cutting, pasting, weaving, hammering and sawing, painting with the fingers or a coarse brush, crayoning, drawing with crayons or pencils, knitting with spools or large needles, sewing with coarse thread and large needles, and putting together puzzles.

There are also certain work skills in the home that young children can learn. They can help in the kitchen by shelling peas or beans, pitting cherries, hulling strawberries, spreading bread for sandwiches, setting the table, wiping dishes, hanging up and taking down the laundry, scraping plates, washing sinks and tables, and so on. They can empty wastebaskets, clean bathtubs and wash bowls, hang up their clothes, assist in making beds, dust, run the carpet sweeper, or mop the floors with a dry mop.

Cautions about Childhood Skills

No young child will perform any of these skills as well as an adult can, but, through constant practice, a child can improve his skills. Meanwhile, he will be learning to control his muscles so that in time finer and more useful skills can be learned.

A very common mistake many parents make is to try to teach young children the finer and more complicated skills before the child is ready for them. If a child dances gracefully when a dance tune is played, the mother decides it is time for the child to go to dancing school. If the child enjoys "picking out tunes" on the piano, many a parent will interpret this as a signal to begin piano lessons.

A premature plunge into a difficult task will fatigue and

The child learns by imitation. It is important to correct him when his imitation is not good so that he will not learn to perform an activity the wrong way and have to relearn it later.

bore a child. Realizing his own limitations will cause him to be dissatisfied and ashamed of his efforts. With this unfavorable attitude, he will try less, and he may even abandon the task completely because he feels it is too difficult for him.

How Skills Are Learned

The child learns to do things by watching others and by imitating what they do. He cannot at first copy perfectly the movements made by another person, and he may not even see just how the movements are made, especially if the person he is copying moves too quickly.

If, however, the person he is trying to copy moves slowly, and if he is checked when he imitates any movement incorrectly, the child will then know how to proceed to train his body to make similar movements. This training will necessitate much practice on his part before anything resembling a skilled movement can be made.

Because children learn by imitation, it is essential that the adult he uses as a model be as good as possible. A poor start, resulting from imitating a poor model, may mean an inferior skill, or it may necessitate relearning the entire skill. It is just as easy for a child to imitate a good model as a poor one, but it is not easy for him to relearn if he gets started in the wrong way.

Clumsiness

No child is *naturally* clumsy unless he is retarded in mental development or is obese, but many children are clumsy in their movements as contrasted with other children of the same age. They stumble over furniture, trip when going upstairs, fall down steps, bump into people, let things slip through their fingers and break, and in general give the impression of being poorly put together or incapable of handling themselves.

As young children, they probably will not become self-conscious about their clumsiness. But as they grow older, it will be a constant source of embarrassment to them. They will begin to compare their behavior with that of their friends and will then realize how far short they fall. Furthermore, if clumsiness is allowed to persist, it will be difficult for the child to take part in the games and sports that make up the principle play activities of older children. Clumsiness is an especially serious handicap in boy-girl relationships during the teens.

How to Correct Clumsiness

Because clumsiness proves to be a liability, not only in childhood but also throughout life, every effort should be made to overcome any tendencies in that direction as soon as they become apparent. Even better, it is wise to assume that every child will show some signs of clumsiness. Efforts can then be made to forestall it before it gets a head start. This can be done by showing the child how to use the different muscle teams for a particular activity when he first begins to carry out that activity.

For example, when the young child first uses a knife for cutting, he should be shown how to use it at the very beginning, and a close watch should be kept on him whenever he uses a knife until he uses it correctly. In the same manner, the child should be shown how to throw and catch a ball. It may seem unnecessary to an adult to spend time showing a child how to do things that he unquestionably will learn to do without adult help, but well-learned fundamental skills will do much to pave the way for good body control later on.

Toilet Training

Learning to control the bladder and bowels is an important part of body control that should be achieved in the early years of childhood. Like all other phases of body control, a state of readiness must be present before learning begins. The age at which readiness occurs will, of course, differ from child to child. One child may be ready to learn bowel control by his first birthday, while another will not be ready until a year later. Bladder control comes later than bowel control.

Before actual toilet training begins, the mother should make daily charts, for at least a week, to indicate the times at which bowel movements and urination have taken place.

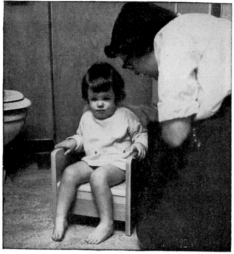

A low toilet chair, placed over a potty, is less fearful to the young child when he is first being trained than a toilet seat placed on the toilet. Both kinds, however, provide adequate back support and ensure safety. Toilet training should never be accompanied by emotional tension or scolding from the parent, and parents should not expect immediate perfection in learning.

SUZANNE SZASZ

If the child is ready for toilet training, these charts will show fairly definite uniformity from day to day.

A toilet chair with a potty under it or a toilet seat attached to the regular toilet gives the child's back and arms adequate support and enables him to relax, thus making toilet training easier. The toilet chair is less fearful to some children because it is closer to the floor. Furthermore, after the child can walk, he can go to the chair alone and does not have to wait to be put on the regular toilet.

By the middle of the second year, most babies are aware that a movement is coming and give some indication of their readiness. Watch for this around the time the baby usually has a bowel movement and put him on the toilet chair. If this proves to be a false signal, take him off after a few minutes. By the time he is two years old, he will prob-ably go to the toilet by himself.

Training the child to urinate follows the same pattern. The times when the child usually urinates should be the times when he is taken to the toilet. They are generally on arising in the morning, after breakfast, after the mid-morning fruit juice, before and after the noon meal, after the nap, before and after supper and around ten o'clock in the evening.

To aid the child in understanding what is expected of him when he is put on his toilet seat so frequently, many doctors recommend turning on the faucet so that the child can hear the sound of running water. Another aid is the substitution of training panties for diapers. The wet panty is uncomfortable and acts as an incentive for the child to control his bladder until he reaches the toilet.

Two important cautions should be remembered in toilet training. The first is that it should never be accompanied by emotional tension, scolding, or punishment. If the child is having difficulty in being trained, he obviously is not ready for it. It is therefore better to drop the whole matter and try again a month or two later.

The second caution is not to expect immediate perfection. Learning to control any team of muscles takes time and practice. This holds true for the muscles that control the organs of elimination. Toilet training, if carried out consistently and systematically, will produce the desired results in time.

For Discussion

1. Since all children try to advance to difficult tasks before they have mastered the simpler ones, how would you deal with this problem of a child who wants "to run before being able to walk"?
2. Explain why it is desirable for a young child to be carefully supervised when he is learning a new skill, such as feeding himself or riding a tricycle.

3. In what ways might a child be helped to overcome clumsiness?

4. How would you determine whether or not a young child was ready to learn to swim, to play the piano, to read, or to learn social dancing?

5. How would you convince a parent who was afraid to allow her child to learn to roller skate that this was unfair to the child, especially if most of the other children are roller skating?

Suggested Activities

1. Study the manner in which a child uses his preferred hand in a number of activities. Then suggest that he try carrying out the same activities with the other hand. Observe not only the results but the emotional tension on the child's part.

2. Observe closely the clumsy behavior of a child. Note what appears to be responsible for his clumsiness and see if, through guidance and help, you can aid him in overcoming the clumsiness.

3. If possible, select a baby for weekly observations. Note the changes that occur in his locomotion and hand control. Keep records of the ages at which different stages in development along these lines occur. Then compare his record with the pattern for the "average" baby.

4. Collect data from parents of young children as to the ages at which they started toilet training, the methods used, and the success or failure they have met. Analyze each technique critically.

5. Make a list of objections your parents have raised from time to time regarding your desire to learn certain skills. How many of these objections seem to be motivated by fear?

CHAPTER 8

Learning to Talk

Every normal baby at birth cries and makes cooing, gurgling sounds. What he has to learn is how to control his vocal mechanism so that he can produce sounds that have meaning and can be readily understood by others. This takes time.

Before a child can speak, he relies upon simple and yet effective means of communication. These are useful as preliminaries to speech; but under no circumstances should they be encouraged beyond the age at which the child is capable of learning to talk.

Crying

The birth cry of a baby differs in intensity, but its tonal quality remains practically unchanged throughout the first month of life. Gradually, changes in tonal quality become apparent, and it is then fairly easy to tell what he wants. A high-pitched wail generally means physical discomfort or pain; a low-pitched moan, broken by yawns and sighs, means sleepiness; angry howls, punctuated by sucking movements, mean hunger.

Since the baby's needs and interests are very limited, his

At about six months the baby has developed an interest in people and has learned that crying is a quick way to get attention. This is called "spoiled crying," and should be discouraged by ignoring it.

repertoire of cries with different tonal qualities proves to be a form of communication adequate to meet his needs.

Around the sixth month, the baby's interest in people has developed to the point at which he wants constant attention. He soon learns that crying is a quick and easy way of satisfying this longing because whenever he cries someone comes to see what is the matter.

In a very naïve manner, he shows his pleasure at gaining the desired end by an immediate cessation of crying and by a broad, happy smile. This type of crying is not a form of language but rather a bid for attention. That is why it is often called "spoiled crying."

Spoiled crying is very different from the crying of the helpless newborn infant who has no other means of communication. It is also different from the crying of a baby who needs attention for some bodily condition, such as hunger, thirst, discomfort, colic, or pain. That is why it is important to be sure that the cry is merely a bid for attention before ignoring it. Only when it is apparent that there is nothing the matter with the baby should his cries go unheeded.

How to Curb Crying

As a young child learns to use words, his need for crying as a form of communication lessens. And, because crying is regarded as an "infantile" form of behavior in a child who is able to talk, the sooner the child learns to substitute speech for crying as a means of communication, the better it will be for his social adjustments.

Showing annoyance, ridiculing the child, or calling him names will not encourage the child to substitute speech for crying. Instead, he should be told firmly and impersonally that he must ask for what he wants, not cry for it. When he finds that this is true and that there are no exceptions to the rule, he will cry less and less.

Gestures

Gestures serve two purposes: (1) They may be a substitute for speech; or (2) they may be a supplement to speech. The young child generally uses gestures because he discovers that he can make others understand him this way.

The gestures he finds most effective are pointing to people

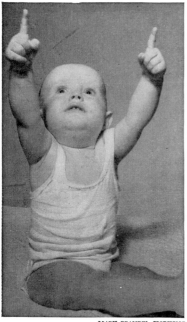

MARY BRANDEL HOPKINS

The child uses gestures as a substitute for speech before he is able to express himself in words. Parents should try to associate words with the child's wants when he gestures so that he may gradually learn to replace gestures with words.

and objects when he wants others to notice them; holding out his arms when he wants to be picked up; stretching out his arms in the direction of an object he wants; shutting his mouth and turning his head when food he does not want is offered him; pushing away food he does not like; and pushing or kicking at people or objects he wants to have removed.

As soon as the child's vocabulary is adequate to meet his needs, the use of gestures should be discouraged. While he is building up a vocabulary, there will be times when he will have to use a gesture as a substitute for a word. At such times he should be told the word he needs and encouraged to use it.

Breaking Up the Gesture Habit

There is no question about the fact that gestures add meaning and emphasis to speech. Since the use of gestures, however, is not recognized as good form in America, it is unfair to a child to permit him to get into the habit of using them.

Most children are unaware of their use of gestures. For that reason it is necessary to call the fact to their attention every time they point, push, or make faces. Gradually they themselves will be on the lookout and can check themselves before the gesture occurs.

Just knowing that he is pointing may not be enough to make the child stop it. He must *want* to do so. This wanting to do so will come only when the child realizes that other people, especially other children, look at him with surprise or scorn when he uses gestures. Thus, you can expect gestures to continue until the school age, when social consciousness becomes a powerful force in the child's life.

Babbling

Babbling is "play speech." It is not a form of communication but rather a kind of play. The baby enjoys making sounds and listening to them. He even laughs at the sound combinations he can produce. The simple gurgling sounds of the newborn become stronger as the baby grows stronger. They are repeated over and over again, often in a singsong fashion. The most common babbling sounds are "eh-eh-eh," "ah-ah-ah," "u-u-u," "i-i-i," and "ow-ow-ow."

Babbling, or "cooing," as it is often called, begins around the third month and reaches its peak when the baby is about nine months old. After that time, the babbling sounds are gradually incorporated into words and are associated with the objects or people they represent.

Since babbling is the basis of true speech, it should be encouraged. Through practice in the use of the muscles of his vocal mechanism, the baby gradually develops control over them. He is thus better prepared to master the difficult task of learning to say words.

Learning to Talk

Learning to talk is a long and laborious task. You cannot expect a young child to pronounce his words as well as you do, to have a very large vocabulary, or to combine his words into sentences without occasionally making grammatical mistakes. Young children, like adults, are lazy about doing things that take effort. If they can get along by using substitutes for speech, such as crying or gestures, or if they are permitted to make grammatical mistakes without being corrected, they will have little incentive to learn to talk correctly.

Learning to talk involves four tasks, each of which is essential. All four tasks are difficult and will take time to master. If the young child shows some improvement from month to month, that is all you can expect of him. As a matter of fact, he will spend the major part of his life improving his speech. By the time he reaches old age, there will undoubtedly still be room for improvement.

Understanding What Others Say

The first task in learning to talk is in understanding what others say. When a baby first hears words, they are completely meaningless to him. In time he gets some idea of what is being said by watching the facial expressions of the speaker. A smile on the face of the speaker comes to mean approval, while an angry look means disapproval.

Also, words said often enough have a familiar sound to the child, but he does not actually know what they mean until some association is made between the words and the people or things they represent. Therefore, in talking to a baby or a young child, it is essential to teach him word meanings by naming things. For example, "cup" becomes a meaningful

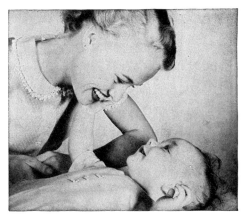

Long before he speaks, the child learns to understand what others are saying. Even facial expressions give him some clue as to what is meant.

PINNEY FROM MONKMEYER

word when the adult points to a cup and pronounces the word "cup" simultaneously.

When adults realize that every word they use is meaningless to a child until the child learns the meaning by association, the three cautions about to be given will be fully appreciated. First, speak slowly and distinctly so the child has time to grasp the meaning of the different words. Second, use a simple vocabulary—the simpler the better. Whenever a familiar word can be substituted for an unfamiliar one, do so. If a child shows that a word is meaningless to him, repeat it and explain its meaning. Third, use the proper words for things rather than substitute words or baby talk.

How Much Does a Child Comprehend?

Studies of large groups of babies and young children give us some clue as to how much comprehension we can expect at different ages. Interpretation of facial expressions and gestures begins around the age of three months. At six months, the baby should recognize his own name, and by the time he is a year and a half old, the meaning of such simple questions as "Are you sleepy?" or "Are you hungry?" should be understood. Six months later, the child should comprehend simple commands, such as "Come to supper" or "Throw me the ball."

From the age of two, the child's comprehension will develop rapidly. At every age, however, his comprehension vocabulary will be greater than his use vocabulary. That is, he will know the meaning of more words than he actually uses. How big his comprehension vocabulary is, in turn, will depend not so much upon his intelligence as upon how carefully the people who are with him help him to learn word meanings.

Building a Vocabulary

The second task in learning to talk is in being able to say words. A child always has more difficulty in expressing himself than in understanding others. His method of learning to speak is similar to that of comprehension. He must learn to associate a word with an object or person as the word is spoken by another.

Then he, in turn, must try to imitate the sounds heard. This is difficult because, even though the child may hear the word correctly, he cannot always control his tongue and lip muscles well enough to reproduce accurately the word he has just heard.

Because of this difficulty, the child should be encouraged to try again and to keep on trying until he can say the word correctly. Before each trial, it is better to repeat the word for him so that he will have the correct sound clearly in mind as a model to imitate. It may require several days of persistent trying on the child's part, with help from the parent, to accomplish his goal.

The adult can help the child learn new words by picking out new words in books and associating them with the objects pictured.

The Child's Vocabulary

Babies learn words as they need them. Nouns are the most useful parts of the vocabulary and for that reason are learned first. Verbs, especially the action verbs, such as "come," "go," "give," and "take," are essential in sentence building and are learned almost as quickly as nouns.

Adjectives to describe likes and dislikes, as "nice," "pretty," "horrid," and "good," gradually creep into the vocabulary but at a slower rate than nouns and verbs. Pronouns and adverbs are less useful because substitutions can be made for them. They are usually the last parts of the vocabulary to be learned. By the age of three, however, pronouns, adjectives, and adverbs should be freely used even though they are often used incorrectly.

How large the young child's speaking vocabulary will be depends partly upon how much interest he has in learning. If the child is helped in this difficult task by being encouraged to learn new words, he is sure to build up his vocabulary rapidly.

Unless there is definite evidence that a child is mentally dull, a small vocabulary means that he needs more help and encouragement in talking. On every possible occasion, the meaning of new words should be explained to him, and he should be encouraged to say the word several times until he can say it correctly.

Combining Words into Sentences

The third task in learning to talk is putting words together into sentences. The child's first attempts are more often incorrect than correct. Before he actually tries to put words together, he may use one-word sentences, in which a gesture is combined with a word, generally a noun. This expresses a complete thought for him. Instead of saying "I want a drink of milk," the baby will say "milk" and point to his cup.

By the eighteenth month, however, most young children are putting several words together to make sentences. The average number of combined words varies from three to five. They are usually nouns, verbs, and adjectives. Pronouns, prepositions, and adverbs are generally omitted. Eventually, of course, all parts of speech will creep into his sentences, with pronouns the last to make their appearance. The average child may be using complete sentences when he is three years old.

Grammatical Mistakes

Grammatical mistakes should never be treated lightly, nor should there be the false hope that the child will outgrow them. The longer he is permitted to speak incorrectly, the harder it will be to break the habit later.

Furthermore, the child's ear will get used to hearing wrong word combinations. He will therefore not be able to distinguish for himself the difference between correct and incorrect speech. That is why he should be corrected every time he makes a mistake. This is essential if a critical attitude toward speech errors is to be developed.

Because young children become intent upon something they want to tell you, and because their enthusiasm carries them along while they are talking, it is usually better to wait until the child finishes his sentence before correcting his mistake. This will avoid the development of a stubborn, resistant attitude on his part.

Learning to Pronounce Words

The fourth task in learning to talk is being able to pronounce words correctly. When you realize that *every* word children use is new to them and that its pronunciation has to be learned, it is quite understandable that children will have even more trouble than adults.

In learning any new skill—and pronouncing words is a skill, just as dancing is—there are certain to be errors at first. These errors should not be overlooked nor should there be the assumption that the child will outgrow them in time. Even more serious, they must never be encouraged because they are "cute." Like grammatical errors, they should be corrected early, and constant attention should be given by the adult to make sure that the child's errors are not repeated often enough to settle into a habit.

Common Errors of Pronunciation

In the early stages of learning to talk, every baby talks "baby talk" to some extent. Baby talk is nothing but mispronunciation. Its common forms consist of omissions of letters or syllables, such as "seepy" for "sleepy" and "buttfly" for "butterfly"; substitutions of letters or words, such as "dat" for "that" and "ticktock" for "clock"; and interchanges of letter, such as "aks" for "ask" and "bicksit" for "biscuit."

Occasionally, as a result of some malformation of the teeth (or absence of the front teeth), jaws, or lips, the young child lisps. Lisping consists of softening the harsh sounds by substituting others for them. Thus, "Simple Simon" becomes "Thimple Thimon," and "tree" becomes "twee."

Slurring or indistinctness of speech comes from inactivity of the lips, tongue, and jaw. The child simply does not put forth enough effort to open his mouth to let the sounds come out. This may result from timidity or from laziness due to fatigue or poor health, but it more often comes from emotional excitement. In an effort to tell something quickly, because he is excited about it or because he wants to finish before he is stopped, he rushes on headlong with his story. The result is a jumble of sounds that no one can make head or tail out of.

When emotional tension is severe, speech disorders of a more serious type, such as stuttering and stammering, develop. In stuttering there is a repetition of a letter, syllable, or even the whole word. The most vulnerable age for stuttering to begin has been found to be at two and a half years; and the next most vulnerable age is at six years, when the child starts to go to school.

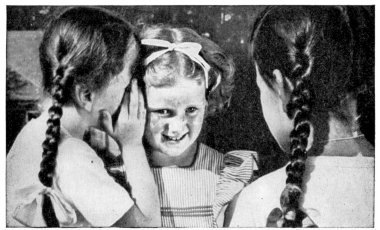

FROM THE MCGRAW-HILL FILM "SOCIAL DEVELOPMENT"

The prime function of speech is communication. To be able to play with other children, the child must be able to speak their language and to understand what they say.

Stammering is a "deadlocking" of speech, caused by the tightening of the vocal muscles. When the muscles relax, the sounds flood out in incoherent words. Then follows another spasm of stuttering. Frequently stuttering and stammering go hand in hand.

How to Deal with Mispronunciations

In the case of baby talk, lisping, and slurring, the best procedure to follow is for the adult to speak words clearly, distinctly, and slowly so that the child can literally hear the sound of every letter in the word. A word that is new to the child should be repeated several times so that he can get a good word-picture of its sound. Then the child should be given a chance to say it.

If lisping and slurring are caused by poor formation of the

teeth and jaws, a dentist should be consulted for advice. When slurring comes from emotional tension and excitement, every effort should be made to encourage the child to calm down and speak slowly. Telling him that you cannot understand what he says when he speaks so fast is generally enough to make him realize how futile it is to rush, since he merely has to repeat what he has said.

Stuttering and stammering are too difficult for the untrained person to try to cope with. The best procedure to follow is to consult the family doctor for his advice. If he feels that a speech-corrective teacher is needed, parents should follow his advice even though they may feel that the expense is unwarranted.

For Discussion

1. In what ways may slang and swearing among young children be regarded as "parrot talk"? How can speech resulting from imitation but without meaning for the user be considered "parrot talk"? Give specific examples to illustrate.
2. Suggest practical methods of attacking the problems of mispronunciations and grammatical mistakes in a young child.
3. List as many arguments as you can in favor of a young child's learning a foreign language. Then list arguments against this. Weigh the two and report your conclusions.
4. Why is baby talk sometimes considered cute by adults? How do older children react to it?
5. Are girls more likely to grow up to be crybabies than boys? If so, do you think it is the result of heredity or cultural pressures?
6. When a child of foreign parentage, who has learned from his parents to use gestures as a means of emphasizing his words, is with children who do not use gestures, should he be encouraged to stop using gestures? If so, how can this best be accomplished?

Suggested Activities

1. Select several children who are in the "toothless stage"—that is, those who have lost their upper front teeth. Ask them to pronounce words with harsh sounds, especially words beginning with "r," "s," and "z." Listen carefully and report your findings.

2. Make a list of babbling sounds used by babies under nine months of age. Study these sounds carefully and then list common words that can be built up from these sounds.

3. Make a list of grammatical errors made by several young children over a period of one week. Then classify these errors according to their types. Where do you find the predominance of errors?

4. Observe a child with any speech defect, such as baby talk, stuttering, stammering, or lisping. How do other children treat this child?

5. Note how children of ages three through ten years react to a child who cries in their presence. Are there age differences in their reactions to a crybaby and what are they?

6. List the words a baby uses when he is first learning to talk. Keep records for a period of at least six months. Then classify these words into different categories. Has he followed the typical "pattern" in learning to talk?

CHAPTER 9

The Child and His Emotions

There is no question about the fact that early childhood is an emotional age. Emotional outbursts are more violent and more frequent at this age than at any similar age span in life. The reason is that the young child has not yet learned to behave as society expects him to behave.

How Children's Emotions Differ from Those of Adults

A young child's emotions are so different from those of an adolescent or an adult that, to understand them, it is essential to know just what these differences are. The most apparent difference is in violence of expression. While an adult tries to control his emotions, a young child makes no attempt to do so.

When he is angry, he lashes out and fights. When happy, he laughs, jumps up and down, and claps his hands. These uncontrolled expressions, though disapproved of by the social group, are far better for the child's physical and mental well-being than is the suppression of emotions which leads to an outward calm accompanied by a state of internal upheaval.

Children's emotions are short-lived. They come, are expressed in violent outbursts, and then disappear almost

152

Unlike the adult, the young child makes no attempt to control or hide his emotions. His outbursts—whether of joy, sorrow, anger, or fear—are violent but short-lived. His moods change so rapidly and he forgets so quickly that tears often give way to laughter before they are dry.

before one realizes what is happening. By contrast, adult emotions frequently drag out over a period of time in a smoldering form known as a "mood." They then gradually die out or end in an emotional outburst.

The explanation behind the short-lived character of children's emotions may be found in the state of development of the child's memory and attention. Typically, a young child's attention is easily diverted from the immediate situation to something else. When, for example, he is angry because he cannot play with mother's prized perfume, he will quickly get over his anger if mother shows him her hand mirror and demonstrates how he can watch himself in it.

The child's memory, likewise, is on a lower level of development than the adult's. The result is that the child quickly forgets even strongly tinged emotional experiences. He will not carry a grudge or brood over matters that worry him because he forgets easily when his attention is attracted to something else.

The rapid shifting of attention and the short duration of memory responsible for the short-lived condition of a child's emotions are likewise responsible for the third major difference between the emotions of children and adults. The child's emotions are transitory. He swings from one emotional state to another as if by the touch of a magician's wand. From laughter to tears, from panicky fear to gnawing curiosity, or from love to hate are common experiences among young children.

Typical Emotions of Early Childhood

Scientific studies of large groups of children have given us much important information about the emotions commonly experienced in early childhood, what is responsible for arousing them, and how they express themselves. From this information we now know what is the typical emotional behavior in early childhood.

Knowing this will help to dispel the belief that the young child who becomes emotionally aroused and behaves in an unsocial way is a "problem child." Furthermore, this information will give clues as to when to expect different forms of emotional expression.

In this chapter each of the emotions of early childhood is discussed, and in each case the usual causes and behavior that normally follow are described.

Anger

The commonest emotion in childhood is anger. A young child finds himself in an environment regulated to suit the whims of adults. He rebels when his wishes are constantly thwarted. The less he is permitted to do as he pleases, the more often he will show his rebellion in an angry outburst.

Having to come to a meal or go outdoors when they are busily engaged in some play activity, having a toy they want to play with taken away from them, having to eat something they do not want, or having to go to bed or remain alone in a room while mother is elsewhere in the house are common causes for anger. In each case the child's wish has been thwarted by having to do something he did not want to do.

In each successive year of the child's life there are more restraints placed upon him. There are also more demands for him to behave in a socially approved manner. This means more anger-provoking situations. Whether the child will express his resentment in angry outbursts or by seething inwardly while remaining outwardly calm will depend upon how well he has learned to control his emotions.

Typical Childish Anger

The typical behavior of an angry child takes the form of a temper tantrum. In his uncontrolled outburst of anger, the young child kicks, stamps his feet, jumps up and down, hits, pounds, throws, bites, screams, throws himself on the floor, holds his breath until he becomes blue in the face, and sobs hysterically.

All these actions are designed to overcome the obstacles in the child's way of doing as he pleases. Because such behavior is annoying and embarrassing to adults, they are prone to give in to the child in order to calm him. Therefore, the

As the child learns that he cannot indulge in temper tantrums, he substitutes sulking, pouting, brooding, negativism, refusal to speak, fussiness, or quarrelsomeness for emotional outbursts. These may be unpleasant but they are not so bad as the temper tantrums.

COURTESY THE CENTAUR COMPANY

child soon learns that a temper tantrum is a quick and easy way to get what he wants.

Violent as they are, temper tantrums do not last long. The time ranges from one to five minutes, depending primarily upon how soon the child gets his wish. The "temper-tantrum age," or the age when every normal, healthy child experiences temper tantrums, begins around the second year and reaches a peak between the third and fourth years.

As the angry expressions are controlled—partly through punishment, partly through the force of social disapproval, and partly because the child discovers that they do not work—the child substitutes sulking, pouting, brooding, "negativism," or contrariness, refusal to speak, fussiness and quarrelsomeness in their place. These substitutes for temper tantrums serve as satisfactory outlets for the child's anger. Unpleasant as the substitutes are, they are less annoying and embarrassing than the temper tantrums.

Fear

Human beings have more fears as little children than they have at any other period of their entire lives. The child's fears disappear as his intelligence develops and he understands that many of the things he formerly feared are harmless and that there is no need to be afraid of them. With increased knowledge, as well as better reasoning, he also realizes that many of the things that he feared might happen in early childhood would have done him no harm.

Causes of Fears

Most fears, however, are the aftermath of a frightening experience. The child who gets beyond his depth in water and has trouble getting back to safety is likely to build up a fear of water. Similarly, fear of high places can generally be traced to some unpleasant experience in a high place, such as climbing a tree and having trouble in getting down or nearly falling out of a window on the upper floor of a house.

As has been pointed out before, it is not the thing itself that the child learns to fear but rather the way it is presented to him. Anything that occurs *suddenly* and *unexpectedly* without the child's being prepared for it will give rise to fear. An animal that appears to be just as harmless as a stuffed toy may suddenly open its mouth and bark or roar. Or it may scratch with its paw. Because the child was not prepared for this, he is frightened.

Common Childhood Fears

Common fears of young children include fear of animals, of being dropped, of being left alone, of falling, of insecurity of footing (such as one experiences when walking on an icy pavement), of strangers, of loud noises—especially of the harsh, metallic sort—and of strange places.

In each instance the fear can be traced to the fact that the child was not mentally adjusted or prepared for it. With each succeeding year, as the child becomes more mature intellectually, he can adjust himself more quickly to the sudden and unexpected. The result will be fewer fears.

Fear Behavior

Fear behavior follows a fairly definite and clear-cut pattern in young children. It is characterized by an attempt to withdraw from the fear-arousing object. Before the baby can creep or crawl, he pulls his arms and legs up to his body, turns his head, and shuts his eyes. He behaves not unlike the turtle who hides in his shell. As the child's power of locomotion develops, he removes his body from the source of fear by crawling, then creeping, and finally by running.

In each case the child is trying to get away from the feared object. Generally a young child will hide when he is frightened. He hides behind a door, a piece of furniture, a tree, a person, or anything that happens to be available. If there is no place to hide, he will turn his head and cover his eyes with his hands so that he cannot see what has frightened him. Accompanying fear is a whimpering type of cry, a temporary holding of the breath, and a checking of the activity the child is engaged in.

Shyness

Shyness is a type of fear that occurs when a child is with a stranger, with a familiar person in an unfamiliar garment, such as the mother wearing a hat and coat instead of her familiar indoor clothing, or when he is in a strange place. Shyness occurs because the child is expecting to see a familiar person or place? He cannot adjust himself quickly to something that is unfamiliar.

There are certain periods in every child's life when shyness is a normal reaction. Between the ages of eighteen months and two years, the so-called "shy age," shyness is not only very common but it is also very pronounced. Another shy age in early childhood comes when the child must first adjust himself to a strange place and to strange people in Sunday school, nursery school, kindergarten, or first grade.

The behavior of a shy child is very similar to that shown in fear. The child runs and hides, puckers up his face in readiness to cry, and whimpers. Strange things, however, arouse his curiosity and he cannot resist the temptation to peek.

When he discovers that there is nothing to hurt him, he becomes bolder and bolder until he finally comes out of hiding. He then adjusts himself to the new situation. This may take five or ten minutes but usually less.

Jealousy

Jealousy is closely related to anger in that the child is annoyed when he believes that his place in the affections of a loved one is being usurped by another. The most common cause of jealousy in early childhood is the birth of a younger brother or sister whose helplessness requires time and attention from the different members of the household.

The jealous child, who has been used to being the center of attention, resents having a baby take his place. Occasionally jealousy is caused by favoritism on the part of a parent for one of the children of the family.

The time when jealousy is most likely to occur is between the ages of two and five years. Before the age of two, the child's mental development is not advanced enough for him to realize that there has been a change in his relations with

others, nor does he realize that he is now getting less attention than he formerly had.

From two to five, he is mentally old enough to recognize
this change; but his comprehension is not developed enough
for him to realize that it is caused by necessity arising from
the helplessness of the new baby, not from lack of interest or
affection on his parents' part.

By the time the child is five years old, his interests broaden.
He finds companionship among children of his own age.
Since he no longer relies entirely upon adults for companionship, he does not miss so much as he formerly did the attention from and association with adults. The result is a gradual
waning of jealousy.

Jealous Behavior

Jealousy is not unlike a temper tantrum in that it is an un-
bridled expression of anger. It differs from a temper tantrum,
however, in that it is always directed against another person,
while anger is not. It characteristically consists of hurting the
offender by hitting, kicking, biting, pinching, or scratching.
Sometimes a jealous child reverts to infantile behavior,
such as bed-wetting, thumb-sucking, refusal to eat, pretend-
ing to be ill, being afraid or helpless in carrying out tasks
formerly carried out successfully. It sometimes shows itself in
general naughtiness. In each case, the young child is bidding
for attention.

Happiness

Healthy children are usually happy. This is true unless the
environment is unfavorable and gives rise to unpleasant emotions. When the young child is in a good physical condition,
it takes relatively little to get a happy response from him.

Studies of young children show that the usual stimuli to happiness include the following: being smiled at, played with, tickled, patted in approval or in love by another person; receiving expressions of friendliness from a pet animal; hearing unusual sounds; seeing funny faces; watching the sudden appearance or disappearance of a person or toy; experiencing slight calamities, such as slipping or bumping into a person; and imitating or watching adults imitate others, especially their speech and gait.

Expressions of Happiness

Happiness is expressed mostly by smiling and laughing. When young children are very happy, they make a lot of noise as they laugh. They open their mouths wide and literally roar. In addition to this source of noise, they frequently clap their hands and jump up and down.

It is not unusual for them to hug the person or thing that gives rise to their happiness. Many young children, after several minutes of uproarious laughter, fall on the floor and roll back and forth like little puppies. Then from sheer physical exhaustion they lie motionless and pant for breath.

Affection

Affection is similar to happiness in that it brings about a happy response. There is no evidence, however, to show that a child has a natural affection for anyone. There is, by contrast, plenty of evidence to show that children learn to love the people, pets, or things with whom they have pleasurable associations. The people who take care of the young child's bodily needs, those who play with him, and those who, in general, are responsible for giving him pleasure are the ones that he will like.

Children express affection easily, spontaneously, and without embarrassment, hugging and kissing the people and animals that they love.

ELIZABETH HIBBS

Family Affection

(As a general rule, little children have greater affection for their mothers than for their fathers.) In American society, especially in cities, the father is away from home at his work for the major part of the day. The child's contacts are therefore mostly with the mother. (It is the mother who, on the whole, takes care of the child's needs and sees to it that life is a pleasant experience for him. By contrast, the father, whose contacts throughout the day are with adults, is very apt to judge the child's behavior by adult standards. Because the child's behavior does not measure up favorably—and logically it cannot be expected to—the father may tend to be impatient.

Naturally this does not make him as popular with the child as does the more tolerant treatment from the mother. It is quite understandable that the child will then have greater affection for the mother than for the father.)

A jealous brother or sister who does not treat a child with

much kindness cannot expect as much affection from that child as if his attitude had been more tolerant. Similarly, a grandparent whose attitude is reflected in the words "I spanked your mother when she was a little girl and behaved like you do" will not receive the same amount of affection from the grandchild as will the grandparent who makes every visit a treat for the child and whose attitude toward misbehavior is one of tolerant understanding.

Expressions of Affection

Childish affection shows itself by the child's wanting to be with the loved one and by his spontaneous patting, hugging, and kissing of the person or thing that he loves. Pet animals are constantly mauled by a young child, and if they do not take kindly to it, the child's affection for them will cease. Likewise, the child's stuffed animals and dolls are hugged and kissed until they literally fall to pieces.

Throughout early childhood, affection is expressed in a spontaneous manner with no indication of embarrassment, nor does the young child show embarrassment when others demonstrate their affection for him. It is not until the child reaches school age that he makes any attempt to control his affectionate behavior.

Curiosity

Little children, like animals, are spontaneously curious about anything new or unusual. If the new is too strange and unusual, it may arouse a temporary state of fear, but this is not likely to last long. When it disappears, curiosity dominates the child, and he proceeds to explore until his curiosity is satisfied.

Young children are curious about many things, the most common of which are (1) *natural phenomena,* such as rain, snow, clouds, the sun, moon and stars, plants and animals and especially how they grow; (2) *scientific phenomena,* such as the workings of clocks, lights, bells, stoves, water faucets, automobiles, and machines of all types; (3) *birth and death,* with emphasis on where babies come from and what happens to people and animals after they die; and (4) *the workings of their own bodies,* such as the excretory organs, their eyes, ears, mouths, fingers, and toes. They are likewise curious to know why the bodies of children differ from those of adults and why boys are different from girls.

Behavior of a Curious Child

When curiosity is aroused, the child's natural tendency to explore leads him to investigate. He handles the object that arouses his curiosity and sometimes is hurt because he does not realize the danger involved. This is true when he wants to "feel" fire or hangs too far out of a window to see what is happening on the street below. If he does not hurt himself, he is very likely to hurt the thing he explores.

Because exploring so often leads to harm, it is very common practice in many families for adults to discourage young children from exploring. This is unfortunate because exploring is one of the important channels through which the young child acquires information about the world in which he lives. It would be far better if the child were encouraged to explore and acquire knowledge under careful supervision so that he does not harm himself or the object he explores.

Effective Use of Emotions

The emotions may be beneficial or harmful, depending upon what use the individual makes of them. That is why it is important that the child learn, as early in life as possible, how to use his emotions as aids rather than as hindrances to

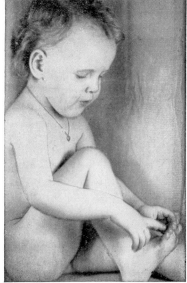

Anything new or strange may frighten the child slightly but it will also make him curious. He will be curious about natural phenomena, such as birds' eggs; about scientific and mechanical phenomena, such as the garden hose; and about the workings of his own body, such as his toes. The child should be allowed to explore, because that is one way in which he learns.

MARY BRANDEL HOPKINS (*top left and bottom*), AND FREDERIC LEWIS (*top right*) his efficiency, his happiness, and his adjustments to other people.

Because the emotions are a part of our hereditary endowment, they cannot be eliminated. Nor would it be desirable to do so, as many emotions not only add pleasure to life but they also aid in our adjustments to life. The child who learns how to use fear, for example, will be cautious in the presence of danger but will not waste emotional energy on things that are not dangerous.

Similarly, learning to direct curiosity into useful channels will provide the necessary motivation to learn about the world in which he lives. If, on the other hand, the child does not learn how to use his curiosity constructively, he is likely to discover that it leads him into dangerous situations or situations in which he arouses the antagonism of others.

One of the greatest helps in learning how to use the emotions effectively is in eliminating the causes of emotional outbursts. It is well for a parent to help a child by avoiding the situations, discussed in the following section, which are likely to cause emotional outbursts. Such outbursts result in behavior that is not beneficial to the child, and they hinder him in making adjustments to other people.

Causes of Emotionality

Studies of children's emotions have shown that a number of factors are likely to cause childish emotionality. Fortunately most, if not all, of these factors can be controlled if adults are willing to watch for them. In the following paragraphs these factors are discussed along with practical suggestions for controlling them.

1. Fatigue. Tired children are inevitably cross and difficult to manage. Fatigue studies have shown that the times of the day when young children are most likely to be tired are just

The parent should realize the time and factors that are likely to arouse a child's emotions. When he is tired, ill, or thwarted, he should be handled with "kid gloves" so as to avoid any emotional outburst. The curbing of emotional outbursts during the early years will help to avoid problems later on as the child grows older.

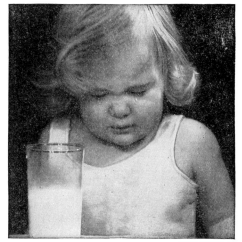

FREDERIC LEWIS

before noon and evening meals, just before bedtime, and just after some unusual activity, such as a shopping trip or a long automobile ride.

2. Poor Health. Good health is reflected in pleasant emotions, while poor health, like fatigue, makes a child cranky and irritable. When the child is very sick, emotional outbursts are relatively infrequent but, as the child convalesces, the tendency to irritability will increase. This, in turn, makes his care increasingly difficult.

3. Association with Emotional People. Little children are mimics. They quickly imitate the behavior they observe in others. The more frequently and the more closely a child is associated with a person whose emotions are uncontrolled, the less likely he is to develop emotional control himself.

4. Thwarted Desires. All young children behave in a selfish manner. They do what they want to do when they want to do it, regardless of how much they may inconvenience others. Society, of course, imposes restraints upon the child's natural impulses. The child, in turn, revolts. The stricter the discipline, the more predisposed the child will be to revolt.

5. *Unpreparedness.* Many times situations for which the child is not prepared give rise to emotional outbursts. Perhaps the emotionality would not have occurred if the child had expected the situation. This fact has already been stressed in the case of fear. It is not the object itself that the child fears so much as the fact that it is presented to him suddenly and unexpectedly.

If unpreparedness is responsible for emotional outbursts, the logical conclusion to draw is that, if the child is to avoid these outbursts which deplete his energy and lead to no useful behavior, he must be prepared ahead of time so that he will be ready for the situation that otherwise would lead to emotionality. Children are too young and inexperienced to be able to anticipate situations that *might* arise.

It thus becomes the responsibility of the adults with whom the child is associated to anticipate situations which commonly lead to emotional outbursts in children of that age and to control them. By doing so, they help the child to avoid establishing patterns of behavior which will prove to be difficult to eliminate later when he discovers how useless or harmful they are. It also helps him to learn how to anticipate troublesome situations so that, in time, he can assume the responsibility for their control without help from others.

For Discussion

1. It is a common belief that emotional parents transmit, through hereditary influences, their emotionality to their children. Give your arguments for or against this belief.
2. Give examples of children's behavior in which anger and fear proved to be helpful to the child.

3. Why is envy or covetousness not a strong emotion in early childhood? What aspects of development must be present before envy will appear?

4. Why is it frequently more desirable to ignore a young child's emotional outbursts than to criticize him? Give specific examples to illustrate this point.

5. Does punishing a child when he is having a temper tantrum teach him not to have temper tantrums in the future? If not, what other methods could be used?

6. Suggest practical ways of helping children to use their natural curiosity in constructive ways.

Suggested Activities

1. Make a list, from your own observations, of the things or situations that cause children to laugh. Then classify these in an orderly pattern and note the most frequent type of causes.

2. Make a list of children's questions. Note the most frequent source of curiosity that gives rise to the questions.

3. Observe a parent on the street, in a store, or in a bus handling an emotional outbreak on the part of a young child. Is the method of handling designed to minimize parental embarrassment or to teach the child emotional control? Report your observations fully to back up your conclusion.

4. Observe as many cases as possible of young children with infant brothers and sisters. Watch closely the parental behavior in dealing with the infant and the child. From your observations, does jealousy on the part of the child seem justified?

5. List situations you have observed that lead to temper tantrums in the home and in the school. Which of these might have been controlled so the tantrums would have been prevented?

6. Observe how teachers handle the child's fear of new situations, of new people, or of tackling a new problem. Which methods seem to intensify the child's fears and which serve to calm the fears?

PART THREE:

The Child's Problems and Habits

CHAPTER 10

Mealtime and Bedtime Problems

Eating and sleeping are natural functions of the human body. As such, there should be no problems connected with them. Little children should naturally eat when they are hungry and naturally sleep when they are tired. Since this is not always possible, problems may arise. When problems arise with children, the trouble can often be traced to wrong training and unwholesome attitudes on the part of the adults who are responsible for them.

There has been so much written and said in recent years about eating and sleeping problems that far too many young parents are dominated by the belief that their child is sure

The artist of the lithograph on the left, Lawrence Beall Smith, is a well-known young American lithographer. Mr. Smith has named this picture *Dustin and His Friends* after his own son, Dustin. The light in this picture, which comes as if from a door opening into a dark room, makes the figures alive and round. (Courtesy Associated American Artists.)

to be a "problem eater" or a "problem sleeper." They are
even on the alert for anything that might suggest the beginning of trouble. The result is that they are often too quick
to interpret a perfectly natural reaction as an eating or sleeping problem.

Importance of Good Eating and Sleeping Habits

Good eating and sleeping habits are essential to good
health. Good health, in turn, is essential to a good disposition and a pleasant personality. A child who does not get
enough to eat nor enough of the right kinds of food has too
little energy for growth and activity.

His growth will sap his strength, and even normal activities will wear him out. As a result, he is constantly fretful,
irritable, and hard to manage. Nothing pleases him and he
pleases no one.

The child who gets too little sleep is an equally difficult
and unpleasant child. Sleep is our way of overcoming fatigue and restoring used-up energy. The child who gets too
little sleep, or whose sleep is of the restless, fitful type, gets
up in the morning almost as tired as he was when he went
to bed.

There are two important suggestions to ensure the establishment of good habits of eating and sleeping. The first
is to assume an outward calm and an attitude of confidence
that all is well. When the adult faces the eating and sleeping situations with a matter-of-fact "I am sure everything is
all right" attitude, the young child will do so also.

However, outward calm and confidence cannot accompany inward apprehension. Worry always shows itself outwardly in tension, irritability, and impatience. Therefore,
the adult who is with the young child when he eats or when
he goes to bed must learn to assume a favorable attitude.

H. ARMSTRONG ROBERTS

When the child refuses to eat, it is important that the mother be pleasant and relaxed. Fear and tenseness on her part are bound to be felt by the child and discourage him from eating.

The second suggestion is as important as the first: Nip in the bud any behavior that may lead to a problem. Before beginning the correction, it is wise to make certain that it really is the start of a problem and not merely a temporary lapse resulting from fatigue, illness, emotional tension, or some other condition of a temporary nature. Whether or not it is a temporary lapse can easily be determined by watching to see if the behavior recurs every time a similar situation is present.

Children have to *learn* to eat. Not only must they learn how to handle tableware and cups, but they must learn how to drink, how to bite, how to chew, and how to swallow. All this takes time and patience on the part of the child and the mother. If the child has learned how to eat well by the time he is four, he is doing well.

COURTESY H. J. HEINZ COMPANY

Eating Problems

There are a number of common eating problems among young children that should be discussed briefly. Practical methods of dealing with them will also be suggested. Not all these problems, of course, will be present in every child's behavior, but few children will escape all of them. Furthermore, it is well to be forewarned of their possible appearance and to know how to diagnose them in their early stages.

Learning to Eat

Strange as it may seem, every child has to *learn* to eat. He will, of course, be able to suck and swallow at birth, but his swallowing will often be accompanied by choking. As he grows older, he will naturally chew and bite; but, once again, learning will do much to improve the natural techniques.

For the first four or five months of life, the child's eating is "infantile" in that food must be sucked into the mouth and swallowed without chewing. For this reason all foods must be in a liquid form.

Biting, Chewing, and Drinking

Biting seems to be a natural form of behavior that occurs even before the teeth cut through the gums. Before the biting can be completely successful, however, the baby must learn how large a bite to take. Otherwise he may bite off too big a piece to handle successfully. Biting normally begins between the fourth and fifth months, but chewing generally does not occur until a month later.

The major problem with regard to chewing is that the baby does not know exactly how to go about it. As a result, he either spits out the food or holds it in his mouth. He can then be shown how to chew. If this does not prove successful, it is best to put him back on a soft diet for a short time. Another problem consists of the tendency to chew "rabbit style," or by using only the front teeth. A larger amount of food placed in the mouth will soon make the baby use his gums as well as his teeth for chewing.

One of the greatest problems in the transition from infantile to more mature forms of eating comes when liquids are drunk instead of sucked. In his early attempts to drink, a baby will invariably suck in air, which will cause choking or even vomiting.

The hungrier he is, the greater will be the baby's tendency to gulp liquids, and, consequently, the more air he will suck in. Thus, the cup should be substituted for the bottle gradually. This should be done only at the end of a feeding period when a baby's hunger is so nearly satisfied that he is less likely to gulp.

The final problem in learning to eat is learning how to swallow solids after they have been chewed. Swallowing liquids is a natural reaction, but swallowing solids, even after chewing, must be learned. If a baby has difficulty in doing this at first, it is best to go back to semisolids for a short time before trying again.

Frequently it helps a baby if his head is tilted back slightly to enable the food to rest on his throat. This stimulates the throat muscles. Also, a swallow of milk will help him to wash down the food after it has been chewed. This method should be used only until the baby gets used to the "feel" of swallowing.

By the time the baby is a year old, he should have mastered all these fundamental problems that arise in connection with eating, but, to be able to master them, he must be given an opportunity to do so. This means that he must not be fed from a bottle longer than necessary, nor should his solids be reduced to liquid form for long when he should be able to bite and chew.

A word of caution in this respect is necessary. A baby must learn the more mature methods of eating very slowly and gradually. Each new eating skill should be introduced separately and be fairly well mastered before the next is introduced. This means that he should learn to drink from a cup with a fair degree of success before he is expected to master the difficult task of biting, and that biting, in turn, should be fairly well mastered before chewing is learned.

Amount of Food Eaten

As a rule, if a specific amount of food, adequate for the child's age, is prepared, the child should eat all of it. However, exceptions should be taken into consideration, such as the fact that a child may not need or want all of that food on that particular day.

Even young babies vary from day to day in the amount of

food they want to eat, but well-meaning parents too often force them to eat all that is prepared for them. Then they are disturbed when the baby spits up part of it.

A young child's appetite will vary from day to day or from meal to meal just as an adult's appetite does. The amount of food he wants or needs will depend to a large extent upon how he feels at mealtime. If he is tired, emotionally upset, excited from being in a crowd, suffering from a slight cold, or hot and uncomfortable, he cannot be expected to be as hungry as if his physical and emotional conditions were more favorable.

A good way to determine whether the child is getting enough food to meet his needs is to observe how he behaves between meals. If he is happy and contented, all is well, but, if he is fretful, irritable, and listless, it may mean that he is hungry. He obviously is not getting enough food to carry him from one meal to another.

Forced Feeding and Overeating

It is far better to throw away food prepared for a young child than to force him to eat it if he revolts. Forced eating is likely to build up a dislike for the particular food that the child has been forced to eat. In time, this dislike will spread to the whole eating situation. The result is that mealtimes will be dreaded not only by the child but by the whole family.

It is far better to remove the uneaten food without comment or show of concern, after a reasonable time, than to bribe, coax, or force the child to clean his plate and drain the last drop from his cup. Should a poor appetite continue for several days, the doctor should be consulted.

Encouraging overeating is almost as bad as forced feeding. It may be a source of satisfaction to a mother to see her child eat with relish everything she prepares for him and even ask for more, but overeating is not good for a child. It can soon develop into a habit and, like all undesirable habits, it will be difficult to overcome when its bad effects become apparent.

Overeating invariably leads to excess weight. A fat child has difficulties in controlling his body or in moving as fast as his thinner companions. Furthermore, fatness in time becomes a source of embarrassment to a child and he resents being called "Fatty" or "Tubby" by his playmates.

Food Likes and Dislikes

Ironical as it may seem, many of us prefer the type of food that we should eat sparingly and dislike the type of food that we should eat in abundance. Such food whims can usually be traced to early childhood experiences.

Scientific studies of taste have shown no inborn food dislikes except for food that is harmful to the human body. We can therefore assume that the majority of our food dislikes are learned. Similarly, we can assume that a child will naturally like all food unless he has learned, in one way or another, to dislike it.

Studies of food dislikes among young children have shown what gives rise to them. The most common cause is being forced to eat a certain food or being punished for not doing so. Some parents even go so far as to require a child to remain at the table until the last mouthful of a food he does not like is eaten.

Some foods are disliked because they are badly cooked. Can you blame a child for not wanting to eat lumpy cereal, watery vegetables, or overcooked meat? Because a child's sense of taste is more highly developed than ours, many foods that are palatable to us have too strong a taste for the child. Salad dressings, highly seasoned sauces and fillings, or highly spiced cakes and pies are disliked for this reason.

Dealing with Food Dislikes

It is usually rather easy to discover why a child dislikes a certain food. Making him like it is another story. Certainly forcing him to eat it will never solve the problem. The most successful approach is to present the disliked food to him in an attractive, well-cooked form, garnished with parsley, watercress, celery leaves, lettuce, raisins, or cherries, depending upon the type of food.

If a child realizes that no one will force him to eat a specific food that he rebels against, it will go far to break down his food dislikes. It may take time for a young child who has been forced in the past to eat disliked food to realize that those days are over. When he finally does realize it, his whole attitude will become more cooperative and willing.

Now, a word of warning about food dislikes. Should a young child persist in refusing a specific food, or should there be evidence of sneezing, hives, or vomiting after eating the food, it is very likely that he is allergic to it. Under such circumstances, the matter should be reported to the doctor at once.

Importance of Food Likes

Strong likes for certain foods are desirable, provided the foods are of the type that are good for a child. The more a child likes a food, the more readily he will eat it. However, if the liking is for food that should be eaten only sparingly—such as candy, rich desserts, and pastry—parents have a real problem to cope with.

The best way to handle this problem is to see to it that the child receives daily a certain amount of these foods. The amount should be determined by the doctor. Under no circumstances should a young child be permitted to eat the foods he likes as much as he pleases or whenever he pleases.

The seriousness of food likes and dislikes is not always comprehended. We do things we like and avoid doing things we dislike. We react in the same way to food. Little children, like adults, are therefore likely to eat too much of the foods they like and too little of the foods they dislike. This results in an unbalanced diet.

Furthermore, the digestive secretions are stimulated when the eater's attitude is favorable to the food he is eating and checked when the attitude is unfavorable. Digestive upsets and vomiting frequently accompany the eating of disliked food. Finally, but by no means of least importance, is the fact that food likes add greatly to the enjoyment of the meal, while food dislikes make the meal an unpleasant experience.

Self-feeding

A tiny baby must, of course, be fed, but he will be able to feed himself for part of the meal sooner than most parents realize. His readiness to do this is shown by the way he tries to hold his bottle and by the way he carries the spoon up to his mouth, even when there is no food on it.

It is desirable for a baby to feed himself as soon as he is able, partly because it is a timesaver for the mother but primarily because it gives the baby a feeling of independence and self-confidence. If he is not permitted to learn to feed himself when he shows a desire to do so, he may get into the habit of depending on others to such an extent that he will later make no effort to feed himself.

It is impossible to give specific ages at which a child can be expected to handle different eating utensils because no two children are alike. However, studies of babies and

The baby's desire to use his own cup comes about the same time as his desire to use a spoon. At first the baby will try to gulp the liquid and may choke. Therefore, he should be trained in how to hold the cup and how to tip it so that he will get the right amount of liquid without spilling it or choking.

COURTESY NATIONAL DAIRY PRODUCTS CORPORATION

young children have revealed average ages for these different activities. They may be taken as criteria of the ages at which one can expect readiness for self-feeding to appear.

Use of Eating Utensils

By the age of six months, a baby will grasp for his spoon and suck it. He will also bang and throw it. If he is encouraged to try to feed himself, by having an adult guide his hand, he will gradually get the feel of it. With practice, he will be able to take over the whole task himself.

When he is eighteen months old, the baby should be able to feed himself with a spoon with relatively little spilling. Left to his own devices, he will grasp the spoon with his hand on top of the spoon handle. This is an awkward way to hold it and encourages sloppiness. He should be shown at

The child's first spoon may be miniature in size, but it should be of an adult type and should not have a curved handle. The first fork should have blunt prongs, and the knife should have a dull edge so that the child will not hurt himself.

first the correct method of holding a spoon and never be permitted to get into the habit of holding it incorrectly.

The desire to hold his own cup shows itself at approximately the same age as the desire to use a spoon. If the cup has a handle, and if the baby is encouraged to support the cup with the other hand, he can avoid many spillings at first. He will have to be shown how to tip his cup to avoid spillings.

Until the skill is well mastered, the cup should be only partially filled. By the time the child is two, a cup or glass without a handle may be substituted for the one with the handle, provided his drinking has been relatively free from spillings for several months.

If a child is allowed to use his spoon for too long a time, he will be delayed in learning how to use a fork. As soon as he has mastered the art of using his spoon, he should learn to eat with a fork. To avoid hurting himself, he should be given a fork with blunt prongs.

The use of such a fork will also discourage the child's tendency to "spear" food. It will encourage him to use a fork correctly by pushing it under the food. Carrying food to the mouth with a fork is more difficult than with a spoon and will therefore require more time for learning. If a child can feed himself well with a fork by the time he is four, he has done as much as anyone can reasonably expect.

Learning to use a knife should begin around the age of two. The knife can be used first for spreading butter or jam. A young child should be given only a dull-edged knife at first because a sharp-edged knife can be dangerous.

It is difficult to cut with a dull knife, but the child can learn first by cutting potatoes, toast covered with creamed meat, or soft, well-cooked meats. He will not be able to cut the tougher meats until he is ready to use a sharp knife. This will not be before he is six years old.

Food Dawdlers

It is not at all uncommon for a baby who eats very quickly to develop into a food dawdler as a young child. He may spend endless minutes over his meal, allowing it to grow cold and unpalatable before he eats a mouthful. This drives his parents to distraction. They bribe, threaten, scold, punish, and nag in an attempt to get him to speed up his eating.

Dawdling generally begins when a young child starts to feed himself. As long as he is hungry, he will eat quickly; but, when the hunger pangs have been satisfied, his interest in eating begins to lag and he turns his attention to something else.

The best way to break up the tendency to dawdle over meals is to give the child a certain amount of time to eat the meal. Then, if he doesn't eat it, quietly and without com-

Attempts to get a food dawdler to "speed up" may only make the matter worse. If the child will not eat within a certain allotted time, his food should quietly be removed and he should not be fed again until the next meal. This way he will soon learn that he must eat at mealtime to keep from getting hungry.

ment or trace of annoyance, remove his plate from the table. Even if he has eaten practically nothing, it will do him no harm to wait until the next meal.

Bedtime Problems

Problems connected with sleep are generally not so serious in the typical American home as are mealtime problems, but they are certain to arise sometime. Unless they are dealt with correctly, they can lead to serious enough obstacles to the child's sleep habits to impair the general state of his health.

Amount of Sleep Needed

Doctors usually inform parents as to how much sleep their child needs, depending upon the child's age and general state of health. There are, however, "averages" for different ages that can be used only as a rough guide to determine the amount needed for each individual child.

From birth to four months, the average baby sleeps from seventeen to twenty out of the twenty-four hours of the day. This is broken into short periods of three to four hours at a stretch because the baby must be fed at frequent intervals. Gradually, as his capacity to eat more at one time increases and as his diet contains more solids, he can sleep for longer periods. By the end of the second month, for example, he should be able to sleep from 10 P.M. to 6 A.M. without waking, and by the age of six months, from 10 P.M. until 7 A.M. By this time, the amount of sleep needed will have decreased to approximately sixteen hours. By the time the child is a year old, he will need only fourteen hours of sleep.

Each year after the first, the sleep time required decreases, on the average, by one half-hour. This means that the average three-year-old will need approximately thirteen hours of sleep; the five-year-old will need twelve hours; and the six- or seven-year-old will need roughly eleven hours.

Naps

Naps are regarded as an essential part of the sleep schedule for babies. During the first year of life the baby has a morning nap just after his bath and feeding, and an afternoon nap just after the midday feeding. Many doctors recommend that this program be followed for at least the first few months of the second year. Then the morning nap may be abandoned.

The average time for naps is one hour in the morning and two hours in the afternoon. During the first two years the naptime is generally spent in sleep. The baby falls to sleep within a few minutes of being put in his crib and frequently has to be wakened when the nap period is over. If he is permitted to sleep until he wakens spontaneously, it is apt to interfere with the next sleep period.

Revolt against Naps

Between the ages of two and three years, it is not at all unusual for a child to spend the entire nap period, even if it has been shortened to one hour, in play instead of in sleep. By the time he is four, he generally begins to revolt against naps by stalling on the way to bed to play with his toys, by getting out of bed as soon as the door is shut, or by pulling off his bedclothes, kicking the wall, or turning somersaults in bed.

He seems to have no desire to sleep, and, because he causes more trouble during the nap period than at other times, his mother comes to the conclusion that he no longer needs a nap. The result is that the nap period is given up.

All children under six years of age, and many for several years longer, need rest during the day even if they do not need sleep. For that reason, when it is apparent that the child does not need sleep in the middle of the day, the nap period should be changed to a rest period.

Preparation for Sleep

Preparation for bed and preparation for sleep are two distinctly different things. Preparation for bed involves undressing, putting on night clothes, cleaning teeth, putting away

Preparation for bed and preparation for sleep are two different things. The time spent in getting the child ready for bed should not be counted as a part of his sleep time.

HAROLD M. LAMBERT FROM FREDERIC LEWIS

toys, going to the toilet, and saying prayers. Each activity must be carried out with a certain amount of effort and a marked degree of concentration on the child's part. This tends to make him alert and wide awake.

Preparation for sleep, by contrast, means relaxing of both mind and body. No one, adult or child, can go to sleep when the body is alert and ready for action.

The best preparation for sleep consists in preparing for bed in a leisurely fashion at least a half-hour before bedtime. Then, during the half-hour, the young child should have a quiet time in which to relax and grow sleepy. This may be spent in story-telling, being read to, looking at pictures, or listening to music.

Under no circumstances should a young child be permitted to engage in a romp or listen to exciting stories just before bedtime. Nor should the time for preparation for bed be so short that he will get tense from a hectic rush to get him to bed on the dot. Anything that tends to excite a child should be avoided at this time.

Bed-wetting

No child can be expected to achieve good enough bladder control to keep dry every night and all night much before he is three and a half or four years old. Some children wet their beds even after that age. Learning bladder control depends upon the development of the nerves and the muscles that control the bladder. It cannot be hurried. As no two children develop in exactly the same way or at exactly the same rate, it is impossible to predict just when a certain child will achieve complete bladder control at night, just as it is impossible to predict when he will achieve complete dryness in the day.

Most children go through periods of short or long duration when they have "accidents." Even a normally quiet, calm child may find bladder control difficult and have an "accident" during times of excitement and nervous tension. These accidents are likely to disturb the child, causing him to be apprehensive and nervous and delaying his learning. His parents can help by trying to convince him that he is learning fast, that he cannot expect to achieve perfection quickly, and that it won't be long now before he will have no more accidents. However, if bed-wetting is a nightly occurrence, it suggests that something is wrong that must be corrected before the bed-wetting will cease. It should not be neglected in the false hope that the child will "outgrow" it.

Bed-wetting by an older child is known as "enuresis." In relatively few cases is it due to a physical cause. For the most part, enuresis stems from some psychological disturbance, such as emotional tension, feelings of inadequacy from adult pressures to do more than he is capable of doing, feelings of rejection—especially when there is a new baby in the family—or excitability. Because enuresis is an individual problem, stemming from some personal need that has not been filled in the child's life, it is wise to consult the doctor about the matter and follow his advice.

Parents should try to find out the cause for the child's tension and work on eliminating *that* rather than putting too much stress on the problem of bed-wetting. The parents' attitude toward bed-wetting has a strong influence on the child's attitude and this, in turn, will influence his success in training. Under no condition should the child be ridiculed, scolded, or spanked for wetting his bed.

A child can be helped to achieve dryness at night by having his liquids reduced gradually after four or five o'clock. To make sure he is getting enough liquids, he should be encouraged to drink additional amounts during the day. He should also go to the toilet just before he goes to bed.

Most doctors today oppose waking the young child during the night to take him to the toilet. This not only breaks the child's sleep, and may cause restlessness for a time after he has been put back to bed, but it also tends to frighten him. However, should he waken of his own accord and call for someone to take him to the toilet, he should be taken.

A child who is used to going to the toilet alone during the day should be encouraged to get out of bed and go directly to the bathroom as soon as he wakens in the morning, without calling for someone to take him. In case it is still dark when he wakens or if he wakes during the night and wants to go, he should have a bed light on a table at the side of his bed and be shown how to turn it on. Fear of the dark or of getting out of bed in the dark keeps many young children from going to the toilet when they need to.

A flashlight can be placed on the child's bedside table for

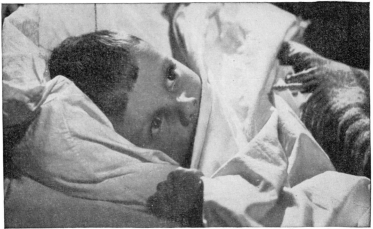

Leaving the door ajar so the child can hear the family is reassuring to him when he has fears at night. Parents should go to a frightened child at once to assure him that nothing is wrong.

use in lighting his way to the bathroom. He should also be shown where the light switch is in the bathroom. It is a good policy to rehearse the trip from the bed to the bathroom, turning on all necessary lights en route, to eliminate any fears or hesitancies that might hold back the child should he waken during the night. To avoid a frightening experience or an accident, the furniture should be pushed aside so there is a clear path from his bed to the bathroom.

Bedtime Fears

It is an exceptional child who is not at some time afraid when he is left alone in bed. Sometimes he is afraid of the dark, sometimes of strange noises inside or outside of the house, sometimes of being left alone, and occasionally of dreaming.

Whatever may give rise to these fears, they are usually genuine and should not be ignored. Ignoring them tends to make them worse. Of even more serious consequence, it builds up a fear of going to bed. Sometimes stalling at bedtime can be traced to a feeling of uneasiness that results from the child's fear of going to bed.

The most successful way to deal with this bedtime problem is to convince the child that he has nothing to fear. If the door of his room is left ajar until he goes to sleep to enable him to hear the familiar sounds of the household, it will tend to reassure him. A night light can be placed in the hall outside his door or in his room, if the child insists upon it. A light in his room may interfere with his falling asleep or it may produce shadows which will frighten him.

Nothing is more important than to encourage a child to talk freely about his fears. This not only helps the parents to realize what the child is afraid of, but it also enables the child to see how senseless the fears generally are. Just talking about a fear helps him to "get it out of his system" and eliminates some of the fear. If his attempts to talk are met with ridicule or indifference, he will brood over the cause of the fear. The more he broods, the stronger the fear will then become.

For Discussion

1. Why are common punishments, such as depriving children of their desserts or sending them to bed for naughtiness, undesirable from the point of view of their after-effects on the child?
2. What suggestions can you offer for handling a child who dawdles over his food?
3. If the child continues to be a sloppy eater longer than usual, what may be the causes? How can this condition be corrected?

4. Discuss the unfavorable effects of the clean-plate policy on the child. Suggest practical methods of handling the problem.
5. How do children of three, four, five, and six years of age feel about bed-wetting? Is there a change in attitude as children grow older?
6. On such special occasions as holidays and week ends, which is better—putting children to bed on the dot, even if rushed, or taking the usual time for preparation, even if this means getting to bed later than usual?

Suggested Activities

1. Make a list of your food dislikes. Analyze each and try to discover the cause and origin of each dislike. You may find it helpful to discuss this matter with your parents for supplementary data.
2. Observe the bedtime preparations of a young child. Analyze his activities to see which foster sleepiness and which predispose him to wakefulness.
3. Analyze some of the traditional children's stories, such as "Little Red Riding Hood," for any terror elements that might cause a child to have nightmares.
4. Observe the eating behavior of several young children. Note the methods of holding cups, spoons, and forks. Does the socially accepted form of eating lead to greater efficiency so far as results and energy expended are concerned?
5. Make a list of different fear dreams you have heard children talk about. Then try to relate these to specific events in the child's life.
6. Observe the relative speed of eating different foods by several children. Do you note a relationship between the speed and the child's reaction to the food?

CHAPTER 11

The Child in the Family

Today's baby becomes a part of the family's life as soon as he is brought home from the hospital. True, a baby's routine must be different from that of the other members of the family. His nervous system is not yet well enough developed to enable him to eat and sleep at regular times as other members of the family do. He is still very helpless and will require attention for all his bodily needs.

Because very few families today can afford outside help to assist in the care of the baby and many do not have relatives nearby to call on, the care of the baby becomes the responsibility of the whole family, not of the mother alone. The father or older children can often substitute for the mother in giving the baby his bath, changing his diapers, or keeping a watchful eye on him while he is having his airing.

Even a child of two or three can have a role to play in the care of a baby. He can assist the mother or an older child with the baby's bath, can play with the baby during the baby's waking periods, or can help to push the baby's coach. Today, fathers lend a helping hand with the care of the baby or young child and play with the older children a*

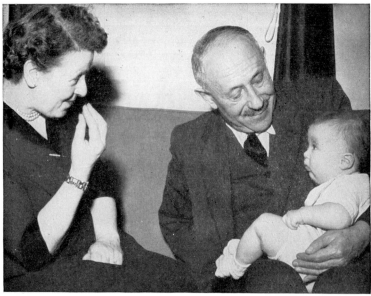

NOTHMANN FROM MONKMEYER

Because a baby is appealing, adults are tempted to play with him during the time he is awake. Too much or constant attention from adults is not good for the baby because it may excite him and cause him to expect companionship too much of the time.

fathers in the past seldom did. No longer do men feel that child care is "woman's work."

Effects of Cooperative Family Relationships

Cooperative family relationships are good for the baby and good for every member of the family. The little child who helps with the care of the baby has little reason to experience jealousy as he might if he were excluded from the mother while she takes care of the baby. As his mother's helper, he has some satisfaction to replace the pleasures he had when he had all of her attention.

To an older child, doing things with and for a baby is often more fun than playing with toys. Unless too much of his time must be devoted to the baby's care, no child will object to doing things for a baby sister or brother. In fact, he will *like* it. And, it is excellent training for him. It teaches him about growth and development of infants, thus helping him to understand and be tolerant of those younger than he, and it gives him training in assuming responsibilities.

The father learns much from assisting in the care of the children of the family. Unless he has an opportunity to help care for them, he doesn't know how to get close to his children. Even more important, he discovers that children are not "miniature adults" and that one cannot, therefore, expect adult behavior from them. Men generally have daily contacts with adults only and therefore are likely to be intolerant of children unless they assume some of the care for the children in the home. They are amply rewarded for this effort in the increased love and attention they receive from the children.

The baby is the chief benefactor of this cooperative type of family relationship. Being a part of the whole family early in his life makes him feel loved and wanted. At the same time he is allowed to be just one unit in the family pattern rather than the most important unit, as babies are when they are cared for by only the mother. From the very beginning he is given the opportunity to adjust to all types of people— something that will be of invaluable help to him when his social horizons broaden to include people outside the family.

The Baby's Place in the Family

While the family is learning to accept the baby as part of the family unit, there must be adjustments on all sides. The older children must realize that a little baby needs more sleep than they do and be willing to be reasonably quiet in their play while the baby is sleeping. They must recognize that the baby needs more feedings than they do, which will sometimes interfere with their plans.

A tactful handling of the situation by the parents will go a long way toward eliminating the possibility of their considering the baby a "nuisance." If each child has his own share of attention and love, and has privileges and responsibilities suited to his level of development, he will accept in a good-natured, matter-of-fact way any trivial inconvenience that the baby's presence in the family may bring.

Likewise, the baby should learn that he is just a part of the family, not the boss of it. His physical needs must, of course, be met. Because his nervous system and muscles are not well enough developed for him to take part in the family's routine, his cries of hunger, pain, and physical discomfort should be met as soon as possible.

However, as has been pointed out before, when it is apparent that there is nothing the matter with him and that all he wants is attention, his cries should not be permitted to disrupt the activities of other members of the family. The sooner he discovers that he cannot demand instant attention from others but must take his turn, the easier his adjustments will be to other people outside the home when he is older.

The Baby's Routine

In order that the presence of a baby in the home does not disrupt the routine of the family for too long, the baby should be put on a routine as soon as possible. For physical and mental efficiency, and for good work habits, everyone needs some sort of routine. This does not come naturally to the baby. It must be learned, but it should not be a schedule of arbitrary standards set by his parents. The routine must fit the baby's bodily needs and the level of his development.

What the baby's routine will be should be determined largely by advice from the doctor. A sample of a daily schedule for a baby during the first year is given below. Each baby, of course, will have his own schedule, suited to his own needs.

Suggested Routine for Child the First Year

BIRTH TO SIX MONTHS

6:00 to 6:30—Feeding
6:30 to 9:30—Sleep
9:30 to 10:00—Bath and exercise
10:00 to 10:30—Feeding

10:30 to 1:30—Sleep, out-of-doors when possible
1:30 to 2:00—Playtime, alone
2:00 to 2:30—Feeding
2:30 to 5:00—Sleep, out-of-doors when possible
5:00 to 5:30—Playtime alone, if awake
5:30 to 6:00—Exercise and play with adults
6:00 to 6:30—Feeding and preparation for bed
6:30 to 10:00—Sleep
10:00 to 10:30—Feeding
10:30 to 6:00—Sleep

SIX MONTHS TO ONE YEAR

7:00 to 7:30—Breakfast
7:30 to 7:45—Preparation for nap
7:45 to 9:30—Sleep
9:30 to 10:00—Bath, exercise, and orange juice
10:00 to 12:00—Play in crib or pen
12:00 to 12:30—Dinner and toilet
12:30 to 3:00—Nap
3:00 to 5:00—Fruit juice, coach ride or play indoors
5:00 to 5:30—Exercise and play
5:30 to 6:00—Supper and preparation for bed
6:00 to 10:00—Sleep
10:00 to 10:10—Toilet (if recommended by doctor)
10:10 to 7:00—Sleep

The baby's routine, established according to his needs and approved by the doctor, should fit as nearly as possible into

A quiet period for the child becomes even more important as he grows older. It helps him to relax, teaches him self-confidence, and makes him less dependent upon others for amusement.

COURTESY H. J. HEINZ COMPANY

the general family routine. It is of little importance, for example, whether the baby is bathed in the morning or afternoon. If it fits into the family schedule better in the afternoon, it should be given then. The important thing is that variations in the routines for the baby and for the whole family should be made to permit every member of the family to have the maximum satisfaction and the minimum inconvenience.

The Young Child's Routine

After the baby's first birthday, his routine will fit more closely into the general pattern of the family's life. The young child will sleep less than he did during the first year. This will give him more time for his own play activities and to do things with the family. Then, too, he will require fewer feedings and will be able to eat most of his meals with the family. His time for play, both indoors and out, will closely approximate that of the other children of the family.

However, as is true of a baby, a young child's routine must be determined more by his physical needs than by family convenience or his own wishes. Of course he will want to stay up as late as the older children do and will rebel against naps if the other children are not required to nap in the afternoons. With the cooperation of the older children in keeping the house quiet when the young child is resting, and the assurance that he will be able to do what they do when he reaches their ages, much of this resistance can be met successfully. Here is a suggested routine for a child of one to five years of age.

Suggested Routine for Child of One to Five

7:00 to 7:30—Toilet, wash, dress	12:30 to 3:00—Nap
7:30 to 8:00—Breakfast	3:00 to 3:15—Toilet, fruit juice and cracker
8:00 to 8:10—Toilet	
8:10 to 9:30—Nap. Substitute play alone after two years	3:15 to 5:00—Play, out-of-doors when possible
9:30 to 9:45—Orange juice and cracker	5:00 to 5:30—Bath
	5:30 to 6:00—Supper and toilet
9:45 to 12:00—Play, out-of-doors when possible	6:00 to 10:00—Sleep
	10:00 to 10:10—Toilet
12:00 to 12:30—Toilet and dinner	10:10 to 7:00—Sleep

The need for quiet periods preceding sleep and eating is more important each year as the child emerges from babyhood. The longer he remains awake, the more apt he is to become tired. The more tired he is, the less likely he is to eat well or go to sleep quickly. A quiet period with no one around helps the child to relax and rest, thus preparing him

FROM THE FILM "FROM SOCIABLE SIX TO NOISY NINE,"
NATIONAL FILM BOARD OF CANADA

Occasional variations in the child's routine, such as allowing him to stay up a little beyond his usual bedtime to be read to or to listen to music, are all right. Often the psychological benefit is greater than any loss of sleep. However, under no conditions should the time be spent in romping or hilarious play.

for his meal or sleep. Furthermore, it teaches him to become self-reliant and to learn to amuse himself.

Variations in Routine

A strictly enforced routine produces nervous tension and resentments. This does not produce a healthy, happy child. Neither does a hit-or-miss manner of handling the child's daily needs produce a healthy, happy child. What the child needs is a routine of some kind but with some leaway and enough variation to break the monotony of sameness day in

The child may have one special treat on special days, such as a piece of cake, candy, or ice cream; but the celebration should not be too exciting, and the usual menu should be followed as strictly as possible.

and day out. When the child is kept on a strict schedule, he feels that he does not have any rights or privileges and that he is being forced to do things that the other members of the family do not have to do.

Variations in the child's routine should be made according to the child's physical and emotional state, rather than on the basis of convenience to some member of the family. If he is rested and in good spirits, that is the time to give him a little treat by permitting him more freedom than he is ordinarily allowed. Shoud he be tired and fretful, it is not fair to him to permit his usual routine to be upset to suit the convenience of another family member. Family living is co-

Holidays usually mean a break in the family routine and in the baby's routine. There is certain to be excitement in the home. The baby is often allowed to eat too much or the wrong kinds of foods, and he may not have the usual amount of sleep. No wonder he becomes cranky and fretful.

STERN FROM MONKMEYER

operative living in which each member must make occasional sacrifices for the other members.

Holidays

Holidays mean breaks in the everyday routine for every member of the family. There is certain to be some excitement connected with the preparation for the holiday as well as with the celebration itself, and there is usually a break in schedule for the day. The family gets up late, breakfast is late, and the usual hours for meals are upset. There are frequently calls from members of the family or friends, or the family may go visiting or riding for the day.

When there are young children in a family, holidays should be kept as nearly like other days as possible. One special treat can be planned for the day, provided it does not interfere too much with the child's routine or involve too much excitement. A plan that upsets the whole day's routine should be avoided when possible.

Special food on holidays is one of the chief sources of trouble as far as young children are concerned. The trouble is especially serious when there are also variations in the time the food is served or when there is in-between-meal eating. Many families provide an abundance of sweets for holidays, such as candy, cake, pie, puddings, and ice cream. Children, of course, are generally very fond of sweets and, because it is a holiday, they may frequently be permitted to overindulge. Overindulgence, when accompanied by excitement and fatigue, leads to stomach upsets, which may necessitate a day or two in bed after the holidays.

Strangers and Strange Places

Breaking the child's everyday routine by going to strange places where there are strange people has much the same effect on young children as holidays do. Adults rarely realize that strange people and places are frightening and exciting for the young child. Such changes break the calm and security of his familiar ways. They make him feel insecure and upset his equilibrium. Emotional tension and excitement are always tiring. Fatigue causes digestive upsets and makes it difficult for the young child to fall off to sleep easily at bedtime.

Of course, young children should not always be kept within the sheltered areas of the home or prevented from seeing new places. No one can grow up in seclusion and hope to be well adjusted to life, but too many strange places or too frequent breaks in the child's routine should be avoided.

Once a day or once every other day is at first sufficiently often for the child to come in contact with strange people or

As the child grows older he can become acquainted with strangers or enjoy new experiences without being frightened. If he is exposed to new experiences gradually from babyhood, he will be better prepared for meeting changes.

COURTESY HARDWARE MUTUALS

strange places. Should the time interval be much longer, it will mean a new adjustment the next time, and the good effects of getting used to strangeness from former experiences will be gone.

For Discussion

1. How would the arrival of a baby in your home interfere with the family routine and what adjustments would have to be made to fulfill the baby's schedule?
2. What reasons have you heard parents give to justify taking young children to evening movies or on all-day outings?
3. How could you tactfully suggest to strangers that they cannot waken a baby from his sleep to play with him or delay his meal schedule?
4. How could you plan the young child's solitary play periods to guarantee that he will be amused at that time?
5. How would the presence of a young child in your household interfere with the usual routine for Sunday or holidays? How could a satisfactory adjustment be made?

6. How did you feel when you were a child about being deprived of doing things your older brothers and sisters did because you were "too young"?

Suggested Activities

1. Sit near parents with a young child at an evening movie. Observe the child and the parents. How much enjoyment do the parents seem to be getting, and how does the child react?

2. Watch a mother with a young child shopping in a large store in the late afternoon. Does she seem to be concentrating her attention on her shopping? What does the child do?

3. Study crowds returning on busses, trains, or subways after a holiday outing. Do the parents of young children show as many signs of having a good time as adults without children? How do the children behave?

4. How would you avoid having a young child stay up too late on holidays or become too cross during the day?

5. List equipment for young children that will encourage solitary play for at least one half-hour daily.

6. Observe the reactions of several children when they are left alone. Compare the way in which they amuse themselves. Ask their mothers if they have a regular time for playing alone, and see if this is related to the way in which they amuse themselves.

CHAPTER 12

Common Behavior Problems

In learning to adjust to the world in which he is growing up, almost every child develops certain kinds of behavior which are annoying or embarrassing to his parents. Parents frequently label such behavior as "problem behavior" and try to correct it. Unfortunately, this usually makes the situation worse rather than better. More often than not, what parents call "problem behavior" is perfectly normal for the child at his age and level of development.

What then, you may ask, is problem behavior? The only behavior which can be correctly called by this name is behavior which interferes with the child's adjustment to life and, as a result, makes him unhappy now or will make him unhappy later on. *Problem behavior is behavior that makes life difficult and unsatisfactory for the child, not for his parents alone.*

The common types of problem behavior may be placed in four groups according to the way in which they endanger the child's well-being.

1. Behavior Which Interferes with the Child's Efficiency. Dawdling is an example of behavior which interferes with efficiency. While it may not be serious in early childhood,

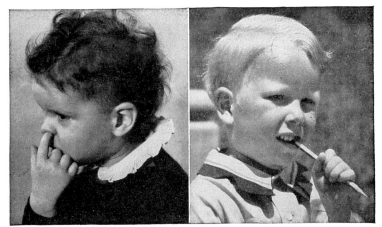

HAROLD M. LAMBERT AND FREDERIC LEWIS

Children have many little mannerisms or peculiarities which show that they are nervous or ill at ease. They should be told about undesirable habits and watched to prevent their recurrence. Read the seven suggestions for overcoming problem behavior on pages 216–219.

when the child has few responsibilities and when he has plenty of time to do different things, it will sooner or later prove to be a great handicap to him.

2. Behavior Which Interferes with the Child's Physical Well-being. Nibbling between meals, gulping food without taking time to chew it properly, or putting up such a strong resistance to going to bed at naptime or nighttime that tenseness preventing sleep results are examples of behavior that interfere with physical well-being. Many of the mannerisms a child develops, such as picking his nose or biting his nails, are not only bad for his physical well-being but they are also socially unacceptable forms of behavior.

3. Behavior Which Interferes with the Child's Social Adjustments. Every child wants to be liked and to have friends, just as his parents want him to. However, if he does things which annoy or antagonize people, he will find himself unpopular with children and disliked by adults. Being rude, selfish, or inconsiderate of the rights and feelings of others will make any child unpopular.

4. Behavior Which Makes the Child Feel Inferior or Inadequate. While no one will accuse a young child of being a "thief" if he takes things that belong to others or of being "untrustworthy" if he divulges secrets he promised "on his word of honor" not to tell, this will not always be so. By the time he starts to school, he will be expected to know better. If he persists in doing things which are regarded as "wrong," he will be criticized, punished, and perhaps ostracized by his classmates. When this happens to a child, he inevitably feels inferior, even to the point of developing guilt and inferiority complexes.

Behavior Is Learned

One very comforting and reassuring fact about a child's behavior is that it is *learned.* This means that a child can learn to behave in a manner that will make adjustment to life easy and pleasant for him just as readily as he can learn to behave in such a way that life will be difficult and unpleasant for him.

However, a child is too inexperienced to *know* what behavior will help him and what will hinder him. So long as he gets momentary satisfaction, that is all that matters to him. He lacks the perspective necessary to know whether a pattern of behavior he is learning will be useful to him as he grows older or whether it will prove to be a serious stumbling block to successful adjustments to life.

Thus it becomes apparent that in establishing patterns of behavior, either for the immediate present or for the future, the child needs guidance to make sure that he will learn the most useful and most desirable patterns. To be most valuable, this guidance should be at the beginning of learning, to start him off on the right track from the very start. Should he, however, get started in the wrong way—and this he may do either by chance or by imitating an adult or another child—it is comforting to know that this behavior can be replaced with behavior that will be more useful to him. This would not be true if the behavior were inherited instead of learned.

Testing for Problem Behavior

To be able to guide a child successfully, it is important to know whether his behavior is normal for his age or not. No matter how annoying it may be to his parents, and no matter how much it may interfere with the child's adjustments at that time, it is impossible to force a child to behave differently if he is incapable of more mature behavior. However, undesirable behavior should not be ignored. If parents are alert to misbehavior, they will be ready to help the child develop more mature forms of behavior as the child is ready to do so. The important thing is for parents to avoid building up a resistant attitude in the child by scolding or nagging.

Most forms of behavior that are likely to lead to poor adjustments on the child's part are those which are carry-overs from infancy. The child persists in behaving in an infantile manner, either because he does not know how to behave in a more mature manner or because infantile behavior gives him satisfaction and meets some strong need in his life. To guide the child, then, he must be shown how to behave more in accordance with his age and level of development. At the same time, if he feels secure enough in his parents' love he will *want* to behave in a manner that will make him happier and better adjusted.

To determine whether the child's behavior is serious enough to need attention and correction, there are certain simple tests that can be applied.

First, the behavior that is troublesome should be compared with that of other children of the same age. If they all behave in much the same way as he does, this would suggest that such behavior is normal for that age.

Second, the behavior should be checked with norms for children of his age as given in any standard book on child development. (See the section which follows on "Common Types of Behavior in Children at Different Ages.")

A third test is to see if the child's troublesome behavior has persisted for a long enough time to suggest that there is something holding him back from the normal progress he should be making. If the behavior gets worse rather than better, there is added reason to suspect that something is holding the child back from progressing as he normally should.

The best and most accurate test is to compare his behavior in this area with his behavior in other areas. Does he lag behind in his development in several areas and, if so, why?

Common Types of Behavior in Children at Different Ages

Most children have a fairly large repertoire of behavior that interferes with good adjustments. Some of this behavior, as has been emphasized before, will be outgrown in time. It is characteristic of the level of development of the child at that age and will change as he becomes more mature, both physically and mentally. Other forms of behavior, perhaps less troublesome at the time, will persist and, in time, settle into firmly embedded habits. These are the ones that need

An activity becomes a habit just as soon as the child is not aware that he is doing it. These children, listening to a phonograph, are so absorbed that they are unaware of their mannerisms.

special attention, preferably before they become so fixed that it will be very difficult to correct them.

While it may be incorrect to label any one form of behavior as "universal," there are many problems that are so common that they might be regarded as universal. The common forms of behavior at different age levels are given in the following classified lists. The ages are also mentioned at which such behavior, if continued, might be considered problem behavior needing correction.

1. Health Problems. From two to four years, the child may bang his head against the headboard of his bed; he will resist being put to bed and call out for something he does not need; he will get out of bed and run around his room; or he will have nightmares. He may dawdle on the toilet; play with toys instead of concentrating on moving his bowels; or he may develop the habit of waiting too long before going to the toilet and wet or soil himself. At meals, he may gulp his food; hold it unchewed in his mouth; spit it out; or fill up so much between meals that he has no appe-'tite at mealtimes. After the child is four years old, many of the same problems may arise, or they may persist from this earlier age. In addition, many children pick at different parts of their bodies, such as their noses and ears, play with their genitals, and bite their fingernails. When sitting or standing, they stoop or shift the weight to one side, thus causing a slight curvature of the body.

2. *Problems of Muscle Control.* From two to four years, the child is likely to be awkward in handling eating utensils, holding crayons and paintbrushes, and he may shuffle his feet when he walks or runs. From four years on, he may shift from one hand to the other instead of using one hand for most things; he may spear his food; or cramp his fingers around a crayon or pencil. He should be shown the right way to do these things before he gets into the habit of doing them in such an inefficient and fatiguing manner.

3. *Speech Problems.* Between the ages of two and four years, the child is too old for baby talk. He should make fewer and fewer grammatical mistakes when he talks, and he should be learning to speak distinctly instead of slurring his words together. Should these speech defects arise, they should be checked. Many children of four or five years start to stutter and stammer when excited, to slur their words together, and to leave their sentences unfinished or run several sentences together. They often make bad grammatical mistakes, and they begin to use slang or to swear.

4. *Emotional Problems.* While no one can expect a child of three or four years not to be frightened at times, not to feel shy in the presence of strangers, not to be jealous of a

brother or sister, and not to have temper outbursts when some wish is thwarted, all of these emotional outbursts should be waning in intensity instead of increasing. The same is true for a child of five or six years. If the child shows the beginnings of emotional control, that is all one can expect. There is no reason for concern unless the emotional outbursts become stronger and more frequent or if he substitutes pouting and sullenness for outbursts.

5. *"Bids for Attention" Problems.* All young children like attention, but some bid for it too much. When a child of three or four years tries to dominate the conversation, interrupts when others are talking, hangs around callers, or

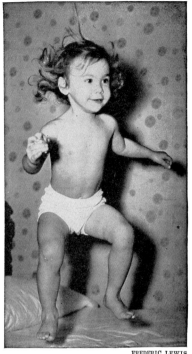

FREDERIC LEWIS

Demonstrations of glee are all right for a very young child, but when the child begins to grow up such unrestrained expressions may seem out of place.

prances around and calls attention to his new clothes, it means that he feels that he is not getting enough attention from his family to satisfy his needs. Likewise, a child of five or six who behaves like a baby by dawdling, crying, or cutting up whenever he has an audience is suffering from similar feelings of neglect. Another common way of showing off is to shout or to use slang or swear words to shock others.

No matter where a child eats, it is important that he learn to eat correctly, for the eating habits formed in early childhood are often carried into adult life and many times are so strong that they cannot be changed. Some parents are so concerned about *what* or *how much* their children eat that they do not notice *how* they eat. It is just as easy for a child to eat correctly as incorrectly, but he must be shown the correct method.

6. Social Problems. No child under four years of age can be expected to behave in a truly social manner. He will push, grab, fight, be rude and discourteous, and will refuse to share his possessions with others. However, after he is four years of age, he should have outgrown this type of behavior. If he still persists in behaving in an unsocial manner, or if he boasts and criticizes others, teases and bullies smaller children, or tattles to adults about other children, he will be out of step with his playmates and will find himself with no one to play with. That is when he will need help in learning to behave in a more mature manner so that other children will want to play with him.

Importance of Parents' Attitudes toward Problem Behavior

Once it is apparent that a child's behavior is not normal for his age and that, if it persists and grows worse he will suffer the consequences in poor adjustments and unhappiness, what should his parents do? The answer is that *what* they do is not so important as *how* they do it. To help the child to meet this problem successfully, the parents' attitude toward the problem and the child is more important than the method they use.

First of all, they must realize that the child is not willfully troublesome. He behaves as he does mainly because he has found satisfaction from doing so. Until the parents ferret out the reason for the child's behavior, they will be at a loss to know how to correct it.

In the second place, the parents should ask themselves if they have been expecting more of the child than he is capable of and, by doing so, have made him feel so inadequate that he has no desire to behave as they want him to. Lack of understanding and intolerance may be the trouble.

Then, third, have they taken a positive or negative approach to their guidance of the child? Many parents spend so much time criticizing and blaming a child for the wrong things he does that they forget to tell him what he should do. Even worse, they neglect to show him their appreciation for his efforts to do what they would like him to do. Can he be blamed for being confused, bewildered, discouraged, and resentful? Such an unfavorable attitude on his part would never have developed had the parents' guidance been positive rather than negative.

And, finally, is there any justification for believing that a child will "outgrow" a troublesome pattern of behavior if they sit back and do nothing about it? The answer is "Yes" only when the behavior is normal for the child's age. If, on the other hand, it is a carry-over of some infantile form of behavior or has been learned by imitating a child or adult who is not a well-adjusted person, the chances that the child will outgrow this behavior are rather slim. Under such conditions, he needs helpful and sympathetic guidance, encouragement, and the feeling that his parents are with him rather than against him if he is to make any improvements in his behavior. Suggestions for guiding children in overcoming problem behavior follow.

Suggestions for Overcoming Problem Behavior

When it is apparent that certain types of behavior are heading the child for trouble, and when a fair testing has revealed that the behavior is becoming so strong that it is not likely to be outgrown as time goes on, then the time has come for parents to help the child overcome this behavior. Studies of learning have shown how this can be done most easily and effectively and with a minimum of strain on the child. From these studies, a few practical suggestions may prove to be helpful in guiding the child.

Suggestion 1. Find out *why* the child is clinging to a form of behavior that is already proving to be a source of trouble in his adjustments. All behavior is motivated by some need. It may be the need for food, warmth, or physical comfort; or it may be the need for love, security, and a feeling of self-importance. If the child is satisfying some need by behavior that is going to lead to poorer and poorer adjustments as he grows older, then a new outlet for this need must be found in behavior that will lead to better adjustments.

Suggestion 2. Help the child to become fully aware of

what he is doing and why it would be better if he behaved in some other way. After a time, some behavior becomes so automatic that the child is not actually aware of what he is doing. Kindly reminders, rather than nagging, will soon put him on guard so that he will be able to check his own acts and not have to be reminded of them.

It is unfair to ask a child to do anything without giving him a reason for it. It is even more important to do this when you are asking him to do something that will be difficult for him. That is why it is important not only to tell the child why what he is doing is undesirable, but also to explain why in terms he can understand. This is especially important if you ask him to refrain from doing something his friends do.

Suggestion 3. Encourage the child to *want* to change the behavior you realize will prove to be a handicap to him as he grows older. Learning cannot take place without effort on the part of the learner. If the child has no desire to change the pattern of his behavior, you cannot help him. When he fully understands why you are asking him to do things in another way and agrees with you that it would be to his personal advantage, then he will cooperate.

Suggestion 4. Encourage the child to begin to replace the troublesome behavior with behavior that will be more beneficial to him as soon as he shows a desire to do so. Don't put it off and allow his enthusiasm to wane. Furthermore, putting it off gives more time for repetition of the very behavior you want to get rid of, thus adding to the difficulty of changing.

Suggestion 5. Replace every act that is proving to be harmful or troublesome to the child with one that will be helpful to him in his adjustments. Not only must the act that is to be substituted for the old be more desirable than the old, but it must satisfy the same need that the old act

When children play games or move about in some activity, it relieves the tension that causes undesirable behavior. The best way to get rid of undesirable behavior is to replace it with desirable activity.

satisfied. As has been stressed before, all behavior satisfies some need in the child's life. You cannot, therefore, expect him to give up a form of behavior that satisfied some need unless its substitute will satisfy that need equally as well as the old.

It is easy enough to tell a child how he should behave. Finding a satisfactory substitute is an entirely different matter. The old behavior is likely to be more satisfying to the child than a substitute because it has been so well learned that it can be carried out with little effort.

Suggestion 6. One sure way of making the new behavior seem more attractive to the child than the old is to associate praise with it. By praising the child for his efforts, even if his achievements are not entirely what you had hoped for, the child will gradually come to think the new behavior is more satisfying than the old. If the child can be motivated by praise in his first attempts to change his behavior, he will gradually gain enough satisfaction from the new behavior so that he will no longer need to be praised for it.

Suggestion 7. Don't overlook lapses. These are almost inevitable, especially if the behavior has been repeated so many times that it has developed into a firmly established habit. But, each lapse means learning to do the very thing he wants to stop doing and this, in turn, makes the job of stopping more difficult and more discouraging.

For Discussion

1. Give some examples of undesirable behavior in adults not commonly found in most children that one should be on guard for lest they develop into habits.
2. Why do parents permit undesirable behavior to develop into habits in their children? What reasons, if any, do they generally give?
3. What substitute behavior of a desirable form can you suggest for temper tantrums, holding the fork the wrong way, or swearing?
4. On the basis of what you know about learning, explain why it is a "vain hope" to expect undesirable behavior to disappear of its own accord.
5. What arguments would you give to a child who claimed that a certain form of undesirable behavior was "all right" and who justified his point of view by saying, "Everyone does it that way"?
6. Give some examples of behavior generally considered as "undesirable" which you consider all right, if not actually desirable. Why, then, does society label it "undesirable"?

Suggested Activities

1. List the different forms of undesirable behavior you observe in a group of young people over a period of one week. Then

classify these according to the classification given on pages 206–208. Which do you find the most common and which the least common?

2. Try to teach a child who holds his fork or pencil incorrectly to hold it correctly. Apply the suggestions given in this chapter for dealing with undesirable behavior. Which is the hardest suggestion to apply?

3. Make a list of substitute activities for several undesirable forms of behavior in each classification referred to on pages 211–215.

4. Decide whether you have allowed any form of undesirable behavior to develop into a habit. Has this proved to be a hindrance to you in any way? If so, how?

5. Then try to substitute some form of desirable behavior for this habit. Keep a record of how long it takes, how often you "slip," and how successful you are at the end of one month, two months, etc.

6. Observe children, adolescents, and adults for mannerisms. Make a list of the mannerisms, and then determine which are the most common forms at different ages.

CHAPTER 13

Discipline, Good and Bad

To most people, discipline means punishment. But the standard dictionaries define it as "training in self-control and obedience" or "education." It also means training that molds, strengthens, or perfects.

True, discipline does involve punishment, but especially in the case of young children, punishment is not all there is to discipline. The educational aspect, in which the child is trained to obey, is paramount in the disciplining of young children. It is not logical, nor is it fair, to expect a child to obey until he knows what is expected of him. In the disciplining of young children, therefore, major emphasis should be put upon educating them to do the right thing, or what society thinks is the right thing for them to do. Then, to make them *want* to behave in a socially approved fashion, good discipline should include rewards for good behavior.

Elements of Discipline

Good discipline should include three separate and distinct, yet closely interrelated, elements: (1) *education* in the form of teaching the child what he should or should not do;

(2) *rewards* in the form of praise and approval for doing what is expected of him or at least for trying to do so; and (3) *punishment* for intentional but never for unintentional wrongdoing.

The first and second aspects of discipline—education and rewards—should be stressed in early childhood. Not until childhood progresses and the child becomes capable of willfully misbehaving should any great emphasis be put upon punishment.

Evaluation of Discipline

In deciding whether a certain form of discipline is or is not effective, one must never judge by the end results alone. Just because a child's behavior is good, or because he can be counted on to behave in a socially approved manner no matter where he is, is no reason to conclude that the methods used to bring about the good behavior are right or that they should be used in the discipline of all children.

It is of far greater importance in deciding about the effectiveness of discipline to observe the attitude of the child who has been disciplined. Of course, it is not so easy to judge the child's attitude as it is to judge his behavior.

When a child's reaction to discipline is favorable, he will behave in a sportsmanlike fashion. He may cry or show signs of hurt feelings, but he will quickly recover from this and revert to his normal, friendly self. There are no evidences of sulkiness, no protests of unfairness, and no indications that he is harboring a grudge against the person who administered the punishment.

Parental Attitudes toward Discipline

Parental attitudes toward discipline are just as important as disciplinary methods. The parents should realize that it takes time for a child to learn what is "good."

When children display unfavorable attitudes toward discipline—such as sulking or resentment—it may be because the parent has placed emphasis on the child rather than on the behavior.

FROM THE McGRAW-HILL FILM "AGES AND STAGES"

The parent's attitude in disciplining should be one of understanding and tolerance. No parent should expect obedience overnight, nor should he be overly disturbed if occasionally a child does something the parent is *sure* the child *knows* is wrong. Instead of punishing him for his "slip," it would be fairer to give him an opportunity to explain his side of the story. Then, if his reason does not seem justified, this can be pointed out to him.

Parents should not be disturbed by the critical attitudes of in-laws, friends, or neighbors about their children's behavior. Most children can be made into "good little" boys or girls, but it requires harsh treatment and leaves its mark on a child's personality. A child who is occasionally naughty will probably be better adjusted as an adult than one who is a paragon of perfection.

The only thing that should disturb parents seriously about the way they are disciplining a child is an unhealthy attitude about it on the part of the child. If the child is rebellious and uncooperative or if he tries to blame others for something he does, then parents have evidence that their own attitudes have been unfavorable and that they have been using methods of discipline unsuited to the child's level of development.

Discipline Must Be Educational

Knowledge of right and wrong must be acquired. The only way that the child can acquire this knowledge is by direct teaching, supplemented by a model of good behavior to imitate. It is just as unfair to a child to neglect teaching him right and wrong as it would be to neglect teaching him how to speak.

Until the child is at least three years old, his vocabulary is so limited that explanations of the whys and wherefores of good and bad behavior are almost impossible. Therefore, a few well-chosen words to describe right and wrong should be selected and used constantly in connection with the child's behavior.

When his behavior is good, the words "good," "fine," or "nice" may be associated with it. In time the young child will learn that his behavior is all right if he hears these words. In the same way, "bad" or "naughty" can be associated with misbehavior, and "hurt" with dangerous actions.

When it becomes apparent that the child's comprehension is increasing, further explanation should be given. Instead of merely saying "naughty" when a child misbehaves, additional information as to why an act is naughty should be given.

Cautions in Educating for Discipline

Two cautions should be kept in mind when explanations are given to a young child. In the first place, it is essential to remember at all times how limited a young child's vocabulary is. Only simple words that are familiar to the child should be used in the explanation.

The second caution to keep in mind is related to the length of the explanation. A young child's knowledge, like his vocabulary, is too limited for him to be able to grasp the meaning of any explanation unless it is brief and simple.

Facial expressions and gestures help to make explanations more meaningful to the young child whose comprehension of words is limited. A smile and a pat

COURTESY NATIONAL SAFETY COUNCIL

The little child does not realize danger. Therefore, he must be protected until he is able to recognize danger himself.

of approval accompanying the words "fine" or "good" tell a whole story to him.

Similarly, a frown, a shaking of the head, restraining the child's body, holding back a childish hand that gets into mischief, a gentle rapping of the fingers with a pencil, or a slight slap on the wrists quickly tells a young child that he is doing something that is either naughty or harmful.

Demonstrations of ways of doing things also have an educational value in discipline. From them the child is given a pattern of behavior to imitate which shows him what to do and what not to do. All little children, for example, seem to be hypnotically attracted by a puddle of water and auto-

Little children learn slowly and forget quickly. It takes much time and patience to teach them what to do and what not to do. They must be told over and over again; then shown; and then told again.

H. ARMSTRONG ROBERTS

matically splash through it. A demonstration of how to skip or dance around it will appeal to them. They will then forget the fun of splashing for the fun of imitating the round-the-puddle dance.

Good Educational Practices in Discipline

All young children, no matter how bright they are, learn slowly and forget quickly. For that reason, good training in right and wrong should include frequent repetitions. The closer together in time these repetitions come, the more quickly the child will learn. Telling a child what to do or what not to do frequently goes in one ear and out the other.

The child must be told over and over again; he must be shown; and then he must be told again. In time he will learn, but, in the excitement of wanting to do something, he may forget what he has learned. Teaching a child right and wrong is a slow and laborious task.

To make sure that a child actually knows what is expected of him, a good procedure to follow is to ask the child to tell what he has been asked to do or to avoid doing. From his repetition of the request, it is possible to discover whether or not he understands what is expected of him. Furthermore, this procedure helps to focus the child's attention on what is said to him.

Finally, good discipline should be consistent. A young child must learn that right is right and wrong is wrong no matter what the situation and no matter who is in charge. Nothing is more confusing to a child than the realization that a certain act is acceptable one time and punishable at another time. If the child is to learn the difference between right and wrong, this confusion must not be permitted to arise in his mind.

Rewards for Good Behavior

Being good is far too often taken for granted. Being bad, by contrast, usually gives the child attention, even though he receives punishment as part of that attention. One can hardly blame a child for not trying to be good when his efforts receive little or no recognition. If he is to have any real incentive to try to do what is expected of him, it should be made worth his while.

Rewards should not be confused with bribery. A bribe is a promise of reward given ahead of time to encourage good behavior. When you say to a child, "If you are good when we call on Aunt Anna, I will buy you some ice cream," that is a bribe. True, it will make the child realize that being good will be to his advantage. Unfortunately, the child will soon

Rewards are not the same as bribes. When a parent tries to make a child behave by promising him ice cream or candy, that is a bribe. But rewards following good behavior are entirely different.

learn to depend upon bribes and will not be good unless he has the promise of a reward.

Effective Rewards for Young Children

1. Praise. Children of all ages love to be praised. It inflates their egos. Praise not only gives them a feeling of satisfaction but, of more importance, it adds to their feeling of security. It helps them to realize that they are acceptable members of the group. For that reason, praise is the best reward that can possibly be given for good behavior.

According to tradition, praise should be used sparingly because it results in conceit on the part of the person praised.

The best reward a parent can give for good behavior or efforts under difficulty is praise. Contrary to usual belief, praise does not spoil the child but encourages him to better actions.

Like so many traditions, there is no scientific evidence to back up this belief. On the contrary, studies of the effects of praise and reproof have shown conclusively that praise does not "turn the child's head" nor make him rest on his laurels. Rather, it incites his desire to be even better in anticipation of a repetition of this very pleasant reward.

2. *Gifts.* In addition to praise, simple little gifts are good rewards for young children. These should never, of course, be promised ahead of time as bribes but, rather, should be given at unexpected moments. When a child has been especially good, or when he has tried to be good under difficult circumstances, rewarding him with a gift in addition to

praise will make him feel that the effort was worth his while because it was duly appreciated.

Giving of gifts as rewards should be spontaneous. The "psychological moment" for giving a child a gift might be at a time when the child's enthusiasm for trying to do what is expected of him is beginning to lag or when he seems to be discouraged in trying.

A gift to a young child need not be costly. The surprise and pleasure accompanying the giving means more to the child than the gift itself. It is a good policy to keep a reserve of useful objects on hand for such occasions.

3. *Treats.* Special treats—like going to the drugstore for ice-cream cones, having a friend for a meal, going to the zoo, taking an automobile trip or boat ride—can likewise serve as rewards for good behavior. Like gifts, they should not be promised ahead of time, even though all arrangements have been made. They should be reserved for a time when the child's good behavior or his efforts to be good deserve some recognition.

Disciplining by Punishment

All good discipline includes punishment for intentional wrongdoing. If punishment is omitted from disciplinary procedures, the child will not learn the full significance of wrong behavior.

Before punishment is administered, there should be definite and conclusive evidence that the child's misbehavior is *intentional.* It is very unfair to punish for ignorance, especially when a young child has no way of knowing that his behavior is wrong unless he has *learned* that it is wrong.

Up to six years of age emphasis should be placed on the educational aspect of discipline and on rewarding the child for trying to do what is expected of him. He is not likely to be naughty intentionally very often unless he has developed an unfavorable attitude toward discipline.

Punishment should never be given because the child has been naughty, however, but because his behavior has been wrong. When a child is punished because he is naughty, the emphasis is placed on the child, and the result is a sullen, resentful child.

If, however, the punishment is given because his *behavior* is naughty, the emphasis is placed on the behavior. The child's attention is, likewise, focused on the behavior. Thus, by shifting emphasis from the child to the behavior itself, there is less likelihood that the child's attitude will be colored by resentment.

COURTESY H. J. HEINZ COMPANY

During the first five or six years, children should not be punished for wrongdoing because they are not misbehaving willfully. After six, when it is clear that the child is willfully misbehaving, punishment is in order.

Unsatisfactory Forms of Punishment

1. Spanking. The stock punishment in most households is spanking. Whenever a young child misbehaves, he is spanked. The severity of the spanking is rarely ever determined by the severity of the misbehavior but rather by the way the adult feels when he administers the punishment.

Should the child misbehave when the parent is tired and irritable or when it is embarrassing or inconvenient, the spanking is apt to be more severe than the misbehavior deserves.

One can hardly blame a child for developing an unfavorable attitude toward discipline and toward all people in authority when spanking is frequently used. In the first place, it puts too much emphasis on the child and too little emphasis on the wrong act, which is sure to lead to unfavorable attitudes.

Then, too, spanking has little educational value. Very few children can tell, after they have been spanked, just why their behavior was wrong. Furthermore, unless the severity of the spanking is carefully controlled, the child will get no clue from this punishment as to how wrong his misbehavior has been.

2. *Other Corporal Punishments.* The criticisms of spanking given above are equally true with regard to all forms of corporal punishment, such as slapping the face or hands or whipping with a hairbrush, stick, shoe, or strap. These methods are likely to establish unfavorable attitudes in the child which result in his not even trying to do what he knows he should do.

3. *Scolding and Nagging.* Scolding and nagging are frequently used by adults who disapprove of corporal punishment. Like corporal punishment, these put too much emphasis on the child and too little emphasis on his behavior. Since no one, child or adult, likes to be criticized and made to feel inferior because his behavior is not acceptable to others, scolding is sure to lead to a resentful attitude.

Resentment is the result of punishment that has little relation to the misbehavior. The punishment should be of a nature that makes clear to the child that what he did was wrong and why it was wrong.

FROM THE MCGRAW-HILL FILMSTRIP "SOCIAL DEVELOPMENT".

Continual scolding and review of past offenses turn into "nagging." The child who resents being scolded is not likely to be favorably affected by nagging. He does not ignore it but rather his resentment grows as the nagging continues. There is no evidence to show that nagging improves a child's behavior. Scientific studies of repeated reproof have clearly shown that the effect is to stifle the individual's willingness to do what he is capable of doing.

4. Locking Up. An old-fashioned method of punishment, which is, unfortunately, still practiced in too many households today, consists of locking a naughty child in a closet or dark room. Because there is no relationship between the child's misbehavior and this form of punishment for it, this method has no educational value.

5. Sending to Bed. Somewhat like the method just condemned is the practice of sending the child to bed without his supper whenever he is naughty. The adult logic behind this practice is that the child must need rest or he would not behave as he does.

Unfortunately, a young child's capacity for reasoning is too limited to enable him to see the relationship between his misbehavior and being sent to bed. However, he is not too young to learn to associate bed with punishment and, therefore, often develops a resistance toward going to bed.

Good Forms of Punishment

When it is necessary to punish a child for willful naughtiness and disobedience, two important facts should be kept in mind in selecting the form of punishment to be used. First, the punishment should be closely enough related to the misbehavior so that even a young child cannot fail to see the relationship between them. Second, the punishment should act as a deterrent to further misbehavior of the same type without, at the same time, arousing an unfavorable attitude on the child's part.

Selecting the right punishment is not so easy as using a stock form, such as spanking, but it will pay big dividends in the improved behavior of the child. The following suggested forms of punishment, if correctly administered, should be helpful in correcting misbehavior.

1. *Making Amends.* From every angle, requiring a child to make amends for his misbehavior is the best form of punishment. When a child intentionally breaks something that belongs to someone else, he should, if possible, offer the other child a choice of his toys or replace the broken toy. For hurting another, he should be required to apologize and ask for pardon.

When a child learns that he will have to do something to

compensate for his misbehavior, and that it frequently takes more time and effort for the compensation than for the original act, he will realize in time that good behavior is easier than bad.

The only criticism that can be raised in regard to this type of punishment is that it is sometimes difficult, on the spur of the moment, to think of a suitable good act to compensate for the bad act. If there seems to be no related compensatory behavior available, the child can always be made to apologize.

2. *Isolation.* Because a young child's misbehavior frequently inconveniences or harms someone else, a second good form of punishment is to deprive him of the pleasure of social contacts until he is willing to apologize and promise better behavior in the future. It is generally more effective to send a child to another part of the room, away from others, than to his own room. While he is in the presence of others, he has an opportunity to realize what he is missing through his own fault.

3. *Depriving the Child of a Treat.* Another good form of punishment is to deprive a naughty child of a special treat. This is especially effective when there are other children in the family or play group who are receiving the treat as a reward for good behavior, for the child has a splendid opportunity to see for himself that being good is far more advantageous than being naughty.

Cautions in the Use of Punishment

Of the three elements of disciplining—education, rewards, and punishment—punishment is the only one that is apt to give rise to unfavorable attitudes. Therefore, it is very important to select punishment with great care to avoid, as far as possible, the establishment of an unhealthy attitude.

Also, the punishment decided upon must be administered in an impartial, objective way just as a judge pronounces a sentence on a guilty person. Never should the child be permitted to feel that punishment is a form of revenge or an outlet for adult anger.

Above everything else, the punisher should remain calm and unruffled, no matter how exasperated he or she may be. This is important because it shifts the burden of responsibility upon the child and makes him realize that he and he alone is to blame.

To ensure the child's realization that the punishment has been deserved, it is always wise, especially in the case of young children, to explain both before and after punishment the reason why it is being given.

By doing this, there is no chance that the child will be confused about why he is punished, nor will there be an opportunity for him to think the punishment was undeserved. If the child is emotionally disturbed, it is best to wait until he calms down before talking over the matter with him.

The final word of caution about punishment is: never allow a child to harbor a grudge. The child should not be permitted to feel sorry for himself or resentful of the punisher. This is far more easily avoided in a young child than it will be when the child is older.

For Discussion

1. Is there any justification for the tradition that children are wicked by nature and that good discipline should consist of driving the devil out of them?

2. Report on cases you know of unfavorable attitudes and cases of favorable attitudes children develop toward discipline.

3. Why is the use of religious fear (fear of the devil, of being sent to Hell after death, etc.) a poor disciplinary technique?

What effect is it apt to have on the child's religious beliefs and on his morals?

4. Why must an impersonal attitude be assumed by the disciplinarian if discipline is to be good?

5. Recall an instance or instances of punishment that you received as a child. What effect did it have on you?

6. When a parent loves a child, how can he or she justify slapping or spanking a child? Do parents act in a fit of temper or do they sincerely believe it is "good for the child"?

Suggested Activities

1. Make a list of punishments you have observed parents and teachers use on young children. Then classify these, using the classification given in this chapter. Note which type is most frequent.

2. While observing the punishments suggested in the first activity, observe also the children's reactions. Note how many are favorable and how many unfavorable.

3. Note the reactions of children following praise or the receipt of a reward for good behavior. Report on how the children reacted.

4. Make a list of bribes used by parents and the circumstances under which the bribes were promised.

5. Question a number of parents of young children to get their reactions to spanking. Question some of your classmates to get their reactions. Then compare the results to see the difference in attitudes regarding punishment before and after becoming parents.

6. Question a child right after he has been punished. List attitudes that indicated the child felt the punishment was justified and those indicating he felt the punishment was unjustified. Which list is longer?

CHAPTER 14

Tests for Toddlers

Ever since the famous Binet-Simon tests of intelligence made their appearance in 1905, intelligence tests have played an increasingly important role in the schools of America. For a number of years intelligence testing was limited to children of school age. There were no tests available to measure the mental development of children under three years of age.

The growing need for tests for the preschool or early childhood years on the part of parents, doctors, and agencies concerned with baby care led a man named F. A. Kuhlmann, in 1922, to devise a series of tests that could be used for babies as young as three months. Since then tests have appeared for babies as young as two weeks.

Why Test Young Children?

Knowledge of the mental development of a baby is essential if his training during the early years of life is to be other than "hit-and-miss." Those who are in charge of young children must know what to expect at every age. Then they should plan the child's daily routine and environment so as to encourage development to take place normally.

Ignorance of what a child can or should be able to do at

different ages is more serious than may seem apparent at first. It is apt to lead to faulty upbringing of one sort or another. It may lead the parents to expect more on the part of a child than he is capable of. This, in turn, results in disappointment to the parents and causes them to nag or prod the child. Disappointment and prodding by the parents foster feelings of inferiority in the child.

Lack of knowledge of what a child is capable of doing may, on the other hand, result in an expectation of too little. The result is that the child is not given an opportunity or incentive to bring out his inherent traits. This is very often the case with quiet children whose real abilities are underestimated.

Value of Early Diagnosis

The real value of an early diagnosis of the child's mental development lies in the fact that it eliminates erroneous impressions on the part of parents as to what a child of a given age should be able to do. Every parent wants to know almost as soon as the baby is born whether or not he is normal in his physical make-up. Doctors can answer this question within a few days after the baby's birth. Questions regarding the baby's mental make-up have, until recently, had to remain unanswered until the child was several years old.

The use of tests has helped to meet this problem. These tests, standardized after studying hundreds of babies and young children, are arranged in such a way as to show what an average child should be able to do at a given age. This gives a basis for education and training by showing when to encourage a child to develop certain traits.

The use of tests in the first years of a child's life makes it possible to predict what his mental development will be. Scientific studies made by retesting children year after year have shown that the intellectual development of the individual is generally consistent—that is, bright children continue to be bright, and dull children continue to be dull, regardless of training or educational influences. The parent of today can, therefore, know from the results of tests given early in childhood years what to expect of a child as he grows to maturity.

What Are Tests for Young Children?

Tests for young children are made up of a series of simple little activities that a normal child of a given age should be able to perform. They measure the characteristic behavior of that age, indicating whether the child is "normal," "above normal," or "below normal" in development.

Tests for the early childhood years are less accurate than tests for the school years because the young child's lack of ability to talk or control his muscles well enough to handle objects makes the choice of materials for the test limited in scope. The tests are, for the most part, performance tests in which the intellectual development of the child is measured indirectly through what he can do rather than directly by his answering questions asked by the examiner.

Although a few of the best tests for the first months of life will be included in the series of tests given in this chapter, intelligence tests are of relatively little value as predictors of later development for babies under three months of age.

During the early years of life the development of intelligence and muscle control are fairly closely related. It is thus possible to test intelligence by testing muscle control. The ability to manipulate small objects and to sit, stand, or walk without support are all aspects of the general growth process; and the age at which the baby can accomplish these tasks gives a definite clue to his mental development.

It is not to determine the child's I.Q. alone that he is given tests, but also to find out if he reacts as hundreds of other children of the same age do. (See pages 238–240.)

Interpreting Test Results

In interpreting the results of the tests given here, no attempt will be made to show the tester how to derive an "I.Q."[1] or "intelligence quotient" score. Because the tests given at each age have come from different sources and are not necessarily equivalent in difficulty, it would be impossible to derive an I.Q. score that would have any degree of accuracy as a measure of a child's brightness. In addition to this, it is generally agreed upon by psychologists that only skilled testers are qualified to use as technical a measure as the I.Q. score.

It is possible, however, to interpret the results of the tests adequately enough to determine in a general way the child's mental level and also how he compares with the "average" child of the same age. If the child can do tests above his age level, it is justifiable to say that he is "above average" or "bright." The further he can go above his age-level tests, the brighter he may be judged to be.

On the other hand, should the child fail several or all of the tests given for his age, it should not be concluded that he is "dull" or "mentally deficient." Only after he has failed the appropriate tests for his age month after month and displayed other signs of backwardness, as analyzed by a competent doctor or psychologist, can it be assumed that the child is mentally deficient. In many cases, the child's failure to pass a test merely indicates that he has not been given the opportunity to learn what he could have learned for his age.

If these tests are used from the point of view of guiding the young child's development wisely and watching his

[1] The I.Q. is a scientific measure of brightness. It is derived by dividing the "mental age" of the child, obtained from his score on a standard test of intelligence, by his chronological, or actual, age.

growth to see how it compares with that of the average baby of his age, they will give a feeling of assurance that all is well. Even more important, they will show where efforts can best be applied to the development of traits in which the child is lagging behind the standard for his age.

Cautions in Testing Young Children

Testing young children is not easy. It may be easy enough to give the tests, but to give them so that they test what they are meant to test and so that the results obtained can be compared with the standards given, the testing instructions must be followed and not changed or modified in any way.

In selecting tests suitable for the child, those corresponding to the child's actual age should be chosen. If, for example, the baby being tested is twelve months old, he should be given the tests listed under the heading "Age, Twelve Months." If he fails any of these, he should be given the tests for the months below twelve until the month is reached at which he passes every test given under the heading. If, on the other hand, he passes every test for his age, he should be given the tests for the months above his age until he reaches the point of failing every test given under a specific age heading.

Instructions for Giving Tests

To make the testing of young children meaningful, the tests must be given as the authors of the tests prescribe. The instructions for giving tests are as follows:

Read over each test carefully before giving it to be sure that you understand it. It is best to practice giving the test without the child to make certain that it runs smoothly. Memorize the instructions, and, if the test calls for verbal requests or questions, such as "Show me your eyes" or "Where

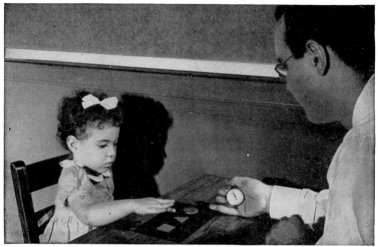

Testing young children is not easy. To give the tests so that the desired results are obtained means following instructions closely and carefully.

is the dog?" memorize these so that you will not have to refer to the instructions in the book.

Because the attention of young children is easily distracted, have all the materials necessary for the test ready before the test begins. Have a few toys at hand to amuse the child if any unavoidable lapses occur. Try to eliminate all distractions from the room in which the test is given.

Follow the instructions exactly as they are given and make no changes or modifications. Do not help the child in any way except to encourage him by saying, "You know how" or "You can do it, I am sure."

If you wish to chat with the child as an aid to keeping his interest from lagging, it is perfectly all right, as long as your conversation has nothing to do with the test.

In giving the tests, take a friendly attitude as if you were playing a game. If the child is obviously not interested in the test or if he wants to do something else, abandon the testing until you can get his cooperation.

Select a favorable time to give the tests, and avoid times when the child is tired and hungry.

Tests for Young Children

In the remaining pages of this chapter, tests for young children from the ages of one month to three years are given. These tests have been taken from standardized series of tests for babies and young children. In most instances the instructions have been rewritten, and technical terms have been replaced by words of everyday usage. The sources from which the different tests were taken are given at the end of the chapter.

No attempt has been made to include tests for children over three years of age. The reason for this is that tests for the older ages are not only technical in form but they also require special materials that would be available only to mental testers. The tests given, however, should prove to be adequate to give a fairly comprehensive idea of how the psychologist measures development during the early years of life.

Test One (Age, One Month)

1. *Reacts Positively to a Mild Noise.* When the baby is fretting or crying from displeasure due to hunger or fatigue, not pain, shake a rattle near his crib and watch his reaction. The test is passed if the baby quiets down during the rattling or immediately afterward.

2. *Horizontal Eye Coordination.* Move a small red light, such as a Christmas-tree bulb attached to a cord, or a flashlight, slowly back and forth several times in a horizontal line

about eight inches from the baby's face as he lies in his crib. The speed of the movement should be about one foot in four seconds. The test is passed if the baby's eyes definitely follow the light through at least two of the back-and-forth movements.

3. Reacts to a Shadow. Place the baby's crib in such a position that your shadow will cover his field of vision when you bend over the crib. While the baby is looking at you, move away slowly. The test is passed if the baby's eyes are held by the moving shadow for a few seconds.

4. Reaction to Unpleasant Stimulation. While the baby is lying quietly in his crib or on a table, rub his nose with a piece of cotton or gauze, using the movements of cleaning the nose without touching the mucous membrane. The test is passed if the baby squirms, moves sideways, or attempts to turn his body.

Test Two (Age, Six Months)

1. Recognizes Name. Place the baby at rest in his crib or on someone's lap. Then call the baby's name and several others, all in the same tone of voice. The test is passed if the baby shows that he recognizes his name by turning his head or smiling.

2. Lifts Cup. With the baby in a sitting position on the mother's lap, near a table, throw a one-inch cube on the table to attract his attention. When he looks at the cube, cover it swiftly with an inverted cup, such as an ordinary kitchen measuring cup. Then, while the cube is covered with the inverted cup, draw it over to the baby, within easy reach of his grasp, and turn the handle of the cup to his right. The test is passed if the baby lifts the cup. It is not necessary that he remove it completely and take it away, nor is it necessary for him to pick up the cube.

3. Hitting a Stationary Object. Hold the baby in a sitting position on your lap and give him a rattle to play with. After he starts to play with it, dangle a small toy attached to a five-inch string close enough before him so that he can hit it with the rattle. Continue to dangle the toy in front of him but do nothing to attract his attention to it. The test is passed if the baby hits at the toy with his rattle. It is not essential that he actually hit the toy, but he must show signs of making a serious effort to do so.

4. Pulls to Sitting Position. Stand at the foot of the crib and lean over the baby while he is lying on his back. Give him your thumbs to grasp and allow him, with this support, to pull himself to a sitting position. Do not do the pulling for him but raise your hands gradually as the baby pulls. The test is passed if the baby pulls himself to a sitting position with this assistance.

Test Three (Age, Twelve Months)

1. Recognition of Object. Place such objects as a ball, a rattle, a bell, blocks, a doll, and a colored picture on a table. Then, after the objects have been arranged so as to be within the reach of the baby, hold him up to the table and see if he reaches for any of the objects. If so, replace the object on the table but in a different position. While replacing the object, screen the baby's eyes with a piece of cardboard or your hand so that he will not see where it is being placed. Repeat this procedure five or six times. The test is passed if the baby selects the same object in at least half of the trials and thus shows preference for it.

2. Says "Bye-bye." While the baby is at rest on someone's lap, or when someone else is in the room with him, leave the room, waving and calling "bye-bye." The person who is in the room with the baby should tell him to say "bye-bye," to you, as waving alone is not enough. The test is passed if the baby says "bye-bye."

3. *Toy-from-second-step Test.* Place one of the baby's favorite toys on the second step from the floor. Put the baby on the floor in a sitting position facing the steps and with his feet one foot away from the riser of the first step. The test is passed if the baby is able to obtain the toy from the step by creeping up, by pulling himself up, or by any other method that gives the desired result.

4. *Standing without Support.* Place the baby on the floor, away from any support. After assisting him to a standing position, move away from him and make him stand unsupported. The test is passed if the baby can stand unsupported for five or more seconds.

Test Four (*Age, Eighteen Months*)

1. *Speech.* Say the following words to the child: "Mama," "Papa," "baby," "yes," "no," "eat," and "man." The test is passed if the child can say three or four of these words distinctly.

2. *Drinking.* Hold a glass of milk or water to the child's mouth and try to make him drink from it. The test is passed if the child takes several swallows in immediate succession without pausing. Be sure that he is actually drinking instead of merely sucking at the glass.

3. *Climbing Three Steps.* Place the child on the floor near a staircase. If he shows no interest in climbing the steps, take one of his favorite toys, call his attention to it, and then place it on the fifth or sixth step. The test is passed if the child is able to crawl up three steps without assistance.

4. *Getting Off Inverted Box.* Place the child in a sitting position on an inverted wooden box, six inches high. The

test is passed if the child is able to get off the inverted box by any method other than falling off by accident.

Test Five (Age, Two Years)

1. Block Building (Tower). Place twelve one-inch blocks in confusion before the child and then build a four-block tower as a model, saying, "See what I am making!" Build this out of his reach and then push the remaining eight blocks to him saying, "You make one like this. Make yours (pointing to a spot) right here." Leave your tower standing for a model while the child builds his. If it is knocked over accidentally, rebuild it. The test is passed if the child builds a tower of four or more blocks that will stand by itself.

2. Walks Downstairs Alone. Put a toy on the lower level of a flight of three steps and encourage the child to come down to get it. The test is passed if the child walks downstairs without support of his hands, standing on each step with both feet before stepping down to the next. The child may not be able to pass this test until he is two and a half.

3. Imitation of Simple Movements. Make the following simple movements and accompany each with the statements given: Raise both arms straight up over your head and say, "Put your arms up like this." Clap your hands several times and say, "Do this." Put your hands on the top of your head, palms downward, and say, "Now do this." Make a circular movement with your hands by turning them around one another in a rather large circle and say, "Make your hands go like this." The test is passed if, in three out of four movements, the child imitates approximately the movements you make.

4. Pointing out Objects in Pictures. Select two pictures from books suitable for the typical two-year-old child. Show

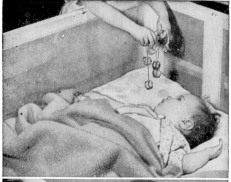

1) A baby of one month will react positively to a mild noise. A fretful baby should quiet down if a rattle is shaken over his crib. (For other tests see pages 245–246.)

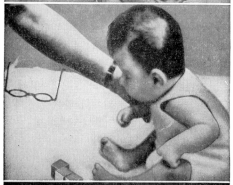

2) A baby of six months should be able to pull himself to a sitting position if he is helped to do so. (For other tests see pages 246–247.)

3) A year-old baby should wave and say "bye-bye" if he is told to do so when another person, leaving the room, waves and says "bye-bye." (For other tests see pages 247–248.)

CARROLL VAN ARK AND "WOMAN'S DAY"; THE
ENCYCLOPAEDIA BRITANNICA FILM "LIFE
BEGINS"; AND GERBER'S BABY FOODS

AND TODDLERS

4) The eighteen-month-old child should be able to climb three steps without assistance. If he shows no interest in climbing, the tester may place a toy several steps above the child. (For other tests see pages 248–249.)

5) The two-year-old should be able to build a tower of four blocks if he is shown how and the tester's tower is left as a model for him to follow. (For other tests see pages 249 and 252.)

6) The two-and-a-half-year-old should be able to walk a few steps on tiptoe when shown how and asked to try it. (For other tests see page 252.)

FREDERIC LEWIS (*top*) AND ELIZABETH HIBBS

the first picture to the child and say, "Show me the dog," "Show me the man," or "Show me the lady." Repeat for the second picture. The test is passed if the child can point out at least five out of eight objects asked for in each picture.

Test Six (Age, Two and a Half Years)

1. Naming Objects. Place on the table before which the child is seated the following objects: a toy chair, a toy automobile, a box, a key, and a fork. Present the objects, one at a time, in the following order: chair, automobile, box, key, fork. Each time, say to the child, "What is this?" "What do you call it?" The test is passed if the child names correctly four of the five objects.

2. Identifying Parts of the Body. Make or buy a large cardboard paper doll. Show the doll to the child and say, "Show me the dolly's hair." Follow this with the requests, "Show me the dolly's mouth," "Show me the dolly's ears," and "Show me the dolly's hands." The test is passed if the child points out distinctly all four parts of the paper doll as requested.

3. Walking between Lines. With a piece of chalk draw two parallel lines, eight inches apart, on the floor. Ask the child to walk between these without stepping on the lines. The test is passed if the child is able to walk eight or ten feet between the lines without stepping on the lines.

4. Walks on Tiptoe. Show the child how to walk on tiptoe and encourage him to imitate you. The test is passed if the child walks a few steps without touching his heels to the floor.

Test Seven (Age, Three Years)

1. Repeating Six or Seven Syllables. Say to the child, "I am going to say some words. Watch me and when I stop and nod my head, then you say the words just as I have said them." Then speak the following sentences one at a time slowly and distinctly: (*a*) "I have a little dog." (*b*) "The dog runs after the cat." (*c*) "In summer the sun is hot." The test is passed if the child repeats at least one of the sentences without a single error or omission after hearing it only once.

2. *Gives Sex.* Ask the child the following question: "Are you a little girl or a little boy?" (for a girl), or "Are you a little boy or a little girl?" (for a boy). To pass the test the child must indicate that he knows the difference by stating that he is a boy or a girl.

3. *Points to Parts of the Body.* Ask the child to show you his nose, eyes, mouth, and hair. The test is passed if the child points correctly to three of the four parts. He may indicate that he knows where these parts of the body are by pointing to them, by winking his eyes, by opening his mouth, or by any understandable method.

4. *Drawing a Vertical Line.* While the child is watching you, draw a vertical line on a piece of typewriter paper. Then, give the pencil to the child and, pointing to a place on the paper below your line, say, "You make one like this. Make it here." Illustrate only once and give only one trial. The test is passed if the child draws a vertical line, even though it is not perfectly straight. It must not be horizontal or circular.

[The tests given in this chapter were obtained from the following sources: Test One: 1, 3, and 4 from Bühler; 2 from Bayley. Test Two: 1 from Linfert-Hierholzer; 2 and 4 from Bayley; 3 from Bühler. Test Three: 1 and 4 from Kuhlmann; 2 from Linfert-Hier-holzer; 3 from Cunningham. Test Four: 1 and 2 from Kuhlmann; 3 and 4 from Cunningham. Test Five: 1 from Terman and Merrill; 2 from Bayley; 3 and 4 from Kuhlmann. Test Six: 1 and 2 from Terman and Merrill; 3 from Cunningham; 4 from Bayley.

Test Seven: 1, 2, and 3 from Terman; 4 from Terman and Merrill.][2]

For Discussion

1. Many parents believe that a child who is more independent of adult aid in his behavior than other children of the same age is, consequently, brighter. Do you agree?
2. Does it help a retarded child to do things for him? If not, why not?
3. Because the level of the child's intelligence remains fairly constant throughout life, is it important to know what the level is in early childhood? Give reasons.
4. Do you think it is wise to inform parents about the intellectual level of their children, as measured by tests? Give arguments for and against.
5. Which of the tests given in this chapter do you think give the most accurate measure of a young child's intelligence? Justify your choices.

Suggested Activities

1. Observe a young child who is obviously retarded in his development. Compare his behavior in different situations with that of other children of the same age.
2. Observe a large group of children of the same age—two, four, six, or any age that is available. See if there is similarity of behavior within the group. Also note any marked deviations that appear.
3. Try giving as many of the tests recorded in this chapter as you can to babies and young children. Report your results and how easy or difficult the giving of the tests proved to be.
4. Try giving tests to a child who is shy, nervous, or tense. Then give the same tests later when he is relaxed. Compare the results. What do your findings suggest regarding the accuracy of intelligence tests in the case of young children?

[2] See Bibliography on page 365 for sources of these tests.

CHAPTER 15

Play and Playthings

Play, which is any activity engaged in for the enjoyment it gives, is a normal accompaniment of child life. Every healthy, happy child plays for a major part of the day. For that reason, early childhood can justifiably be called "The playtime of life."

After the child reaches the age when he has definite responsibilities and when he is expected to do whatever he undertakes seriously and well, his attitude changes. The end result then becomes more important to him than the activity itself. This changed attitude is, in time, reflected in his play activities.

Because the enjoyment of the activity is the essential element of all play, the child engages in a given play activity only as long as it amuses him. When he becomes bored, he drops what he is doing and turns his attention to something that, for the moment, he finds more enjoyable.

In time, as his interest in the new activity begins to lag, he will drop it, even though he may be only in the middle of it Half-finished activities are characteristic of childhood play. They demonstrate how unimportant the end result is as compared with the enjoyment that accompanies the activity.

Essential Features of Play

The following essential elements in play must be understood if one is to have a complete comprehension of the child's play life.

1. Surplus Energy. A child must have more energy than he needs for daily living if he is to use it for nonessential activities like play. Studies of the starved children of Europe during the Second World War show that children who have barely enough energy for everyday existence because of malnutrition show no inclination to play.

Furthermore, children who have to assume too much responsibility at home or work extra hours to earn money in after-school jobs have less energy left for play than they did when they were younger. As a result, they play less and their play is of a less energetic sort.

2. Time. To be enjoyable, play must be free from pressure of responsibilities. Whether in childhood or adulthood, the individual must feel leisurely and must not have to watch the clock constantly to be ready for the next engagement. After the routine duties of bathing, dressing, eating, and going to the toilet are completed, the young child's time is his own to do with as he chooses, and he generally chooses to use his free time for play.

3. Equipment. Very little play can be carried out without some equipment, no matter how crude and simple it may be. A young baby plays with his hair, ears, toes, or fingers. After exploring his body, he will then need something else to play with.

Few children, even those of very poor parents, are completely lacking in play equipment. The trouble more often lies in the fact that the play equipment is not suitable for, nor satisfactory to, the child. He is too young or too old for

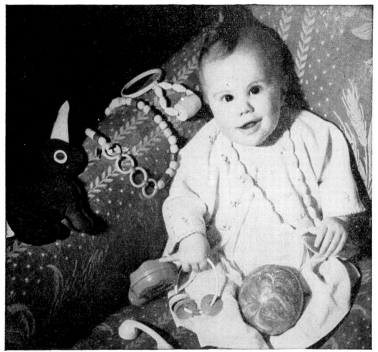

During the first year, the child sleeps so much of the time that he has little time for play. His only play needs are a cuddly toy, rattles, blocks, beads, and a big rubber ball.

it; it is too complicated for him to play with without adult help; there is not enough variety to it to stimulate different kinds of play; or it has to be gotten out and packed away every time the child wants to use it.

4. *Space for Play*. Very few play activities can be carried out in cramped quarters. The child should have room, both indoors and out, where he can play with safety to himself and without danger of harming the family possessions. The

child who lives in a small town or country district with large houses and yards has a distinct advantage in this respect as compared with the city child. Space alone, however, is not enough. There must be play equipment in the area where the child can play safely.

5. *Knowledge of How to Play.* Giving the child space and equipment for play is, in and of itself, not enough. The child must know how to use it. The only ways he can learn are by being shown how to use it or by watching other children play with similar equipment. Left to his own devices, a young child may chew his crayons, thinking they are sticks of candy, or scribble on furniture or wallpaper to see the pretty colors they make.

6. *Playmates.* Solitary play is no more pleasurable for a child than for an adult. Part of the fun that comes from playing is the opportunity it offers for social contacts. Even though young children actually play very little with others, they like to know that there are other children present who are playing also.

They may watch their playmates; they may play with them for a time; or they may ignore them and play alone. Whatever they choose to do is of little consequence. They like to know that there is someone to play with or to watch, should it please them to do so.

Values of Play

Play is not a waste of time or a method of keeping little children out of the mother's way while she attends to the household chores. It has distinct values which cannot be overlooked in the child's development.

First and foremost, it is an outlet for excess energy. In modern life, with its many laborsaving devices for use in the home and with smaller families in which much is done for

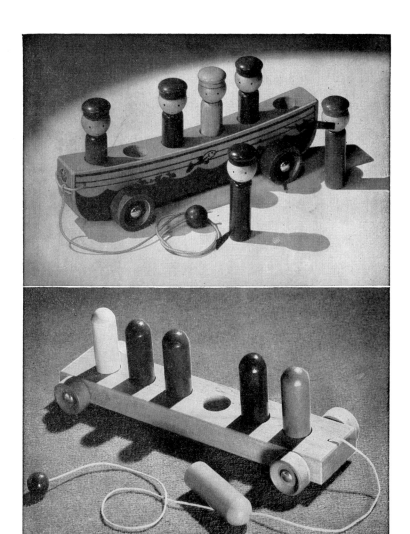

At about the time he is starting to walk, the baby will enjoy playing with some of the pull-type, pegboard toys. Many of these are constructed with the child's safety in mind. They have no sharp edges or small pieces; they are made of wood that will not splinter and are covered with paint that will not chip.

the child, the normal, healthy child has more energy than his daily living requirements make use of. If he does not siphon off some of this surplus energy in play, the chances are that he will turn it into less desirable channels by getting into mischief.

Play offers an opportunity for exercise, which promotes a good appetite and encourages healthful sleep. This is especially true of outdoor play. Through play activities, the child learns to do many things and acquires skills that prove to be useful to him throughout life. Many a woman's skill in sewing was learned when, as a child, she wanted to make clothes for her dolls.

The final, but by no means the least important, value of play is its socializing influence. Through their play activities, children learn to get along with other children, to share their possessions, to be fair and play the rules of the game, to cooperate, and to wait for their turn. Learning to be a good sport and a good loser during childhood will fit the child for many of the difficult social adjustments he will have to make as he reaches maturity.

Varieties of Play Activities

Play is a pleasurable activity, but different types of activity can give pleasure to the child. At one time, he enjoys running; at another, he likes to read; and, still another time, he may want to color a picture. Because the pleasurable activity varies in the form it takes, not all play is of the same type. For this reason, children's play from the angle of the different types that are normally found during the early years of childhood will be discussed in this chapter.

So that play is well-rounded, every child should engage in all the types described, although the amount of time devoted

Blocks are the "perfect" toy because they fulfill the three requirements for a good plaything: 1) simple enough to require no outside help; 2) durable enough so that no amount of handling will harm them; and 3) stimulating enough to offer unlimited opportunities for play.

FROM "ALL THE CHILDREN," NEW YORK BOARD OF EDUCATION

to each will, of course, vary from child to child, depending partly upon the child's interests and abilities and partly upon the opportunities offered by his environment.

1. Exploratory Play. Young children love to play with toys. At first their main interest is exploratory. They look at a toy; they shake it or pound it to see what noise it will make; they suck it; they squeeze or pat it to see how it feels; and they smell it.

Frequently, in the process of exploration, they break the toy or change its appearance so that it is barely recognizable. However, it has served its purpose and has not only given the player enjoyment but has also given information to add to the child's rapidly growing fund of knowledge.

2. Construction Play. By the time the child is three, he is too old to limit his toy play to exploratory actions. He wants to make things, no matter how simple and crude his efforts may be. His playthings are now used for construction. He no longer throws or bites his blocks but builds them into towers, houses, or bridges. Instead of chewing on his crayons or scribbling at random with them, he colors pictures in a book or draws his own pictures.

Clay and sand are used to construct all sorts of objects—people, houses, flowers, or ashtrays—and not merely patted, pounded, or thrown. The finished product is not important to the child. For him the making is an enjoyable experience and quite adequate reward for the energy expended.

3. *Dramatic Play.* Just about the time the child begins to use his toys to construct things, he discovers that it is fun to dramatize with them. To a little girl, a doll is not merely a doll but a baby. To a boy, tin soldiers are real soldiers, stuffed animals are real animals, and toy trains are real trains.

The child engages in make-believe play in which the playroom, with a few changes, becomes a house, a robber's den, a schoolroom, or any other background needed for the play. With the aid of a few articles of clothing, the boy or girl can quickly turn into a character in his play world, and his toys may become the other players.

4. *"Mother Games."* Before the baby is two, he likes to play simple little games with his mother, father, some other adult, or an older child. In this type of game, generally referred to as "mother game" because the mother is most often the other player, there are simple rules. Each player must take his turn. Peekaboo, I Spy, This Little Pig Went to Market, and Guess Which Hand? are the young child's favorite games.

Not only are games of this sort a source of real pleasure to the child but, of greater importance, they are good training for playing games later on with other children. Through

COURTESY H. J. HEINZ COMPANY

At about three or four, children discover that it is fun to dramatize. A toy telephone is a real telephone to them; a doll is a baby to a little girl; and toy soldiers are the real thing to a little boy.

them the child learns that he must obey the rules of the game, must take his turn, and must be a "good loser."

5. *Neighborhood Games.* By the age of four or five years, children have outgrown mother games. They now want to play with children of their own age. The games they play at first are very similar to those played with adults except that the rules are slightly more exacting, the play a little more complicated, and the players are of their own age.

This latter fact has given rise to the name "neighborhood games." Two or more children, or even a whole group, can play Tag, Hide-and-Seek, Cops and Robbers, Follow the Leader, Hide the Thimble, or other popular games of the early childhood years. The rules are elastic enough and the plan of play flexible enough to allow for any number of players.

6. *Amusements.* Amusements are forms of entertainment in which the player is more or less in the role of a passive participant. The enjoyment comes from watching or listening to others. This is the ideal kind of play for times of the day when the child is tired and yet needs something to occupy his attention, such as the periods just before meals or bedtime.

If used for such occasions, amusements are an ideal form of play; but, if the child is encouraged to engage too extensively in play of this type, he loses the advantage that comes from toy play or from games.

7. *Amusement from Watching Others.* There are different forms of amusement that appeal to young children. Watching others, whether children or adults, is a constant source of entertainment not only for children but for adults as well. No matter how simple, humdrum, or repetitious an activity may be, a child seems to be fascinated by watching other people's activities.

Washing dishes, ironing clothes, fixing a broken table or light fixture, cleaning a stove, washing the windows, cutting the grass, or the thousand and one jobs of a home are all interesting to a child and keep him amused indefinitely.

Watching animals, whether household pets or animals on a farm or in the zoo, provides unlimited entertainment for a young child. He never seems to grow tired of watching a cat wash himself with his tongue, a dog chew on a bone, the monkeys climb up and down in the cages in the zoo, or the cows being milked on the farm.

8. *Amusement from Pictures.* Looking at pictures in magazines or books is a favorite amusement of young children.

Play has many advan-
tages aside from pure
enjoyment. It is an out-
let for surplus energy,
it offers an opportunity
for exercise and, partic-
ularly if outdoors, it encourages appetite and
healthful sleep. In ad-
dition, through play ac-
tivities children learn
skills that may last
them throughout life.

COURTESY NATIONAL COLLEGE OF EDUCATION
AND "CHILDHOOD EDUCATION"

Pictures with bright colors and little detail in the drawings, which depict simple, everyday people in everyday settings, are more understandable to them than fine art. That is why they like the pictures in advertisements, in children's story books, or in the "comics."

Judged from the point of view of artistic merit, these pictures might not be considered "good." However, their simplicity and lack of detail makes them comprehensible to a young child and, because of this, he enjoys looking at them. He looks at the same ones over and over again, each time discovering something that he did not see before or some new meaning to the picture.

9. *Amusement from Stories.* Before a child can actually understand words, he likes to have stories told or read to

The child likes the rhythm of music, whether he has talent or not. A phonograph is better than a radio for children because they can hear the same records over and over until they are familiar with the words.

him. But the story must be told or read so that the child can understand it if his attention is to be held. This means that the teller must use facial expressions to give significance to words, must put emphasis on the meaningful words, must speak slowly so that the child has time to grasp what he hears, and must use simple words that the child knows.

Frequently in reading a book to a child it is necessary to substitute a simpler word for one used by the author. This is especially true of books written a number of years ago, such as the classic fairy tales. Authors of the past were not as word-conscious as they are today.

The themes of stories for young children should be simple, homey, and close to their everyday lives.[1] Stories about children their own age, about the people they know outside the home—such as the policeman, the milkman, the postman, the butcher, or the grocer—and the animals on the farm or in the city—such as cows, pigs, chickens, horses, cats, and dogs—are what children like to hear about.

They also like to hear about themselves. It fascinates them to have a simple story built up around them as the central character. It is not until the child is approaching five years of age that he really enjoys fairy tales or stories of adventure that take him off into a world unknown to him. When a child likes a story, he wants to hear it over and over again, just exactly as he has heard it before.

In addition to stories, children like poems, but the poems must be simple in theme and structure. The classic nursery rhymes that are passed down from one generation to another and the more modern poems for children, such as those by A. A. Milne, have the strongest appeal. The more jingle there is to poetry, the better the young child likes it.

Pictures in books appeal to the child as much, or sometimes more, than does the story. Children like to look at the pictures while the story is being read and later, if no one is available to read to them, they enjoy opening the book and studying the pictures. Even before a child can read, he enjoys looking at comics. The bright colors appeal to him, and the simple drawings with plenty of action fascinate him. In the preschool years, he likes comics about animals, children, and families.

10. Amusement from Music. Music that is simple and has a definite rhythm appeals to all children whether or not they

[1] A librarian can give you a list of books suitable for any age level.

have musical talent. They like to sing to accompany the music. After hearing a tune several times, they will sing without the musical accompaniment. Piano music, orchestral music over the radio, or music from the phonograph are all common sources of musical enjoyment.[2]

The chief advantage of phonograph records is that the music can be played over and over again. This the child likes. Furthermore, most phonograph records of music for children have vocal accompaniments with the words so clearly and distinctly enunciated that the child can understand them. From hearing them he can learn the words so that he, too, can sing the songs. With radio music he cannot learn the words nor hear his favorite tunes when he wants to hear them.

11. Amusement from Television. Young children of today are fascinated by television. If permitted, they will sit for hours before the television screen. Even when they do not understand what the program is about, they enjoy the action, the music, and the sounds of words. Most television networks have programs appropriate for preschool children at times of the day when the child is likely to be indoors— right after breakfast, before dinner, and in the late hours of the afternoon. If the programs are properly selected for the child's level of development and if he is not permitted to watch for too long at a time, television watching is an educational, relaxing, and enjoyable experience for the child.

Essentials of Playthings

Play requires equipment. However, not all equipment labeled "toys" or "playthings" is adequate. Because play is an activity, the play material must be such that the child can do

[2] New records are being made for preschool children every year. Consult your local music store for titles.

something with it. The more different activities it will stimulate, the more satisfactory it is. For example, a toy automobile that actually works offers the child opportunities for many hours of enjoyable play. On clear days he can ride in his automobile outdoors, can share rides with his playmates, and can even build a "garage" in the yard from boxes covered with a cloth or boards for a roof. On rainy days the hall or his room can be used for his daily "rides." If his automobile is equipped with a horn, this will add to the fun he can have with it.

Playthings must be safe so that a child can play with them without harming himself. The numerous plastic toys available today are less expensive and safer than many of the toys made of metal or wood. Sharp edges on metal toys can cut or bruise if the child falls on them; soft wood will splinter; and paint will chip off if the child bites or picks it.

Playthings that Appeal to Children

While each child has his own favorite playthings, there are certain toys that have a universal appeal to young children. It is from these universally popular toys that the child selects his favorites. He then concentrates the major portion of his playtime on them.

As a general rule, the child's favorite playthings are those used in his favorite play. His favorite play, in turn, is closely related to his ability. A little boy, for example, who prefers his engines to every other toy he possesses will, as he grows older, in almost every instance show an ability along mechanical lines.

It is never possible to predict what kind of play equipment will prove to be most pleasurable to a young child. For that reason, it is far better to encourage a well-rounded play program than a narrow, one-sided one. To make this possible,

COURTESY LIBRARY OF CONGRESS AND (*left*) "ALL THE CHILDREN," NEW YORK BOARD OF EDUCATION

Children should have access to larger equipment (*top*)—such as swings, slides, seesaws, and other playground facilities—to help muscle development. They should also have constructive toys (*left*)—such as scissors, crayons, paints, and pegboards—for using in creative handwork.

270

Every child should at
some time or other have
a tricycle, roller skates,
a wagon, a sled, or a
doll carriage (*top*). For
quiet hours, he should
have books, magazines,
scrapbooks, and post-
cards (*right*).

the playthings of a young child should be chosen so that there is some equipment for every type of play—exploratory, dramatic, and constructive—games, and amusements of all kinds.

Playthings that Promote Development

To foster muscular coordination, which is still undeveloped in early childhood, and to encourage construction play, the young child will need blunt scissors, colored papers, paste, crayons, pencils, paints, clay, blocks, pegboards, strips of paper for weaving, odd bits of ribbon, pieces of wood, and clothespins.

Imaginative play requires dolls that represent people, stuffed animals, and tin soldiers, but the child will also need a supply of castoff clothing and pieces of bright cloth that can be used for costuming his dramatizations.

In a city, much of the needed outdoor play equipment, such as swings, slides, jungle gyms, seesaws, sandboxes, and wading pools, is provided in the public parks. Children who grow up in a small community generally do not have the use of a well-equipped playground provided by the community. Each child, however, will need at some time a tricycle, roller skates, wagon, jump rope, garden tools, boxes of all sizes to climb on or push around, sled, ball, doll carriage and, when very young, push-and-pull toys.

For the quiet hours children need plenty of books with brightly colored pictures, old magazines, phonograph records, and homemade scrapbooks containing odds and ends gathered from every source and brought together for their amusement. Collections of Christmas cards, birthday cards, and postcards are good to while away the quiet periods that every young child's daily program should include.

For Discussion

1. Would it be bad to encourage boys and girls to play with similar toys or to play the same games much after they are five years old? Give examples to prove your point.
2. In what kinds of play will poor health be the greatest handicap to the child? What can he do to compensate for this?
3. Why are games more important for the shy, retiring child than for the aggressive one?
4. Why does television have more appeal than radio to children? What type of program appeals most to children under six years of age?
5. Suggest some homemade substitutes for ready-made toys that can be used when a family budget is limited.

Suggested Activities

1. Visit the toy department of a large store, preferably near Christmas. Make an itemized list of play equipment for a child of three, four, or five and total the cost.
2. Note the workmanship of the play materials. List those which would hold up under the impact of a child's play and those which would not.
3. Make a list of the items displayed for babies that might be dangerous and the source of danger in each toy.
4. Go to the children's division of your local library. Ask the librarian to show you books suitable for children under six years of age. Examine some of these books critically to see whether you think the pictures and words would be comprehensible to a young child. If not, give your reasons.
5. Go to a record store and check the records listed "For Children." Try to make your own list of records you think children at various age levels will like.

PART FOUR:

Alice Harold Murphy

The Child as a Person

CHAPTER 16

The Child's Companions

A natural craving for companionship is apparent in little babies before they are six months old. Whenever they are awake they look around for someone to watch, and, if they find they are alone, they put up a protest in the form of a loud wail. Each successive month, as they spend more and more time awake, the craving for human companionship becomes more marked.

The Importance of Companionship

Every child, no matter how young he may be, needs companionship. It is through companionship with others that the child learns to be a socialized being and finds out how to make the necessary adjustments to enable him to get along with other people.

The young artist portrayed in the etching *Artist at Work,* on the opposite page, is so absorbed in her own drawing that she is unaware that she is posing. The etcher, Alice Harold Murphy, is well known in graphic arts, her work having been included many times in collections of the year's best prints. (Courtesy Associated American Artists.)

275

Should the child be deprived of human companionship during the early years of life, or should that companionship be limited to a few adults in his home environment, the child will become so used to being alone or with adults that he will become too self-sufficient.

Furthermore, he will be uninterested in his contemporaries and, unless corrected, will develop into a shy, retiring, self-conscious personality.

It is not only important that the child have plenty of companionship and have it early when the natural craving for it appears, but it is equally important that his early social relationships be pleasant. No one can blame a child for preferring his own company if the children with whom he has come into contact have bossed him, teased him, or neglected him.

If the child has unpleasant experiences when he first seeks the companionship of other children, it generally dampens his interest and throws him back upon his own resources or upon adults. In adults he generally finds pleasant companionship because the adult more often than not will pamper, pet, and give him the attention he craves.

Young children imitate others in a parrotlike fashion. They mimic the mannerisms, speech, play interests, thoughts, and morals of the people with whom they happen to be. For that reason the child's companions have a profound influence on his behavior and on the development of his whole personality.

Parent-Child Relationships

Through the helpless months of babyhood, the child's major social contacts are, of necessity, limited to the adult members of the household. The helplessness that is responsible for limiting his contacts is also responsible for putting him in the limelight of adult attention. Not only is he the

Because the young child is so helpless, he is almost completely dependent upon adults. Parents should help the child to become less and less dependent upon them as he grows, so it will not be too difficult for him to get along with other children when the time comes for him to do so.

COURTESY "TODAY," INTERNATIONAL HARVESTER COMPANY

apple of his parents' eyes but of his doting relatives' as well. Even the friends of the family give him their undivided attention when they are permitted to peek at him or, as a very special favor, to hold him in their arms and play with him. If he is the first-born baby of the family, he is likely to have every whim recognized and satisfied, especially when he puts up a fuss and demands it. It is not surprising, then, if he develops an exaggerated idea of his own importance.

Even when the months of helplessness have passed, some parents find it difficult to adjust their attitudes toward the

COURTESY H. J. HEINZ COMPANY

Pleasant relations between children of the family are highly desirable
for harmony in the home and for the adjustment of the younger child
to other playmates when he is ready to make friends outside the
family.

child who was once their "baby." Instead of helping him to
grow up and gain the independence he is capable of, they
keep him dependent on them. This makes adjustments outside the home difficult for the child and places an added
burden on him.

Naturally, the child finds the companionship of his parents
very pleasurable. Every child, to a certain extent, no matter
how large the family group may be, gets some pampering.

The seriousness of pampering by adults lies in the fact that
it makes adjustments to other children more difficult. Other
children cannot be expected to pamper a child as his parents
and relatives do.

Brother-Sister Relationships

Should the family group include other children, the young child's early companions will, of course, be his brothers and sisters. If they are older than he, they may pamper and pet him. They may even go so far as to humor his every whim. More likely, however, they will boss him around, show open contempt when his behavior falls below their standards, or even make him feel unwelcome.

Parents should be on the alert for such treatment and should explain to the older child why the younger behaves as he does. In addition, giving the older child some responsibility for the care of the younger adds to his feeling of self-importance and helps to foster in him a favorable attitude toward the younger.

As a result, the younger child will, in turn, be more likely to have a favorable attitude toward children born in the family later who are younger than he is. He will want to do things for and with them. He will want to teach them as his older brothers and sisters have taught him. In this way, brothers and sisters learn to find pleasure in one another's company, thus solving the problem of companionship for them when outside friends are not available.

Neighborhood Friends

The young child's immediate neighborhood supplies most of his playmates. Sooner or later he will come in contact with the children who live on his block, who go to the same park to play, or who attend the same preschool or Sunday-school group. From these neighborhood children he will select as congenial companions the children of his own age whose development is such that their interests and abilities are on approximately the same level as his.

The immediate community generally supplies the child's first play-mates. From these children in the neighborhood he learns how to do many things and acquires general information that broadens his outlook and prepares him for socializing in larger groups later on.

To the young child, the social and economic status of his companions is unimportant. He can have just as much fun playing with a child whose parents are poorer than his as he can with a child whose father's income is many times that of his father's. Nor does the position his friend's family holds in the community matter to him so long as he and his friend have fun together.

Similarly, religion, racial origin, and color of skin are unimportant. The young child is not a snob in the usual sense of the word. He judges his friends on the basis of their merits, not on the basis of standards often considered important by older members of society.

Preference for companions of the child's own sex does not appear much before the age of six years. Until this time, little boys will play happily with little girls; and little girls, in turn, will have just as much fun with the boys of the neighborhood as with the girls.

Value of Neighborhood Friendships

The value of neighborhood friends to a child's development is tremendous. From them he learns how to do many things — such as climbing trees, throwing balls, playing all kinds of games—and gains a great deal of general information. True, he might learn these same things from associating exclusively with adults or brothers and sisters, but the chances are that he would not.

Association with others gives him a broader point of view about life in general. Each child will talk quite frankly to his friends about everything that interests him. He will, in turn, get his friends' point of view. Many of their ideas may differ from his, and, in time, he may change and perhaps liberalize his own opinions.

By far the greatest advantage of neighborhood friendships is the socialization that they encourage. To get along with others, to be accepted in the group, and to be liked by his friends, each child must learn to give and take, to share, to be a good sport when he loses and not a boaster when he wins, to feel sorry for his friends when they are in trouble, and to lend a helping hand in times of necessity.

Substitute Companions

Many children are lonely. While it is true that they have adults on whom to draw for companionship and sometimes even brothers and sisters, this is still not adequate to satisfy their needs for companionship. There may be a number of reasons why a child cannot find adequate companionship outside. First, there may not be other children of his age or level of development living in the neighborhood who can be counted on for companionship.

Second, even if there are plenty of children, the child may not be welcome in the neighborhood group because of his unsocial behavior or for other reasons. Therefore, it is not the only child alone who is lonely. Many children are lonely for one reason or another.

The lonely child compensates for his loneliness in a number of ways. The two most common ways are by constructing "imaginary companions" to play with and by playing with pets. If everyday life does not offer him companionship, the child will construct companions of his own in his imagination and play with them.

These imaginary companions will, of course, be to his liking. He may, in time, develop such an affection for his imaginary playmates that he will give them names, attribute to them all the qualities he most admires in real children, and play with them so constantly that companionship with real children is unnecessary.

An offhand judgment might lead one to believe that this is an easy and satisfactory solution to the lonely-child problem, but it is really far from satisfactory. True, it fills the child's immediate need for companionship, but it in no way contributes to his social development.

On the contrary, it has exactly the reverse effect. The imaginary playmates are always docile, easily led, nonaggressive creatures whom the real child can dominate without fear of retaliation. He can have everything his own way and can even cheat or play out of turn without a protest from them. How different this imaginary play is from play with real children!

If a child is lonely because there are no children around or because he is not welcome in the group, he may find substitute companions in the way of pets or imaginary playmates. It is all right for a child to have a pet, but playing with a pet does not teach a child to get along with other children.

MARY BRANDEL HOPKINS

Pets

Pets, such as dogs, cats, ponies, birds, fish, or turtles, are frequently given to only children or to children who, for one reason or another, are lonely. They fill a gap in the young child's life and satisfy his craving for companionship.

Dogs, cats, and ponies are more satisfactory companions for the child than are birds, fish, and turtles, because they are more responsive and will actually play with a child. This is especially true of the animals that are not too highly pedigreed.

Like imaginary companions, pets do not have a socializing influence on the child. He does not learn from playing with them how to get along with other children. If they happen to be docile pets, they will permit the child to have his own way in play, even if it means pulling their ears and tails, sitting on their backs, dressing them up in clothes, or doing any one of the many things that children delight in doing when playing with a pet.

Unsocial Behavior

In spite of a strong desire for the companionship of other children and for popularity among his playmates, every child displays from time to time behavior trends that can be labeled by no other term than "unsocial." This unsocial behavior results from a conflict within the child created by a desire to do what he wants to do and, at the same time, to be one of the group.

A few of the most common forms of unsocial behavior frequently found among young children follow.

1. Quarreling. Between the ages of two and six, nearly all children quarrel when playing together. After a few minutes of harmonious play, one child decides he wants a certain toy; immediately the other child decides that that is the very toy he not only wants but must have. The result is a quarrel.

Quarreling nearly always occurs because of the desire for some material object—generally a plaything. The form it takes is a knock-down, drag-out fight for the desired object. The best of friends will quarrel as will casual acquaintances. The worst quarrels generally take place in the home between the children of the family.

Owing to the fact that young children have little if any emotional control, they can inflict real harm on one another when they quarrel. Therefore, constant supervision is necessary when young children are together. An adult should always be ready to step in and stop an argument before it reaches a point where it might be dangerous.

In spite of its disagreeable aspects, quarreling has a distinct educational value that no child should be deprived of. Through quarreling, every child learns that he cannot have his own way all the time and that he must respect the wishes of others. He also learns how much other people will tolerate from him and that he must curb his selfish interests if he wants to have friends.

2. *Bullying and Teasing.* Bullying and teasing are alike in that they both inflict pain. They differ, however, in the fact that the pain inflicted in bullying is physical, while in teasing it is mental. In physical bullying the body is hurt, and in mental bullying the feelings are hurt.

Every child, at some time or other, gets satisfaction in the feeling of superiority that comes from the realization that he has the power to inflict pain on others.

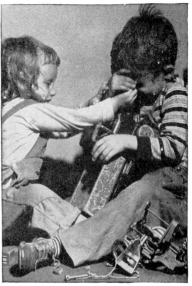

FREDERIC LEWIS

All children quarrel because, invariably, what one has the other wants. In spite of its disagreeable aspects, some amount of quarreling is educational for the child. He learns that he cannot always have what he wants and that he must respect the rights of others.

Boys as a rule are more subject to this type of unsocial behavior than are girls, but girls are by no means free from it.

Bullying and teasing result from the child's natural tendency to want to assert himself. This tendency is sometimes exaggerated by the realization that his playmates do not give him the opportunity for self-assertion that he craves. He therefore forces them to pay attention to him by bullying in the form of tripping them as they walk, pinching, pulling away chairs as they start to sit down, pulling hair, slamming doors in their faces, or any one of dozens of little mean tricks that children can play on their friends.

Hurting feelings, a child may discover, is a more effective way of commanding attention than is bullying. The child who is a bully or a tease will find out what are the sensitive spots in other children and point them out for public ridicule. If another child is fat or skinny, has red hair, is slow in learning, is shy and sensitive, or is clumsy in his movements, he will hear about it time after time.

There is no educational value in being teased or bullied, nor does the child who engages in the teasing or bullying mend his ways even when he learns that others resent it. He is more likely to continue his unsocial behavior as a compensation for his unpopularity. The only cure for a tease or a bully is isolation from other children.

3. *"Parallel" Play.* It is quite unusual for children under four years of age to play together, even though they are in the same room or the same play yard. Each child goes his own way, apparently quite oblivious to the fact that there is another child near him with whom he might play.

The child plays as he wishes, with a toy of his own choosing, and frequently talks out loud, not to the other child but to himself. It is a form of "thinking aloud" rather than of communication. Any other child who happens to be around behaves in the same manner. This is known as "parallel" play because the children are playing side by side but not together.

4. *Watching Others.* All young children enjoy watching other children at play. Frequently it is difficult to persuade the child to join the group, in spite of the fact that he watches them in a way that suggests he longs to be one of them. He is held back by fear and lack of self-confidence.

COURTESY "CHILDHOOD EDUCATION"

Until he is about three, the child does not play with other children, even if they are near by. Often, however, he will engage in parallel play—that is, playing by himself but with other children playing around him. Parallel play is good for the child because he becomes acquainted with other children and overcomes any tendency he may have to be lonely.

At the same time he is gaining satisfaction from being with a group of other children. In most instances, several days in the role of spectator are all the child needs to overcome his timidity and to satisfy his longing to become an active participant in the group.

Leadership in Childhood

Contrary to popular belief, leaders are made, not born. True, few little children show real leadership characteristics, although many try to dominate others in a tyrannical fashion. Seldom do the tyrants of early childhood prove to be the leaders as the children grow older.

Studies of leaders, not only in childhood but in adolescence and maturity as well, have shown that leaders have intelligence slightly above that of the group as a whole; they show initiative and are aggressive; they use imagination to plan; they get along well with others by respecting their rights and wishes, by being cooperative and sympathetic; and, above all, they are not self-centered and egotistical.

Training for Leadership

Whether or not the potential leader will develop into a true leader will depend to a large extent upon his early social experiences. A child who is pampered and spoiled by adults, who is permitted to become self-centered to the extent of wanting everyone to humor his whims as he has been accustomed to being humored at home, has little chance of becoming a leader unless he mends his ways.

By contrast, the child who has been expected to conform to others in his home life and has had plenty of opportunity to play with other children learns to get along well with others and to consider their wishes and rights.

Ability to get along well with others is, alone, not enough. The leader must have initiative and a degree of aggressiveness that will enable him to take the lead not only in suggesting what the group will do but also in showing the others how to carry out the suggestion.

Initiative and aggressiveness, while dependent to a certain extent upon intelligence, are by no means universally found in children of high intellectual levels. Whether or not a child will develop these leadership qualities will depend primarily upon his opportunities to develop them, especially in the early years of childhood.

If he is permitted to make decisions for himself, if he is encouraged to plan his own activities in his playtime, to as-

sume simple responsibilities, and to assert himself in regard
to his wishes, he will be laying the foundation for these traits.

Social Responsibilities

Companionship with others carries with it certain responsibilities that the young child should learn as soon as he begins to associate with other people. This means in the home,
when his earliest companions are his parents. If he does not
learn then the responsibilities he must assume, he will find
himself unpopular outside the home.

1. Cheerfulness. One of the most important responsibilities
that everyone, child as well as adult, has to others is to be
agreeable. No one likes a "grouch" who complains and finds
fault with everything and everyone. Children whose home
environment is pleasant and who are accustomed to being
with people who are cheerful will imitate this attitude.

There are times, of course, when every child is "grouchy."
These generally occur when he is tired or not feeling well.
To make him realize how unsocial his behavior is, he should
be sent to his own room until he can be cheerful. He will
learn through this that he must be cheerful if he wants to be
with other people.

2. Good Manners. Closely related to cheerfulness are good
manners. No one likes a "boor" any more than he likes a
"grouch." For that reason the young child must learn that
politeness is an essential responsibility to others. Furthermore, he must realize that rudeness will not be tolerated. If
he learns a few courtesies, such as "thank you" and "please";
to say "I am sorry" when he interferes with or hurts another;
to allow adults to walk through doorways in front of him;
and to wait until grownups start to eat before he begins—
that is all you can expect of a young child.

If good manners are stressed at home, they will become so

habitual that the child will automatically treat outsiders with the same degree of courtesy that he shows to the members of his family.

3. *Respect for Rights of Others.* In a group, whether it be composed of members of a family or outsiders, everyone has certain rights. The young child must learn to respect the rights of others and not to expect everyone to give in to him constantly.

Whether he fights with his fists or by calling people names, he is acting unsocially and showing lack of social responsibility. Social responsibility, by contrast, demands that he take turns, share what he has with others, and not only recognize but also respect the rights of others.

4. *Respect for Possessions of Others.* Not only must the child respect the rights of others but he must also learn to respect their possessions. This means that he must come to realize that he cannot harm the property of others, that he should not even touch it without asking permission first, nor should he, under any conditions, appropriate it.

5. *Respect for Privacy of Others.* Every individual, whether adult or child, is entitled to some privacy in the home. Whether the time is spent for bathing, dressing, relaxing, reading, working, engaging in a hobby, listening to the radio, or watching television is an individual matter. Because few young children are given privacy, they do not realize that others expect it and are apt to be annoyed when their privacy is encroached upon.

The best way to teach a child to respect the privacy of others is to respect his own privacy. Every day, preferably during the afternoon rest period or the before-supper quiet period, the child should be given his "private time." He should be told that no one will disturb him unless something very important turns up. The door of his room should be shut, and if any member of the household has to go into his room during that period, he or she should knock on the child's door and ask permission to enter.

6. *Accepting Blame.* Accepting the blame for one's acts is likewise a form of social responsibility. It is easy to blame others and thus free oneself from scoldings or punishment, but it is unfair and unsportsmanlike. To help the child develop this form of social responsibility, scoldings and punishments should be avoided until the child has had an opportunity to tell his side of the story and until it is evident that he knew that what he did was wrong. In this way, the child is less likely to want to blame others.

7. *Self-evaluation.* A final aspect of social responsibility which every young child should be trained to assume is that of understanding his own position in the group. Many little children, often through no fault of their own, get an exaggerated idea of their own importance.

This leads them to demand attention, to dominate the conversation, to interrupt when others are talking, or in some other way to thrust themselves into the limelight. A child cannot, of course, have enough social experience to realize that demanding attention is regarded unfavorably by others. Nor does he realize that it will cause him to be disliked. Therefore, it is the responsibility of the adults with whom he is associated to see to it that these attempts to gain attention are checked at once.

For Discussion

1. Why is too much adult companionship, as in the case of only children, bad for a child? What advantages does it have for the child?
2. Why do young children more frequently quarrel over possessions than over uncomplimentary comments?

3. Suggest practical ways of developing leadership qualities in a shy, retiring child.
4. In what ways does moving from one neighborhood to another or from one community to another interfere with the socialization of a child?
5. How do the relationships the child has with his parents and with his brothers and sisters influence his behavior when he is with other children?
6. Why are leaders in early childhood often not leaders when they reach the high school age?

Suggested Activities

1. Observe the parallel play of several young children. Note the frequency and form that social interaction takes. From your observations, would you conclude that parallel play is a good preliminary to real socialization?
2. Observe the behavior of a child who is the leader of a play group. Note what traits he displays that are responsible for his leadership. Then, by contrast, list the traits characteristically displayed by the children who follow him.
3. Select a child who is devoted to some pet. Watch him as he plays with his pet. Is there any indication of the development of attitudes that would be helpful in social adjustments with people?
4. Try to recall any imaginary playmates you had as a young child. Recall and list as many facts as possible about your imaginary playmate.
5. Observe a quarrel among young children. What started the quarrel? What form did the quarreling take? How did it end?
6. Rate three children—a popular, a moderately popular, and an unpopular child—on the difference of their characteristics for social responsibility.

CHAPTER 17

A Place of His Own

Children, like plants, need space in which to grow. During early childhood, when the most rapid physical growth is occurring, space is most important to the child. Young children, like puppies and kittens, want to romp and play, and because of their poor muscle coordination they are likely to bump into furniture and trip over the legs of chairs unless the room is large enough to allow free space for romping.

The Ideal Home for a Child

Ideally, for a young child, the home should be a large rambling house. Many old-fashioned houses are better suited to the needs of a young child than are modern homes that are designed primarily for efficiency in homemaking. Neither is an apartment with small rooms and no inside stairs an ideal home for a young child, who likes to run around, climb up and down steps, or run in and out of doors to play.

No matter how small and cramped the family living quarters are, every child from infancy should have a space set aside for him which he can think of as his own. To an adult, the sharing of living quarters with the other members of the family is quite satisfactory, but a young child wants to have a room of his own, or at least a part of a room, set aside for

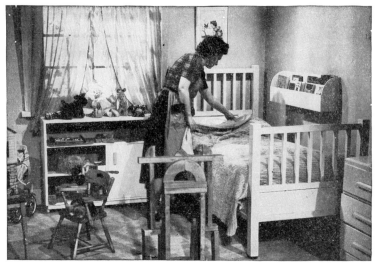

COURTESY CRAWLEY FILMS

If the child cannot have a room of his own, he should have a place of his own somewhere in the house.

him. In addition, he wants a place in the bathroom where his towel, washcloth, and toothbrush will always be found; a place in the dining room or kitchen which is his place for eating; and a place in the yard or garden where he can do as he pleases.

Security Resulting from Ownership

You may wonder why it means so much to a young child to have a place of his own. The reason is that it helps to foster a feeling of security and certainty that every little child lacks. In a place of his own he feels secure; he feels that he is being recognized as an individual; and he has a sense of pride from realization of ownership.

In addition to this, young children are not gregarious

enough to want to be part of a group all the time, nor has their social development advanced far enough for them to be able to share with others what they have. They like to be alone at times when they can feel that their possessions are their own to do with as they please.

Value of Permanency

If the child is to be "master of his domain" and derive the psychological benefits that come from this, his domain must be as permanent as possible. The more permanent it is, the greater will be his feeling of security.

To achieve this end, the room selected for a young child or the space set aside for him in a room shared with another child should remain his as permanently as possible. Nothing will make a young child resent the arrival of a new baby in the household more than being put out of his room or having some of the space allotted to him taken away from him and given to the new baby.

What is true of the child's room is equally true of all other spaces in the home which he comes to regard as "his." If his towels are hung on a certain rack in the bathroom and his toothbrush is hung on a certain hook, they should continue to be placed there.

As long as he eats at a small table, that table should have a special place reserved for it in the kitchen, dining room, or nursery. When the child is old enough to eat at the family table, his place should remain his place, and he should not be shifted from one side of the table to the other.

The Child's Room

The usual practice in American homes is to reserve the largest bedroom for the parents and to assign one of the other bedrooms to the first child. As new children arrive, they are given the remaining room or made to share a bedroom with an older child. Doubling up is nearly always necessary in city apartments or small modern homes.

Generally, the rooms given to children are smaller than the one the parents have, and frequently they are not so light or well ventilated. This is unfortunate because a young child usually spends more time in his bedroom than his parents do. Good lighting and ventilation, as well as space, are therefore more important to him.

Whenever possible, each child should have a room of his own rather than having to share a room with another child. Children develop at different rates. The interests and activities of two children several years apart in chronological age are so different that sharing the same room will not be a pleasurable experience for either.

If the family is large, it is a better arrangement to put the oldest child with the youngest child, rather than to put two children of nearly the same age together, because an older child generally has a more tolerant attitude toward the youngest child than the child who is more nearly the same age.

An Ideal Room for a Child

An ideal room for a child is not likely to be found in a ready-built home or apartment. However, the room which the child occupies should contain as many features of the ideal room as possible. Some of the important features for a child's room are these:

1. *The Windows.* The windows of a young child's room should receive the morning rather than the afternoon sun. This makes the room bright and sunny in the morning when the child plays indoors. Furthermore, it does not interfere with the afternoon nap.

The walls of a child's room should be light and cheerful. Patterned, washable wallpaper or washable paint are ideal.

If possible, the windows should face on a street where there is not enough traffic to disturb the child at naptime or in the early evening, but where, nevertheless, there are enough interesting things for the child to watch as he looks out of the window.

2. *The Walls.* For the bright, cheerful atmosphere that should prevail in every young child's room, the walls and ceiling should be light in color, preferably a pastel shade of blue, pink, green, or yellow.

There are many wallpaper patterns with nursery designs that are excellent for a young child's room. He not only enjoys looking at the pictures on his walls, but does not have to be so careful of finger marks because patterned paper does not show spots easily. Washable wallpaper is ideal for a child's room, especially when it has a brightly colored pattern. If the child's room is to be painted, washable paint should be used so that finger marks or crayon marks can be washed off.

3. *The Floor.* All young children are "floor sitters," so the floors in their rooms should be protected with carpets, preferably with pads under them. This will help to keep the child from taking cold during the winter.

Carpets, like wallpaper, should be patterned rather than plain. If made of cotton, nylon, or Orlon, they can be kept clean very easily with home washings. Every child, no matter how careful he may be, will at some time spill food, paint, crayons, or water on his carpet.

4. *The Lighting.* Special attention should be given to the lighting of a young child's room because his eyes are delicate and easily strained. The best type of artificial lighting is indirect. In indirect lighting, light is thrown on the ceiling or walls and from there diffused through the room.

Few homes at the present time have indirect lighting systems, but table and floor lamps of the indirect type are good substitutes. The important thing to remember is that there must be plenty of light. It is poor economy to save on electricity used in a child's room.

5. *The Closets.* The final feature of the ideal child's room is the closet. This should be large enough to store the child's clothing and also the toys that are not in constant use. To encourage habits of neatness and responsibility, there should be plenty of hooks within easy reach of the child so that he can learn to take down and hang up his own clothes.

The closet should also contain open shelf space, low enough for the child to reach, where toys can be kept. It is important that there be ample space on the shelves to spread out the child's toys. When toys are stacked up, the child often

ELIZABETH HIBBS

Furniture for the little girl (or boy) should be scaled to her size. If she has a low bureau where she may keep her own clothes, she will gain a feeling of security and independence and learn to be neat.

hesitates to play with them because of the effort involved in getting them out and putting them back.

Equipment for the Child's Room

Young children grow so quickly that they soon outgrow baby furniture. A bassinet is good for only two or three months. For that reason, it is an expensive luxury. The child of three is generally too big to sleep comfortably in a crib and is ready for a bed.

The child's room should be supplied with low, open shelves for the keeping of toys that are in constant use. Shelves should be adequate enough to allow room for the toys to be spread out, for when toys are stacked up one on top of another, the child becomes discouraged in getting them out and putting them away.

COURTESY H. J. HEINZ COMPANY

The important thing about cribs and beds is not the nursery designs painted on them but the kinds of mattresses they have. If cribs and beds have good, heavy springs and thick, hard mattresses, the child's sleeping posture will be good. There will then be little likelihood of spinal curvature because of soft mattresses.

If the young child is to learn independence in dressing at an early age, he must have a low bureau with drawers that are not too heavy for him to open and close. Such a bureau can be used for many years. If a mirror is hung over the bureau, it will encourage the child to see that his clothes are on straight and that his hair is well groomed.

In addition to a bed and bureau, every child should have a large, stuffed chair in which he can curl up and relax when he looks at books. There should also be a small table for eating, playing games, pasting, crayoning, and many other play activities. In addition, having two straight-backed chairs in the room may encourage cooperative play with another child.

Open shelves, where toys and books in constant use may be kept, should also be provided. These shelves, like those in the closet, should be ample enough so that the toys can be spread out and do not have to be piled one on top of another.

The Child's Playroom

Few homes of today are large enough to allow setting aside one room exclusively for a child's playroom. A playroom is not necessary if the child's room is large enough to give adequate space for play. Actually, even though the child has a playroom, he may prefer to play in his own room because he feels more "at home" there.

Unless the child's room is very small, it should be possible to arrange all furniture needed for sleeping and dressing in one part of the room and all equipment for play in the other part. Then, while the child is playing, the furniture not needed can be pushed against the wall to give the maximum possible space for play.

At naptime and bedtime, toys can be "put to bed" and the playroom converted into a bedroom again. If a screen is put between the child's bed and the toy shelves, he will not see the toys and will not be tempted to get out of bed to play with them.

Outdoor Play Space

All children need outdoor play space, and, especially for young children, it is important that the play space be safe. Most older houses have a small backyard where the child can play. Children who live in apartments or small houses

Children need space. Many city children who do not live near a park are forced to play in the street. If possible, the child's outdoor play should be in his own back yard, where he can have his own equipment.

frequently have to be taken to a city park or use the sidewalks or streets for play.

A back or front yard, where outdoor play equipment and toys can easily be brought from the house, gives the child a feeling of security and possession which does not exist when there is no play space he may call his own.

As the child reaches the sixth year and begins to crave the companionship of other children in his play, a yard has little appeal for him unless the neighborhood children come there to play with him.

All young children should have a garden, no matter how small, where they can plant seeds and watch them grow. If the family has a garden, the child should have a place in that garden allotted to him which he can regard as "his garden" and should be given an opportunity to plant seeds of his own choice in it.

It should be his responsibility to water, weed, and take care of his garden with adult guidance and supervision. A child of three is old enough for this. From the garden he can

All young children should have some sort of garden, for which they have full responsibility. If there is no space in the yard for a child's garden, he should be taught to cultivate a garden in a window box.

learn a great deal about growth in addition to enjoying the
rights of ownership.

Responsibility for His Domain

Much of the pleasure as well as much of the psychological
value of a place of his own will come from the child's assumption of responsibility for it. Of course, a young child
cannot be expected to assume full responsibility for his
room, his play space, his part of the bathroom, or even of his
garden, but most young children are capable of assuming
more responsibility than they are given an opportunity to
assume.

Any child who is able to take toys from a shelf is likewise
able to put them back on the shelf. If hooks are low enough
in a closet for a young child to reach, he can, when he is
three or four years old, hang up his pajamas and put away
his bedroom slippers.

In time he can be given the responsibility of hanging
coats on hangers and putting clean clothes in the bureau
drawers. By the age of six, every child should assume complete responsibility for putting away and taking out all his
clothing and toys.

Other responsibilities for a young child in the care of his
room include picking up scraps from the floor, daily empty-
ing of the wastebasket, watering plants in his own room,
hanging up his towel, washcloth, and toothbrush, and putting away his outdoor play equipment.

Every child feels that the family home is *his* if he has some
responsibilities in it. Thus, small duties should be assigned
to the child for which he and he alone is responsible. These
duties should be performed daily so that the child will have
the daily reminder of the role he plays in home life.

If possible, the child's responsibilities should be such that he is thrown in contact with other members of the household. This will give him the added feeling of sharing the work of the home with others. Assisting in setting the table, drying dishes, or sorting laundry can all be "community" activities.

For Discussion

1. What effect does it have on you to shift from one room to another or from one house or apartment to a new place? Explain why shifting of this sort is equally serious for a young child.
2. Why do young children generally prefer to play in their own rooms rather than in a playroom?
3. What compensations can you suggest for lack of space that the young child may regard as his very own?
4. Why do little children like to have gardens of their own?
5. How old should a child be before he is permitted to decide what color or colors he wants his room to be decorated in? Why did you select the age you did?

Suggested Activities

1. Visit a child's room. Suggest improvements that are practical in the furniture, arrangement of furniture, curtains, etc.
2. Draw a diagram of an ideal room for a young child.
3. Make a list of home responsibilities that a child of three, four, five, and six can be expected to assume.
4. Visit the furniture department of a large store. Inspect critically the nursery furniture. See how sturdy it is and compare it with small-sized adult furniture. Make a list of necessary furniture, secure prices, and estimate the cost of furnishing a child's room.
5. Visit a furniture department and ask to see furniture built for the child to "grow into." For how many years and at what ages would this furniture be suitable and appeal to a child?

CHAPTER 18

The Child and His Clothes

To a baby, clothes are a nuisance, but by the time a child reaches the age of three, clothes are the source of much pleasure and pride. Like his room, the child's clothes give him a feeling of security. They do much to build up his confidence in himself.

Furthermore, they become a part of *him*. When he is wearing clothes that he likes, especially if they are admired by others, his ego expands. He then feels secure, even in a world where he is a midget by comparison with others who tower over him.

Readiness to Dress Himself

A baby dislikes clothes. Because of this, he stiffens his body when it is time to be dressed and thus makes it difficult for others to dress him. The peak of resistance to clothing comes toward the end of the first year. By that time the baby's muscle coordination is well enough developed so that he can pull off a garment nearly as soon as it has been put on him.

Because undressing is easier than dressing, and because the baby gets keen delight from pulling off his garments, his

The child's interest and delight in pulling off his own clothes should be encouraged as a background for his learning how to dress himself later on.

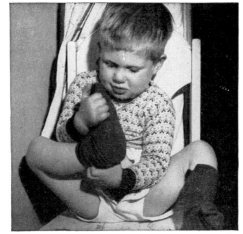

MONKMEYER

interest in undressing should be used as a starting point for teaching him how to dress himself.

When it is time for the baby to be undressed, he should be given a chance to take off his clothes. The one-year-old can easily pull off his cap, mittens, shoes, and socks, but he will be a year and a half or two years old before he can take off all his garments.

When the baby's desire to remove clothing is satisfied, and when his muscle coordination is good enough to make it possible for him to start to learn to dress himself, his interest should be tested by asking him to hand the adult the different garments, one at a time.

If he finds this fun, he might be asked if he would like to try putting on his socks or his cap. If he shows an interest in this suggestion, he should be allowed to try. If not, the matter should be dropped until there is more definite evidence of interest. Occasionally he can be asked if he would like to try, but he should never be forced.

Obstacles to Self-dressing

Expecting a young child to learn to dress himself before he is ready will surely result in failure. Even more seriously, it will build up an antagonistic, rebellious attitude which will militate against the child's willingness to learn when his development has reached the level where learning would be easy.

Equally bad is the failure to recognize the fact that the child is ready and able to dress himself. His spontaneous interest in doing this will quickly be stifled if he is not given the opportunity. When interest is gone, the child will make no effort to help himself. He will even be content to allow others to do things for him that he can easily do for himself.

Pattern of Self-dressing

The order in which a young child learns the different tasks involved in dressing himself follows a fairly definite and predictable pattern. If the child's muscle coordinations are good, his self-dressing pattern will of course be slightly accelerated. Similarly, with retarded muscle coordination, one can expect retarded self-dressing.

Between the fifteenth and the eighteenth month, the average young child should begin to show a real interest in putting on his clothing. By that time he can take off all his clothes, with the exception of loosening such fastenings as buttons and shoelaces. Undressing is an old story to him, and he now wants to do something new.

With opportunity and encouragement, he will first try to put on his socks or his cap. Of course he will not get them on straight at first, but this will not bother him, since he will be content just to have put them on.

Several months later, the young child will try to put on

The child learns first how to put on simple things, such as his cap or his socks; he next learns how to put on his shirt, sweater, or panties; and then he learns how to put on all his other garments except shoes, which he usually cannot put on until he is two and a half or three years old.

COURTESY NATIONAL DAIRY PRODUCTS CORPORATION

his shirt or sweater or panties. A little girl may even try to put on her dress by this time. At first the garment is just as likely to be put on backwards or turned inside-out as it is to be put on correctly.

The interest in putting on these garments will be fitful and spasmodic. One day the child will insist upon putting on his own shirt; the next day he may refuse to try. But, with encouragement and opportunity, the child should be able to put on all his garments except his shoes by the time he is two years old.

Owing to the complication of telling which is right and which left, putting on shoes or rubbers is one of the most difficult tasks of dressing. Most children are two and a half or three years old before they can learn this part of self-dressing. It is generally another year before they even try to buckle the buckles or tie the bows on the shoelaces. Few children under six can lace their own shoes tightly enough

ELIZABETH HIBBS

To encourage self-dressing, buttons and fasteners should be large and located in positions that are not too hard for the child to reach.

or tie their laces securely enough so that the shoes fit snugly.

Fastening Garments

Learning to fasten garments follows a fairly definite pattern also. The child between one and a half and two years of age enjoys fumbling with buttons. He likes to pull them out of their holes. Likewise, he finds it amusing to zip and unzip zippers or to pull open snap fasteners.

Opening a fastener is easier than closing it and, for that reason, opening always precedes closing. After several months of experimenting with opening fasteners, the child begins to show an interest in closing them. He tries to put buttons into their holes, put the snap fasteners together, and zip up the zippers.

By the age of three most children can fasten different types of fasteners, provided they are not too small and are not located in positions that are difficult for the child to reach. Ability to handle large buttons always precedes that of handling small buttons. Buttons placed in the front of a garment can be manipulated earlier than those under the arms or in the back of a garment.

The young child buttons first the buttons he can see. This means that he fastens first the buttons that are near the waistline. Later, when buttoning skill has been acquired, the buttons which are just under his chin and which he can see only when he looks in a mirror can be handled successfully.

Appropriate Clothes for Young Children

Appropriateness in clothing, as far as young children are concerned, has nothing to do with style. Children are not style-conscious, nor does it trouble them in the slightest if their clothes are out-of-date. For a young child, "appropriate clothes" are clothes that fit his needs and interests.

There are six criteria that must be kept in mind in judging the appropriateness of clothing for young children.

1. Clothing Must Give Freedom for Action. Because the young child's life is filled with activity, he should not be hampered by clothing that is too large or too small for him. This is especially important in the case of trousers, panties, sleeves, and shoes.

2. Clothing Must Be Sturdy. The child's active life and his lack of knowledge about care make sturdy clothes of serviceable materials absolutely imperative. As they will need constant washings, the material should be preshrunk and preferably require no ironing. Corduroy, gingham, pima cotton, and many of the new fabrics, such as Orlon and nylon, combine these features.

3. Clothing Must Allow for Self-dressing. Appropriate clothes for young children should have a minimum of fas-

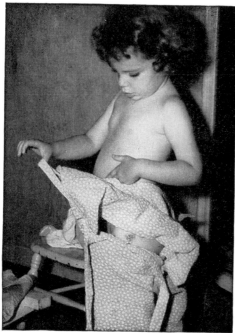

Clothes that are too complicated make it difficult for a child to dress himself, even though he is old enough to know how. Poor motor development, lack of opportunity to try, and lack of practice may be other reasons why a child over five cannot put on his own clothes.

FREDERIC LEWIS

teners, located in areas of the garment that the child can reach easily. Preferably, clothing should be of the slip-over-the-head variety. It should always create the impression in the child's mind that dressing himself will be an easy job.

4. Clothing Should Be Suited to the Temperature. Young children are much more subject to colds than are adults. Therefore, children's clothes should be selected to meet changes in temperature. Most homes and schools in America today are warm enough so that cotton clothing is adequate.

5. Clothing Must Be of Suitable Weight. Because young children are active, they should not be weighted down with heavy clothing. Cotton clothes are light in weight and, therefore, very appropriate. Outer garments made of nylon or Orlon give adequate warmth and are much lighter in weight than wool. Furthermore, they will not shrink when washed.

Shoes are the heaviest single item of clothing and therefore should be made of lightweight materials, even though they may not be as durable as heavy materials. Most young children outgrow their shoes before they are worn out anyway, so it is not so essential to consider durability for this item.

6. Clothing Should Promote Good Posture. Garments for children should be large enough to permit the child to sit and stand correctly. Clothing that is too tight or too short for the child encourages him to slump forward. Shoes and socks that are too short or too tight interfere with good posture in standing and walking.

What Children Like in Clothing

The adult likes clothing that is in style regardless of its becomingness or its aesthetic merits, but a child is neither style-conscious nor aware of the becomingness of his clothes.

To him clothing serves much the same role as it does in the life of a savage. It is a form of ornamentation, a medium through which he attracts attention and admiration to himself. Until he is two years old, clothes are a source of irritation to the child. After that, he begins to show keen interest and delight in his clothes. The following items with regard to his clothes are important.

1. Ornamentation. What the child likes in clothing is its ornamentation. Buttons, lace, embroidery, monograms, buckles on shoes, and feathers, ribbons, or flowers on hats are all focal points of the child's interest in a garment. As long as there is some ornamentation, it does not disturb the child if the

Children love to be admired in something they have just acquired, whether it is new or not.

material is old and faded, the style out-of-date, or the garment a hand-me-down from an older brother or sister.

2. *Newness.* All young children like new clothes or hand-me-downs that are new to them. They want to wear their new clothes at once. They frequently beg to wear new shoes or hats home from the store. The pleasure they derive from wearing new clothes is greatly enhanced when they are recognized as new by others and admired.

3. *Color.* The color of a garment is so important to a young child that he usually refers to it by its color rather than its style or type. What adults might refer to as a "sport coat," the child would call a "red coat." Patent-leather shoes are "black shoes," and a pink silk party dress is a "pink dress."

Because children like colors, they develop definite color preferences. Frequently they ignore the becomingness or the appropriateness to the occasion in their choice of colors in clothing. Even worse, they are likely to put together their favorite colors whether or not they harmonize.

4. *Texture.* The texture of a garment means more to

FROM THE MCGRAW-HILL FILMSTRIP "CHILD CARE AND DEVELOPMENT"

Children are fascinated by color and design in their clothes. They also like the texture of clothes.

a young child than most adults realize. The child likes the "feel" of soft materials, such as fur, velvet, and silk.

5. *Similarity to Clothes of Their Friends.* Finally, a young child likes garments similar to those of the other children of his acquaintance. The garments do not have to be identical but they should be alike either in color or style.

Clothes and Personality

As soon as the child begins to be conscious of his clothes as an asset rather than a liability, he begins to identify himself with them. Clothing that he likes or is proud of bolsters his morale and adds to his self-confidence. Clothing that he dislikes or that he is afraid other children will make fun of does much to undermine his confidence in himself and gives rise to feelings of inferiority.

For the timid and retiring child, the selection of clothing

Of more importance than anything to children is that their clothes
are similar to the clothes worn by other children. Quality and quantity
do not mean nearly so much as similarity.

is particularly important. With the new fabrics that dry quickly and require little or no ironing, a child can have clothes of any color or style that appeal to him without causing extra work for his mother. Such clothes will do much to build up his confidence in himself.

What does disturb a child, however, is having other children ridicule him because his clothes are different from theirs. If they do not actually make fun of him, he is equally sensitive about being asked why he "has to wear" long stockings or dressy clothes or anything, in fact, that is different from what they wear.

The Child's Bath

To a child, as to an adult, bathing is a pleasant, relaxing experience. The young child thoroughly enjoys playing in the water. His water toys are among his favorites. A tired, fretful child comes out of a warm bath relaxed and refreshed. All irritability vanishes, and the child's face is rosy and wreathed with smiles.

If the bath is given in a leisurely manner, bathing will be regarded by the young child as a pleasant experience, and he will have a strong desire to learn to bathe himself when he is able to do so. Bathing is far easier for a child to master than dressing. The only serious obstacle to the child's learning is unwillingness. This is not likely to be present unless the bathing situation has been made unpleasant for the child.

It is very easy for the child of two or two and a half years to get at least part of the dirt off his legs, feet, arms, and hands. When he is provided with a large bath sponge and a nail brush, he thoroughly enjoys rubbing soap and water over his extremities, and, for the most part, he can get them clean. By the time he is three, he should be able to wash his stomach and chest also.

Hard Spots in Bathing

Washing the face, neck, back, and ears are the difficult tasks in bathing. Few children can do them well until they are five. The child's early attempts generally are very superficial. They consist of rubbing the washcloth over the ears without bothering to wash inside them, and rubbing the cloth over the front center of the neck.

The child's muscle coordination must be fairly well developed before he can be taught to wash the back of his neck, the insides of his ears, and the sides of his face. The task is difficult for him because he must guide his movements by feel rather than by sight.

The back is unquestionably the most difficult part of the body to bathe. Not only is the back difficult to reach but it cannot be seen. A long-handled bath brush will help the child to reach most of the parts of his back. Using such a brush is fun for him, and by demonstrations of how it is used the child will eventually get the "feel" of washing his back.

However, the child cannot be expected to bathe all areas of his body until he is six or seven years old. To avoid giving the child the impression that he is not doing a good job, the adult may tactfully suggest that she will "rinse off the soap."

Grooming

Early childhood is none too soon to learn standards and habits of good grooming. No young child can be expected to assume the responsibility of being well groomed, but he can be making a good start, and, of even more importance, he can learn what good grooming means.

If at six years old the child has learned how to put on his clothes with a reasonable degree of neatness, if he tries to keep his nails clean and his shoes tied, and if he objects when his clothing is not clean, he shows an understanding of the principles of good grooming. No more than this can be expected of him until he is older.

As an aid to good grooming, the young child should be provided with a mirror, preferably a full-length door mirror, in his bedroom or bathroom. Furthermore, he should be encouraged to look at himself in the mirror while he is dressing or certainly after his dressing has been completed.

Another incentive to good grooming is the "inspection test." Before going to meals or before leaving the house, a young child should be required to go to the mother or some other adult in the household for inspection. This should include a critical examination of the child's clothing, hands, hair, knees, and shoes.

No healthy, active child can be expected to remain neat and clean. Actually, he should not have to, for to do so he could not play as all children like to play nor could he do what other children do. But he should learn at an early age the necessity for being neat and clean when he starts out to play, when he comes to the table, when he goes to bed, or when he is with adults.

For Discussion

1. Recall any experience you had regarding favorite clothes and try to account for it.
2. Is the child's liking for clothes similar to those of other children tied up with his desire to be one of the social group? Justify your point of view.
3. Why are young children often careless about their clothes? How can adults encourage them to assume more responsibility for their care?
4. Do you recall being ridiculed, as a child, for wearing certain

garments, such as a particular type of shoe, hat, or dress? If so, how did you react to the ridicule?

5. If a child is given clothes by friends or relatives that are not the same as those of his playmates, should he be forced to wear them?

6. Should a child be permitted to wear clothes that are unbecoming, even if he likes them and they are similar to those worn by his playmates?

Suggested Activities

1. Make a visit to the children's clothing department of a store. Examine the different articles of clothing for young children for their appropriateness as discussed in this chapter.

2. Observe the clothing of young children on the street or in a play group for the same purpose.

3. Watch a child put on different articles of clothing, especially outer garments like snow suits and rubbers. Keep a record of the time required and count the random movements used for each article.

4. Observe young children of two, four, and six in their baths. Note the different reactions toward the bath at these different ages. Observe how much or how little responsibility for bathing himself the child assumes at different age levels.

5. Observe the "self-help" clothes available in stores today. What features in these clothes enable the child to dress himself?

6. Find children who are dressed alike—twins, brothers and sisters, sisters, or brothers. Question them and see how they feel about the matter.

CHAPTER 19

Personality Building

"Personality" is a word so loosely used in everyday speech that its true meaning is not always understood. When we speak of personality, we do not mean some vague, intangible quality inherent in a person but rather the quality of his behavior as it affects us. We say that a person has an "attractive personality" if the way he behaves is to our liking. If, however, his behavior displeases or irritates us, we say that he has a "mean" or "unattractive personality."

The Critical Age of Personality Building

Because personality is developed through learning and is not the result of heredity, early childhood is the critical period in its development. It is at this time that the foundation of personality traits is established, and from this foundation the traits continue to develop as the child grows older.

Before the child is ready for school, the dominant characteristics of his personality are so well set that they show up in the expression on his face, even when it is in repose. A cross, surly disposition, a timid, frightened outlook on life, or a sunny, happy one can readily be spotted by looking at the child's face.

The old saying that the child is "a chip off the old block"

Before the child is ready to enter school, the dominant character-istics of his personality are so well set that they show up in the expression on his face.

PINNEY FROM MONKMEYER

implies, as far as personality is concerned, that a child inherits a certain type of personality from one of his parents. Furthermore, it is assumed that there is nothing one can do about this matter.

True, many children do show personality traits similar to those of one or another of their parents. But experimental studies of personality have shown fairly conclusively that this similarity is the result of imitation, acquired from the constant contact of the child with his parents. There is little or no evidence to show that it is hereditary.

Since personality traits are learned and not inherited, adults who assume the responsibility for the upbringing of a child should guide his development so that there will be a predominance of desirable personality traits. They should also check undesirable ones as soon as they appear. Leaving personality development to chance may produce good results, but the reverse is just as likely to be the outcome.

Environmental Influences in Personality Development

Inasmuch as most personality traits are learned, the child's early environment plays an important role in determining what they will be. Also, because the child's environment during the early years of his life is limited to his home, the members of the household are the people who are of primary importance in determining what sort of person he will be. The only other influence on the child's personality development during the early years is the nursery school or kindergarten.

The influence of the children in the neighborhood is of secondary importance to the child's personality development because in these early years the child does not actually play *with* other children; he plays parallel to them. Furthermore, his contacts with them are few and short, as compared with his contacts within the home.

As the child progresses in years, however, playmates become progressively more important in the development of his personality, and the influence of the home decreases in importance.

Home Influences in Personality Development

There is ample evidence to show that similarities in personality between parent and child are the result of learning by imitation. Thus, the mother with a cheerful and happy outlook on life presents a desirable pattern of behavior to her child. The father who comes home tired and irritable will not only present an undesirable pattern of behavior but, of even more seriousness, he is likely to shroud the atmosphere of the whole household with sullen gloom. It is inevitable that, in time, these patterns will be reflected in the child's personality.

H. ARMSTRONG ROBERTS

The members in a child's family are of prime importance in determining the sort of person he becomes, since his early years are limited to contacts with the people in his home.

While the mother and father unquestionably have the greatest influence on the personality development of the child, other members of the household also exert some influence. Brothers, sisters, grandparents, uncles, aunts, and servants all play a role in determining what type of personality a young child develops. How great an influence they will have will depend upon two facts: first, how much time any one of them spends with the child; and, second, how great the child's affection for that person is.

The ideal home environment for personality development is one in which all members are happy, contented, and har-

Relatives broaden a child's relationships, but care should be taken that they do not pamper the child or interfere with established patterns of discipline.

COURTESY H. J. HEINZ COMPANY

monious; in which each individual is respected and given rights, privileges, and responsibilities suited to his age; and in which there is no domination by either or both parents nor by older children who are permitted to boss younger ones.

The presence of too many relatives who spend much of their time in the home does not make for an ideal home for the young child. Relatives tend either to pamper and spoil the child or to interfere with the home discipline. This results in divided authority and uncertainty on the child's part concerning what is expected of him.

Above all, the ideal home should give the child a sense of security and a realization that he is a loved and welcome member of the family group. His efforts to do what is expected of him should be encouraged and praised so that he may develop confidence in himself.

Constant criticism will quickly undermine what little self-confidence a young child possesses. On the other hand, the feeling that he is not wanted or that he is regarded as a "nuisance" is one of the quickest ways to lay the foundation for a deep-rooted feeling of inferiority in a child.

Finally, for an ideal home environment, there should be a complete family—that is, a mother, a father, and at least two children. A marriage broken by death, separation, or divorce is an unfortunate situation for a young child. In families broken by separation or divorce, every effort should be made to allow the child to experience some companionship with each parent so he does not feel that he is totally missing what other children with both parents are experiencing.

An Attractive Personality

An attractive personality is one in which socially desirable personality traits predominate. It is impossible to find a person in whom only pleasing traits exist. But it is possible to develop in a young child traits that are regarded as attractive by others.

An individual who has an attractive personality is well adjusted. This means that he gets along with all types of people with more than average success. The better adjusted he is, the more attractive his personality.

Criteria of an Attractive Personality

The standard to keep in mind in the development of the personality in childhood is whether or not the traits being developed will be serviceable to the child, not only while he is a child but also throughout his life.

Extremes of any trait, whether good or bad, should not be encouraged. Just because a desirable trait proves to be attractive in a moderate form is no justification for assuming that in a well-developed form it will be even more attractive. As a matter of fact, the reverse is true.

Take unselfishness as an example. A moderate amount of

unselfishness goes far in helping the child to get along well with other people, but extreme unselfishness results in the child's being taken advantage of by others. He is not respected for this and might be considered weak, spineless, and completely lacking in ability to stand up for and demand his own rights.

Attractive Personality Traits

There are certain traits that are regarded so universally as being desirable for an attractive personality that their development should be encouraged early in childhood. With the pattern set at this early age, further development can then be fostered as the child grows older.

They may develop of their own accord, without guidance and control, but the matter is too important to leave to chance. For that reason it is valuable to know what personality traits should be fostered in early childhood and what procedures have been found satisfactory for developing them.

1. Cheerfulness. In any environment, no matter how favorable or unfavorable, cheerfulness is always a pleasant trait. Everyone admires it, and most people envy those who can be cheerful even in the face of adversity. All children should be encouraged to be cheerful, no matter what befalls them.

There are three aids to the cultivation of cheerfulness. First, a good, healthy condition. Being sickly or not feeling well colors a child's outlook on life. By contrast, it is not hard for healthy children who feel well to laugh and frolic. Life seems pleasant to them, and they show their enjoyment through their sunny dispositions.

Second, because all children are mimics, being surrounded by cheerful people helps in the cultivation of cheerfulness.

Cheerfulness is contagious. A healthy child cannot elude the effects when he is in constant association with others whose outlook is happy.

Third, the avoidance of all unnecessary restraints and frustrations aids cheerfulness. Restraints and frustrations tend to irritate the child and throw him into a state of temporary gloom.

2. *Enthusiasm.* Nothing is more refreshing than spontaneous and genuine enthusiasm. Boredom, even though it is obviously a pose, is never regarded as "smart" or attractive— certainly not in a young child. Furthermore, enthusiasm adds to the individual's own enjoyment and makes even trivial experiences seem important to him.

Like cheerfulness, enthusiasm can be learned, but a healthy physical condition does much to pave the way for it. Also, like cheerfulness, enthusiasm is contagious. A young child quickly mimics the enthusiasm of those around him and experiences it as vividly as if it had originated with him.

A good way to foster enthusiasm in young children is to talk about, plan for, and anticipate the pleasure to come from even the simplest experiences. Then, at the time of the experience, emphasize all the pleasant aspects concerned with it. All unpleasant aspects should be ignored or minimized.

3. *A Sense of Humor.* The American people have the reputation for having more sense of humor than the people of any other nation. There is no question about the fact that having a sense of humor is a great asset. It helps one to meet the irritations and troubles of daily life. However, like other personality traits, the ability to see the funny side of life is not hereditary nor will it develop of its own accord. It must be cultivated.

A young child should always be encouraged to see the

funny side of a difficult or irritating situation. This can be done by pointing out to him anything that seems humorous in the situation. At the same time, the sober, irritating aspects should be ignored or minimized.

Like enthusiasm and cheerfulness, humor is contagious. Being with people who can laugh and see the amusing aspect of anything gives the child a pattern of behavior that he will find easy to imitate. A sure way to make the development of a sense of humor difficult, however, is to be with people who take themselves or their activities too seriously.

4. *Courage.* No matter how highly civilized life becomes, there will be times when courage is needed to meet the problems and adversities that arise. A time comes in every child's life when he must stand on his own feet and fight his own battles. He must accept defeat and disappointment with a willingness to accept the inevitable and to make satisfactory adjustments to it rather than give way to his emotions.

All children can learn to be courageous, provided they are given an opportunity to learn. Instead of hovering over a child and showing concern for his safety, it is far better to do everything possible to see that his environment is safe and that the chances of his hurting himself are reduced to the absolute minimum.

In this way parents and other adults who are responsible for the child's safety can assume a more confident attitude toward him. This confident attitude is quickly felt by the child himself, so that he, in turn, behaves with more courage and self-assurance than he does when he feels that others are worried about his safety.

The child should always be praised unstintingly for even a slight display of courage. Criticism of cowardice, by laying emphasis on the fact that the child is a "baby" or a "fraidy cat," will not foster courage. It will cause the child either to

DESIRABLE PERSONALITY TRAITS

1) *Cheerfulness*. There are three aids to the cultivation of cheerfulness in the child: good health, a cheerful atmosphere, and a minimum of restraint or frustration.

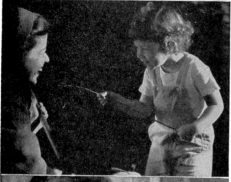

2) *Enthusiasm*. A good way to foster enthusiasm in the child is to talk about, plan for, and anticipate with him simple experiences.

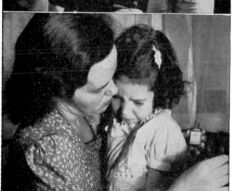

3) *Courage*. An "all is well" attitude on the part of the parent when the child is hurt will help to build a courageous attitude in the child.

TO BE DEVELOPED

4) *Unselfishness.* All young children are selfish and self-centered. Being encouraged to share toys or to contribute to others will help to foster unselfishness in the early years.

5) *Self-confidence.* Allowing children to do things for themselves and praising them for accomplishments of the smallest kind will build self-confidence.

6) *Self-assertiveness.* The child should be allowed to express his opinions about different matters and be given a chance to make decisions about his likes or dislikes in order to encourage self-assertiveness.

develop a resentful, antagonistic attitude toward his critic
or to withdraw into his shell and try to cover up his timidity,
thus intensifying it through lack of expression.

5. *Unselfishness.* The helplessness of a baby or a young
child necessitates constant attention and aid from others. It
is not surprising, therefore, that all young children are selfish and self-centered. The first-born and the only child are
the most common victims of selfish behavior because it is
possible for their parents to give them more attention than
could ever be lavished on other children.

Selfishness, however, is never a serviceable personality
trait, even though it may be understood and tolerated in
early childhood. As the years pass, understanding and tolerance will wane. The selfish individual will find himself
ignored and disliked by those who have learned to think of
others.

Unfortunately for the child, selfishness usually gives more
satisfactory immediate rewards than does unselfishness.
Through selfish demands, the child's immediate wishes are
fulfilled. That, to him, is more important than the respect or
love of other people.

As the child grows older and esteem from the group becomes increasingly more important to him, he gradually realizes that selfishness makes him unpopular. He then does one
of two things: He tries to mend his ways by attempting to
curb his desire to satisfy his wishes even at the expense of
others; or he continues to behave in a selfish manner and
ignore the people who show disapproval of his selfishness.

On the positive side, encouragement in sharing his toys
and possessions, in doing little kindnesses for others, and in
making some contribution of his toys, clothes, or money to
those less fortunate than he will go a long way toward focus-
ing his attention on others and away from himself.

Unselfishness should always be rewarded if the child is to believe it is worth his while. Certainly no one can blame a child for being resentful if his sharing of a favored toy with another child results in nothing more than the appropriation of that toy by the other child. Satisfaction from recognition of his unselfishness, whether it takes the form of thanks, praise, or an actual reward, will encourage the child to continue to be unselfish in his relations with other people.

6. *Sympathy.* Sympathy and unselfishness go hand-in-hand. The sympathetic person is one who is interested enough in others and their affairs to be able to imagine himself in their places. Furthermore, he can imagine how he would feel if he were to experience what they are experiencing.

There is no question about the fact that sympathy is essential to all true friendship. No one can hope to get along well in human society unless he shows at least the rudiments of sympathy in his behavior. All young children, however, because of their selfish tendencies and limited imaginative powers, lack the ability to sympathize with others.

As a matter of fact, they go to the opposite extreme and actually gloat over others who are in trouble. This is readily apparent when another child is punished for misbehavior. Some children even go to the extreme of making others suffer by teasing and bullying because it gives them a feeling of superiority to realize that they have this power.

Development of sympathy must wait upon the development of imagination, but, through careful direction, its development can be fostered slowly in the early years of childhood. Asking a child how he would feel if some calamity befell him, such as having his pet dog killed by an automobile or his favorite toy lost, helps to stimulate the child's imagination. At the same time it directs his attention toward the difficult task of projecting himself into the place of another.

In young children it is sometimes necessary to introduce actual demonstrations to supplement the child's imagination. When a child is asked, "How would you feel if someone stepped on your tin soldier?" and responds that he "wouldn't care," he obviously is still unable to project himself into the place of the owner of the tin soldier. If he is given a practical demonstration by having his own favorite toy stepped on, he will quickly be convinced that he, too, would feel very badly about it.

7. *Calmness.* Excitable, nervous people not only wear themselves out but they wear out everyone with whom they come in contact. By contrast, the calm individual is restful to be with. Furthermore, he is able to do more with less effort and fatigue.

The most satisfactory method of fostering calmness in a young child is to control his environment so that there will be a minimum of exciting experiences. The country, of course, offers a quieter environment than the city. For that reason country living is especially desirable for young children. If, however, for one reason or another, it is impractical for the parents to live in a country or suburban environment, the young child's room should be located in a quiet part of the house or apartment to eliminate as much as possible the noises, bustle, and confusion of city life.

As a final aid to the cultivation of calmness, the young child should associate as much as possible with people who are calm. A young child will quickly imitate excitability in others and will just as quickly calm down when he is with calm people.

8. *Self-confidence.* One of the most common causes of maladjustment in adults is lack of self-confidence, with its

usual accompaniment—a feeling of inferiority. Very few young children are confident of themselves. This may readily be seen in their embarrassment in the presence of strangers or when they are asked to sing or recite before others, even before their kindergarten or Sunday-school classmates. In every case, lack of self-confidence is traceable to fear of oneself and of one's capacities.

Self-confidence can never be built up in an atmosphere of constant faultfinding and criticism. This merely accentuates the child's fear of self and leads him to believe that his abilities are even less than he thought they were. There are three constructive approaches to building up self-confidence in a young child, not one of which will fail if used properly.

The first consists of the lavish use of praise for the child's efforts to do what is expected of him, whether it be his attempt to put on his clothing, to build a tower of blocks without help, or to be polite. This will not make him conceited, as many believe, but will merely tell him that he is doing what others approve of. If he is praised frequently enough, he will begin to believe in himself. This, in turn, will build up a self-confident attitude.

The second way to build up a young child's confidence in himself is to give him plenty of opportunities to evaluate his abilities *favorably*. This can be done only by comparing his abilities with those of other children. Naturally, if the comparison is primarily with older children, the young child will show up unfavorably. Therefore, he should occasionally be given a chance to do things with younger children with whom he will show up favorably by comparison.

The third constructive approach to building self-confidence comes from teaching the child to do things for himself as soon as he is capable of doing so. Helplessness tends to break down self-confidence, while independence fosters it.

This good effect can be accentuated by repeated reference to the fact that "Johnny is a big boy because he can tie his own shoes" or "Mary is no longer a little girl because she can now hang up her own coat."

9. *Self-assertiveness.* The days when it was believed that "children should be seen and not heard" have passed. We now know that a child brought up to be seen but not heard gets so into the habit of behaving in that fashion that, as an adult, he lacks the self-assertiveness necessary for success in American life today. His behavior as an adult reflects the submissive attitude he was forced to assume as a child, and by the time he is mature enough to realize his handicap, he may be unable to overcome it.

Every child should be given opportunities to assert himself. Furthermore, he should be encouraged to do so within reason. When possible, he can be asked to tell his preference for one of several foods that are equally good for him, one of several garments that are equally suitable, one of several activities that he might engage in, or one of several children available for him to play with. This forces him to face a problem involving choice and to make his own decision regarding it.

In addition to this, the child should be given opportunities to express himself on different matters. If, for example, he does not like to play with his next-door neighbor, he should be encouraged to say why instead of being told that he is "foolish" or "unneighborly."

Simple as these approaches may seem at first, they go a long way toward stimulating the child's ability to assert himself, to stand on his own feet, to express his opinions, and to make him realize that others recognize him as an individual. It is excellent preparation for the role he will play in society as a mature person.

For Discussion

1. What evidence can you give to prove that the saying "A chip off the old block" is not applicable to personality? Give specific examples.
2. What persons are most influential in the personality development of the individual in early childhood, in late childhood, and in adolescence? Illustrate from your own experiences.
3. Give examples to illustrate the fact that extremes in either direction in personality traits are not serviceable.
4. How do you react to unattractive personalities? How does a young child generally react to them?
5. What evidence is there that every child can have an attractive personality?

Suggested Activities

1. Make a list of good and bad personality traits in a child whom you have observed carefully over a period of time. Weigh and evaluate the results in terms of pleasant or unpleasant personality.
2. Study the expressions on the faces of a group of children who are strangers to you. Do the same with a group of adults. In which group is it easier to guess what the dominant personality traits are?
3. Observe the outstanding personality traits in several children. Then study their parents. Do you find any similarity in the personalities of the children and their parents?
4. Study several children who are said by others to have attractive personalities. What traits do you find to be dominant?
5. Ask several children of different ages what it is that they do not like in other children. Compare disliked traits at different ages for similarities and differences.

CHAPTER 20

Getting Ready for School

Going to school may be an exciting adventure or a terrifying one, depending upon the child's preparation for it. To all young children, however, going to school means "growing up." They look forward eagerly to the day when they will be grown-up enough to be known as "school children."

Their eagerness, however, may be stifled if, when they enter school, they find themselves unprepared for it. Fear and feelings of inadequacy quickly overcome the pleasure they anticipated.

Unfortunate early experiences in school are serious because the child's whole attitude toward school for years to come may be influenced unfavorably by a wrong start. As the days go by, his dread of school may become stronger and stronger. In time, he may revolt so vehemently against going to school that his parents will find it necessary to take him out of school.

Going to School—An Adjustment

Going to school is for most children the first real break with the home environment. This means a serious adjustment to new people, new surroundings, and new modes of behavior.

To a young child, whose experiences and worldly wisdom are limited, any adjustment is difficult. This is true of even so slight a change as having a visitor in the home or moving to another house.

The ability to make adjustments to new situations depends partly upon intelligence. More important, however, are the child's previous experiences in making adjustments. Until the fundamental physiological, motor, and social habits are established, the child's environment should be kept as stable and unvaried as possible so that he can become "set in his ways."

Any slight change is apt to upset the child under three; but from that age, variations in routine, if not too great, are more helpful than harmful because they help the child to make adjustments to changed conditions which, sooner or later, he will have to learn to do.

The important thing to keep in mind is that it is the *child* who should make the adjustments. Too often adjustments are made for him. This, of course, gives him no training or experience along these lines.

Preliminary Adjustments Are Helpful

All this preliminary training in learning to adjust to new situations and people is an invaluable preparation for school. Young children should be gradually trained to adjust themselves—particularly during the six-month period before they enter school—to help cushion the shock that is bound to come when the child enters school for the first time.

There are several ways in which a child can get preliminary experience in making adjustments that will help him when he is ready to enter school. He may go to a nursery

school or kindergarten for a year or two before he is ready to
enter first grade. Or a play group of neighborhood children
may be organized by mothers who take turns in supervising
the children's play. Attendance at Sunday school for a year
or two before going to school also does much to pave the
way for satisfactory school adjustment.

The more time the child has to learn to make adjustments,
the easier it will be for him. Concentrated training in making
adjustments rarely produces as good results as gradual training over a longer period of time.

Emotional Tension Accompanying Adjustment

Every adjustment to new people or new situations is accompanied by a certain amount of emotional tension. This is
true of adults as well as of young children. Getting used to a
new job, living in a new city or a new neighborhood of the
same city, and even adjustments to marriage are always a
strain on an adult and require a certain amount of time to
accomplish.

In the case of young children, where the adjustment is
more difficult because of the child's lack of experience, the
emotional tension is far more pronounced. It shows itself in
many different ways, the most common of which are general
irritability, tendency to cry without adequate reason, loss of
appetite, difficulties in falling asleep, vomiting, loss of
weight, and speech disorders, such as slurring, stuttering,
and stammering.

Preparing the Child for School

A splendid preliminary to preparing the young child for
his entrance into school is for the mother to familiarize herself with the school by visiting for a day before she enters
her child. Careful observation of the school's routine and

Any type of preliminary experience that the child has in preschool groups, such as Sunday school, nursery, or kindergarten, will be helpful in preparing him for adjusting to school successfully.

H. ARMSTRONG ROBERTS

By visiting the school for a day to find out about the routine requirements, the mother can help her child to make a good adjustment.

what is expected of a child will give the mother a good idea of what she must do to prepare her child to meet the requirements of the school.

Schools in some communities have a preliminary adjustment period in the spring or when school begins in the fall when mothers and children go to school together. This helps the mother to find out what will be expected of her child in school and, at the same time, it helps the child to make the first, difficult adjustments to school.

Skills Needed by the School Child

To be able to adjust successfully to school, a young child must be independent as far as self-care is concerned. He must be able, without help, to put on and take off his outdoor clothing—such as hats, coats, gloves, rubbers, or galoshes; he must know when to go to the toilet without wait-

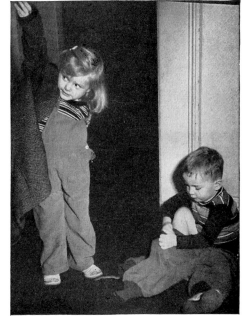

By the time he goes to school, the child should be able to put on and take off his own clothing, because there will be nobody there to help him.

ing to be told; he must be able to wash his hands and face and comb his hair; he must be able to feed himself, even to cutting his own meat, in case he has to remain in school for lunch; and he must be able to keep his possessions in a neat, orderly fashion in the space assigned to him.

Because nursery schools, kindergartens, and the early grades of elementary school devote a great deal of time to construction and play skills—such as painting, crayoning, drawing, cutting, clay modeling, weaving, tossing and catching balls, jumping rope, hopping, skipping, and racing— plenty of time should be set aside for the development of such skills before the child goes to school.

If the child has learned some of the common skills at home before entering school, he will have less difficulty in adapting himself to school activities.

Each day the young child should be encouraged to practice these skills. Furthermore, he should be so directed in his practice that he has at least average mastery of them. The better developed his skills are when he enters school, the better able the child will be to adjust himself to school activities requiring the same or similar skills.

Social Adjustments Needed

In addition to knowing the skills, the young child must be prepared to make many social adjustments when he goes to school. The social contacts of most young children before they enter school consist of members of the family, relatives, children of the neighborhood, and various adults whom he meets in his daily life, such as neighbors and family friends, the postman, a policeman, clerks in neighborhood stores, or workmen employed in and around the home and community.

Going to school presents for the young child problems in social adjustment that are new to him. First and foremost, he must learn to get along with other children of his own age, most of whom are complete strangers to him. He will have to learn to stand on his own feet and to get along with the other children as best he can. If he does not measure up, the other children will ignore him. Even more serious, they will probably ridicule him. There will be no adult to intervene and suggest that the other children include him in their play or that they stop teasing him.

For the first time, the young child will find himself with adults other than members of the household. He will find that they have authority over him just as his parents do, but they will not be the easy prey to his pleadings for special privileges or for forgiveness for wrongdoing that his parents might be. He cannot expect the attention or affection from his teacher that he has been accustomed to have from the adults with whom he has been associated before. No teacher has time for special attention for individual children, nor will she show affection for any one child.

To ease the task of making satisfactory social adjustments to school, the young child needs plenty of opportunity beforehand to be with people of all types, young and old, and of different home backgrounds. Whenever possible, these contacts should be free from parental domination, thus giving the child a chance to learn to get along with people alone.

Occasionally, a day's visit with neighborhood playmates without an accompanying member of the family or a visit with relatives away from home will do wonders in aiding the child to solve the problems of social adjustment later on.

Learning to Serve Others

The helplessness of the young child results in his having more done for him than he is able to do for others in return. Even as he grows older and is capable of doing things for himself, his parents far too often continue to do things for him either through habit or because they find it the quickest and easiest way. All this results in making the young child self-centered, selfish, and dependent. He expects things to be done for him with little or no thought of reciprocation.

In school he will find a very different condition prevailing. Certainly no teacher will wait on him as his parents have done, nor will his classmates. He will soon discover that he is expected to do things for others. He will be asked to perform little duties for the teachers and for his classmates. Furthermore, he will be given small responsibilities for which he will be held accountable. For many young children, doing things for others and assuming the responsibility for these tasks will be a new and exacting experience. It will be a difficult adjustment for them to change their attitudes from one of expectation of being served to one of serving others. It is helpful, therefore, for the child to have preliminary training in running errands for the different members of the household and in assuming complete responsibility for certain tasks every day.

Adjusting to School Discipline

In many cases, school discipline is stricter, more consistent, and fairer than the discipline used in the home. Many young children are brought up in homes where the discipline is lax and where, unfortunately, they discover that they can do almost anything they please if they put up enough fuss about it.

They also learn that exceptions are frequently made for their misbehavior because reproof or punishment might prove to be embarrassing to their parents. This is true when their misbehavior occurs outside the home or when outsiders are present.

Young children who have had a haphazard discipline in the home will find it difficult to adjust to school discipline. They will find there that right is right and wrong is wrong. There will be no special exceptions made for them. They will discover that they cannot do as they please no matter how much fuss they make.

At least six months, but preferably a year, before the child is to enter school, his parents should examine their disciplinary techniques in a critical fashion. This examination is likely to show up laxities and discrepancies between their ideals of discipline and the methods they use. Then, with firmness and determination, the parents should proceed to discipline the child as he will be disciplined at school.

Intellectual Adjustments

All school activities, whether in nursery school, kindergarten, or in the grades, require concentration of attention. This is a difficult adjustment for most children because they have not learned to concentrate before they entered school. When a child gets bored playing with a certain toy at home, he puts it aside to play with another. Similarly, if his attention lags while a story is being read to him, the adult usually stops reading or reads another story of the child's choosing. None of this promotes the development of concentration. Rather, it encourages mind-wandering and distractability.

To prepare the child for what the school will expect of him, careful attention should be given to this problem. Since lack of interest is at the root of all cases of poor attention, the first step in improving concentration is to try to increase the child's interest in whatever activity he undertakes.

One way to encourage concentration is to force the child to pay attention whether or not he is interested, but it is not a satisfactory way because it encourages the child to pay attention only when someone is with him to force him to concentrate.

Memorizing is another mental ability that is new and difficult for the young child when he enters school. Children are expected to memorize the words of songs, of poems, and even of simple prose passages. They must learn the fundamental number combinations and how to spell simple words. To help the child develop the skill of learning easily, simple games of counting, learning names of objects, and of spelling simple words can be played at home. This training will be invaluable for the child and he will find it "fun" because it is part of a game.

A third important mental ability that school expects of young children is reasoning. In the early school years, the reasoning required for successful achievement is very simple. It consists primarily of the ability to make decisions in relatively easy situations or in easy subjects. However, for the young child who has rarely been faced with the problem of making a choice, or who has had his decisions made for him, this proves to be a difficult task.

To avoid this stumbling block to successful school adjustment, the young child should be given plenty of opportunities at home to make his decisions. He can decide, for example, which of two, three, or four suitable garments he wishes to wear; what toys he wants to play with; whether he wants carrots, beets, or peas for dinner; whether he wants to play on the porch or in the yard; and whether he wants to hear a story or look at a book. In fact, in any situation in

Learning to read is often a laborious task. Many children are ready for it when they enter school because of stimulation at home. Encouraging a child to look at the pictures in a book and to follow the printed word will make him better able to read when he enters school.

PINNEY FROM MONKMEYER

which choice is involved, he should be given the choice whenever possible.

However, the child must learn to abide by his decisions. If he knows they cannot be changed, he will be less likely to make snap judgments.

Readiness to Read

Many young children are mentally ready to read at the time they enter school, but their lack of interest in learning may prevent them from learning. This lack of interest can be traced, in most cases, to lack of stimulation. Young children who are read to constantly but are not encouraged to look at pictures, tell the meaning of the pictures, or even look at the printed words on the page while they are being read to are the ones who generally lack an interest in learning to read.

Test of Readiness for School

The following questions will serve as an index to determine how adequate this preparation has been. If all these questions can be answered according to the word given in parentheses at the end of each question, there is no doubt about the fact that the child's home preparation for school has been complete enough to make the transition to this new form of life relatively easy for him.

If, however, only a few of the questions can be answered as indicated, it will show where the weaknesses in preparation lie. The more incorrect answers there are, the more certain it is that adjustment to school will be a difficult experience accompanied by emotional tension and feelings of inadequacy on the child's part.

1. Does the child go to the toilet without being told to do so? (Yes)
2. Does the child blow his nose when he needs to, without being told to do so? (Yes)
3. Can the child put on his rubbers or galoshes without assistance? (Yes)
4. Can the child put on his coat, snow suit, hat, and gloves without assistance? (Yes)
5. Can the child eat his entire meal without assistance and without urging? (Yes)
6. Does the child eat the food placed before him without complaints that he "doesn't like it"? (Yes)
7. Does the child dress like the other children of his age? (Yes)
8. Is the little girl's hair style similar to that of other little girls of her age? (Yes)
9. Can the child crayon an outline picture without going over the lines except occasionally? (Yes)

10. Can the child cut well enough with blunt scissors to be able to cut out large figures? (Yes)
11. Can the child paste pictures on pieces of paper? (Yes)
12. Can the child handle paint without too much smearing? (Yes)
13. Can the child throw, catch, and bounce large balls? (Yes)
14. Can the child roller-skate? (Yes)
15. Can the child jump rope? (Yes)
16. Can the child get along with other children with only occasional quarrels? (Yes)
17. Does the child want to play with other children when they are present rather than be an onlooker? (Yes)
18. When children and adults are present, does the child show a preference for being with the children rather than with the adults? (Yes)
19. Does the child adjust quickly to new adults? (Yes)
20. Does the child react in an emotionally upset manner to adults when left alone with them? (No)
21. Does the child get along better with children of his own age than with older or younger children? (Yes)
22. Does the child volunteer to do little tasks for others? (Yes)
23. Does the child graciously carry out any task he is asked to do? (Yes)
24. Does the child have any duties for which he alone is responsible? (Yes)
25. Does the child carry out his responsibilities without constant reminders? (Yes)
26. Is the child obedient most of the time? (Yes)
27. Does the child "put up an argument" when he is told to do something or when he is reproved for wrong-doing? (No)

Going to school will be an exciting adventure for the child if he is prepared beforehand for the social, mental, and skill adjustments that he will have to make. The factors that determine whether a child is ready are listed in the "Test of Readiness for School" on page 350.

352

28. Does the child try to shift the blame to others to try to avoid punishment? (No)
29. Does the child react favorably to discipline? (Yes)
30. Does the child rebel against discipline when administered by others than members of the family? (No)
31. Does the child's attention wander easily from the task at hand? (No)
32. Does the child make any attempt to concentrate on a subject, even though he is not interested in it? (Yes)
33. Does the child like to tell stories which have been read to him? (Yes)
34. Does the child ask questions about the stories which are in his storybook? (Yes)
35. Does the child show a tendency to repeat poems which he has enjoyed? (Yes)
36. Does the child make his own decisions rather than rely upon someone else to make them for him? (Yes)
37. Does the child want to change a decision he knows is right when he finds it difficult or unpleasant to carry out? (No)
38. Does the child of his own accord study the pictures in his books and tell their meaning? (Yes)
39. Does the child voluntarily follow the printed matter on the page while he is being read to? (Yes)
40. Does the child show any interest in learning to read, such as asking the meaning of words, asking what a printed word is, or asking to be taught how to read? (Yes)

For Discussion

1. Why does the child's clothing play so important a role in his school adjustment? Give specific examples.
2. How does some physical handicap, such as a poor heart or

partial deafness, handicap the child in his adjustment to school?

3. How does a general condition of babyishness prevent a child from getting along in school, not only at first but as his schooling progresses?

4. What skills are of greatest value to successful school adjustment in kindergarten, in first grade, and in high school? Explain the reason for each.

5. When is being different from the group the biggest handicap to a child's school adjustments—in nursery school, kindergarten, or first grade?

6. Is it wise for a child to begin music lessons when he starts school? Why or why not?

Suggested Activities

1. Visit a nursery or first grade during the first week of school. Observe the adjustment of several children very closely. Analyze each case and list the factors responsible for satisfactory or unsatisfactory adjustment.

2. Apply the test given at the end of this chapter to several children who will enter school within a year. How diagnostic do you find it?

3. Test the reading readiness of these children by the procedure suggested in the chapter.

4. Observe several children who are different because of clothing, awkwardness, speech defects, or any other cause. Note how their being different affects their adjustment throughout at least one full school day.

5. Observe a group of children during the first week of school. How does the teacher handle children who are having difficulties in making adjustments? What improvements could you suggest?

6. Observe the children whose mothers remain in school for part of the day during the first week of school. How do the children behave while the mother is present and when she leaves?

Bibliography for Students

Books

Aldrich, C. A., and M. M. Aldrich, *Babies Are Human Beings*. The Macmillan Company, New York, 1954.

Baber, R. E., *Marriage and the Family*. McGraw-Hill Book Company, Inc., New York, 1953.

Bacmeister, R. W., *All in the Family*. Appleton-Century-Crofts, Inc., New York, 1951.

Bacmeister, R. W., *Your Child and Other People*. Little, Brown & Company, Boston, 1950.

Baruch, D. W., *New Ways in Discipline*. McGraw-Hill Book Company, Inc., New York, 1949.

Baxter, L., M. M. Justin, and L. O. Rust, *Sharing Family Living*. J. B. Lippincott Company, Philadelphia, 1951.

Beasley, C., *Democracy in the Home*. Association Press, New York, 1954.

Better Homes and Gardens Baby Book. Meredith Publishing Company, Des Moines, Iowa, 1951.

Cherner, N., *How to Build Children's Toys and Furniture*. McGraw-Hill Book Company, Inc., New York, 1954.

Duvall, E. M., *Family Living*. The Macmillan Company, New York, 1950.

Duvall, E. M., and R. L. Hill, *When You Marry*. D. C. Heath and Company, Boston, 1953.

English, O. S., and C. J. Foster, *Fathers Are Parents, Too*. G. P. Putnam's Sons, New York, 1951.

Faegre, M. L., and J. E. Anderson, *Child Care and Training*. University of Minnesota Press, Minneapolis, 1947.

Force, E. S., *Your Family—Today and Tomorrow*. Harcourt, Brace and Company, Inc., New York, 1955.

Frankel, L., and G. Frankel, *What to Do with Your Preschooler.* Sterling Publishing Company, Inc., New York, 1953.

Goodspeed, H. C., E. R. Mason, and E. L. Woods, *Child Care and Guidance.* J. B. Lippincott Company, Philadelphia, 1953.

Groves, E. R., E. L. Skinner, and S. J. Swenson, *The Family and Its Relationships.* J. B. Lippincott Company, Philadelphia, 1953.

Gruenberg, S. M. (ed.), *Our Children Today.* The Viking Press, Inc., New York, 1952.

Gruenberg, S. M., *The Wonderful Story of How You Were Born.* Hanover House, New York, 1952.

Harris, F. L., and T. E. Kauffman, *Young Folks at Home.* D. C. Heath and Company, Boston, 1953.

Hartley, R. E., *Growing Through Play: Experiences of Teddy and Bud.* Columbia University Press, New York, 1952.

Hatcher, H. M., and M. E. Andrews, *Adventuring in Home Living.* Book 1. D. C. Heath and Company, Boston, 1954.

Hostler, P., *The Child's World.* Roy Publishers, New York, 1953.

Hurlock, E. B., *A Guide and Record for Your Baby's Early Years.* The C. R. Gibson Company, Norwalk, Conn., 1952.

Hurlock, E. B., *Guideposts for Growing Up.* Standard Education Society, Chicago, 1954.

Jenkins, G. G., H. Schacter, and W. W. Bauer, *These Are Your Children.* Scott, Foresman & Company, Chicago, 1953.

Justin, M. M., and L. O. Rust, *Today's Home Living.* J. B. Lippincott Company, Philadelphia, 1953.

Katz, B., *How to Be a Better Parent.* The Ronald Press Company, New York, 1953.

Kenyon, J. H., and R. K. Russell, *Healthy Babies.* Little, Brown & Company, Boston, 1951.

Kepler, H. C., *The Child and His Play.* Funk & Wagnalls Company, New York, 1952.

Kepler, H. C., and E. O. Hesser, *Food for Little People.* Funk & Wagnalls Company, New York, 1950.

Landis, P. H., *Your Marriage and Family Living*. McGraw-Hill Book Company, Inc., New York, 1954.

Little, G., *Design for Motherhood*. The Ronald Press Company, New York, 1953.

Lowndes, M., *A Manual for Baby Sitters*. Little, Brown & Company, Boston, 1949.

McCullough, W., *Illustrated Handbook of Child Care: From Birth to Six Years*. McGraw-Hill Book Company, Inc., New York, 1954.

McDermott, I. E., and F. W. Nicholas, *Homemaking for Teen-Agers*. Chas. A. Bennett Company, Inc., Peoria, Ill., 1954.

Manwell, E. S., and S. L. Fahs, *Consider the Children*. The Beacon Press, Boston, 1951.

Meek, L. H., *Your Child's Development and Guidance*. J. B. Lippincott Company, Philadelphia, 1951.

Montgomery, J. C., and M. J. Suydam, *America's Baby Book*. Charles Scribner's Sons, New York, 1951.

Moore, B. M., and D. M. Leahy, *You and Your Family*. D. C. Heath and Company, Boston, 1953.

Moore, M. F., *The Baby Sitter's Guide*. Thomas Y. Crowell Company, New York, 1953.

Parents' Institute, Inc., *Parents' Magazine Book of Baby Care*. McGraw-Hill Book Company, Inc., New York, 1952.

Parkhurst, H., *Exploring the Child's World*. Appleton-Century-Crofts, Inc., New York, 1951.

Pemberton, L. L., *Stork Didn't Bring You*. Hermitage House, Inc., New York, 1948.

Smart, M. S., and R. C. Smart, *Living and Learning with Children*. Houghton Mifflin Company, Boston, 1949.

Spock, B., *The Pocket Book of Baby and Child Care*. Pocket Books, Inc., New York, 1946.

Spock, B., and J. Reinhart, *A Baby's First Year*. Duell, Sloan & Pearce—Little, Brown, 1955.

Strain, F. B., *Being Born.* Appleton-Century-Crofts, Inc., New York, 1954.

Thomson, M. M., and J. M. Simpson, *Talk It Out with Your Child.* McGraw-Hill Book Company, Inc., New York, 1953.

Zabriskie, L., *Mother and Baby Care in Pictures.* J. B. Lippincott Company, Philadelphia, 1953.

Pamphlets

Baruch, D. W., *Understanding Young Children.* Bureau of Publications, Teachers College, Columbia University, New York.

Children's Bureau, *Infant Care.* U.S. Government Printing Office, Washington, D.C.

Children's Bureau, *Your Child from One to Six.* U.S. Government Printing Office, Washington, D.C.

Dearborn, N. H., and B. Andrews, *Your Safety Handbook.* Science Research Associates, Chicago.

Eckert, R. G., *What You Should Know about Parenthood.* Science Research Associates, Chicago.

Faegre, M. L., *Your Own Story.* University of Minnesota Press, Minneapolis.

Flander, J., *Baby-sitters' Handbook.* Science Research Associates, Chicago.

Hymes, J. L., *Enjoy Your Child—Ages 1, 2, and 3.* Public Affairs Pamphlet No. 141, Public Affairs Committee, New York.

Kirkendall, L. A., *Understanding Sex.* Science Research Associates, Chicago.

Mayer, J., *Getting Along in the Family.* Bureau of Publications, Teachers College, Columbia University, New York.

Neugarten, B. L., *How You Grow.* Science Research Associates, Chicago.

Pfeiffer, J., *Genetics—The Science of Heredity.* Public Affairs Pamphlet No. 165, Public Affairs Committee, New York.

Whiteside-Taylor, K., *Getting Along with Parents.* Science Research Associates, Chicago.

Bibliography for Teachers

Books

Arlitt, A. H., *Psychology of Infancy and Early Childhood*. Mc-Graw-Hill Book Company, Inc., New York, 1946.

Biber, B., L. B. Murphy, L. P. Woodcock, and I. S. Black, *Life and Ways of the Seven-to-Eight Year Old*. Basic Books, Inc., New York, 1952.

Bossard, J. H. S., *Parent and Child*. University of Pennsylvania Press, Philadelphia, 1953.

Bossard, J. H. S., *The Sociology of Child Development*. Harper & Brothers, New York, 1954.

Bossard, J. H. S., and E. S. Boll, *Ritual in Family Living*. University of Pennsylvania Press, Philadelphia, 1950.

Bowman, P. H., *Studying Children and Training Counselors in a Community Program*. University of Chicago Press, Chicago, 1953.

Breckenridge, M. E., and E. L. Vincent, *Child Development*. W. B. Saunders Company, Philadelphia, 1955.

Bühler, C., *Childhood Problems and the Teacher*. Henry Holt and Company, Inc., New York, 1952.

Carmichael, L., *Manual of Child Psychology*. John Wiley & Sons, Inc., New York, 1954.

Charles, E. N., *Understanding the Mind of the Young Child*. William C. Brown Company, Dubuque, Iowa, 1952.

Crow, L. D., and A. Crow, *Child Psychology*. Barnes & Noble, Inc., New York, 1953.

Cunningham, R., *Understanding Group Behavior of Boys and Girls*. Bureau of Publications, Teachers College, Columbia University, New York, 1951.

Cutts, N. E., and N. Moseley, *Better Home Discipline*. Appleton-Century-Crofts, Inc., New York, 1952.

Del Solar, C., *Parents and Teachers View the Child*. Bureau of Publications, Teachers College, Columbia University, 1949.

Dennis, W., *Readings in Child Psychology*. Prentice-Hall, Inc., New York, 1951.

English, H. B., *Child Psychology*. Henry Holt and Company, Inc., New York, 1951.

Forest, I., *Child Development*. McGraw-Hill Book Company, Inc., New York, 1954.

Frank, M., and L. K. Frank, *How to Help Your Child in School*. The Viking Press, Inc., New York, 1950.

Garrison, K. C., *Growth and Development*. Longmans, Green & Co., Inc., New York, 1952.

Garrison, K. C., *The Psychology of Exceptional Children*. The Ronald Press Company, New York, 1950.

Gesell, A., *The Child from Five to Ten*. Harper & Brothers, New York, 1946.

Gesell, A., *Infant Development: The Embryology of Early Human Behavior*. Harper & Brothers, New York, 1952.

Gesell, A., *Studies in Child Development*. Harper & Brothers, New York, 1948.

Griffiths, W., *Behavior Difficulties of Children as Perceived and Judged by Parents, Teachers, and Children Themselves*. University of Minnesota Press, Minneapolis, 1952.

Gruenberg, S. M. (ed.), *Encyclopedia of Child Care and Guidance*. Doubleday & Company, Inc., New York, 1954.

Gruenberg, S. M., *Parents' Questions*. Harper & Brothers, New York, 1947.

Hartley, R. E., L. K. Frank, and R. M. Goldenson, *Understanding Children's Play*. Columbia University Press, New York, 1952.

Havighurst, R. J., *Developmental Tasks and Education*. Longmans, Green & Co., Inc., New York, 1952.

Havighurst, R. J., *Human Development and Education*. Longmans, Green & Co., Inc., New York, 1953.

Hurlock, E. B., *Developmental Psychology*. McGraw-Hill Book Company, Inc., New York, 1953.

Hymes, J. L., *Understanding Your Child*. Prentice-Hall, Inc., New York, 1952.

Ilg, F. L., and L. B. Ames, *Child Behavior*. Harper & Brothers, New York, 1955.

Jersild, A. T., *Child Psychology*. Prentice-Hall, Inc., New York, 1954.

Jersild, A. T., E. S. Woodyard, and C. Del Solar, *Joys and Problems of Child Rearing*. Bureau of Publications, Teachers College, Columbia University, New York, 1949.

Joseph, H., and G. Zern., *The Emotional Problems of Children: A Guide for Parents*. Crown Publishers, Inc., New York, 1954.

Kuhlen, R. G., and G. G. Thompson, *Psychological Studies of Human Development*. Appleton-Century-Crofts, Inc., New York, 1952.

Lightfoot, G. F., *Personality Characteristics of Bright and Dull Children*. Bureau of Publications, Teachers College, Columbia University, New York, 1951.

Martin, W. E., and C. B. Stendler, *Child Development*. Harcourt, Brace and Company, Inc., New York, 1953.

Martin, W. E., and C. B. Stendler, *Readings in Child Development*. Harcourt, Brace and Company, Inc., New York, 1954.

Midcentury White House Conference on Children and Youth, *A Healthy Personality for Every Child*. Health Publications Institute, Inc., Raleigh, N.C., 1951.

Peck, L., *Child Psychology*. D. C. Heath and Company, Boston, 1953.

Podolsky, E., *The Jealous Child*. Philosophical Library, Inc., New York, 1954.

Reynolds, M. M., *Children from Seed to Saplings*. McGraw-Hill Book Company, Inc., New York, 1951.

Rochford, E., *Mothers on Their Own*. Harper & Brothers, New York, 1953.

Rudisill, E. S., *For Fathers Only*. The Muhlenberg Press, Philadelphia, 1953.

Stephens, A. D., *Providing Developmental Experiences for Young Children.* Bureau of Publications, Teachers College, Columbia University, New York, 1952.

Strain, F. B., *New Patterns in Sex Teaching: A Guide to Answering Children's Questions on Human Reproduction.* Appleton-Century-Crofts, Inc., New York, 1951.

Teicher, J. D., *Your Child and His Parents.* Little, Brown & Company, Boston, 1953.

Thompson, G. G., *Child Psychology: Growth Trends in Psychological Adjustment.* Houghton Mifflin Company, Boston, 1952.

Woodcock, L. P., *Life and Ways of the Two-Year-Old: A Guide for Parents and Teachers.* Basic Books, Inc., New York, 1952.

Pamphlets*

Bacmeister, R. W., *Your Child's Manners.* Science Research Associates, Chicago.

Bettelheim, B., *Overcoming Prejudice.* Science Research Associates, Chicago.

Child Guidance Leaflets, 1 to 7. U.S. Government Printing Office, Washington, D.C.

Child Study Association of America, *When Children Ask about Sex.* New York.

Children's Bureau, *Home Play and Play Equipment for the Preschool Child.* U.S. Government Printing Office, Washington, D.C.

Children's Bureau, *When You Adopt a Child.* U.S. Government Printing Office, Washington, D.C.

Del Solar, C., and M. J. E. Sen, *Readings on the Psychological Development of Infants and Children.* Children's Bureau, U.S. Government Printing Office, Washington, D.C.

English, O. S., and S. M. Finch, *Emotional Problems of Growing Up.* Science Research Associates, Chicago.

* It is suggested that you have your name placed on the mailing lists of the Children's Bureau and the U.S. Government Printing Office for information about new pamphlets as they are released.

Foster, C. J., *Developing Responsibility in Children.* Science Research Associates, Chicago.

Gallagher, J. R., *Your Children's Health.* Science Research Associates, Chicago.

Grant, E. H., *Parents and Teachers as Partners.* Science Research Associates, Chicago.

Grossman, J. S., and E. LeShan, *How Children Play—For Fun and Learning.* Science Research Associates, Chicago.

Hunnicutt, C. W., *Answering Children's Questions.* Bureau of Publications, Teachers College, Columbia University, New York.

Hymes, J. L., *Being a Good Parent.* Bureau of Publications, Teachers College, Columbia University, New York.

Hymes, J. L., *Discipline.* Bureau of Publications, Teachers College, Columbia University, New York.

Josselyn, I. M., *Emotional Problems of Illness.* Science Research Associates, Chicago.

Keeping the Well Baby Well. U.S. Government Printing Office, Washington, D.C.

Kirkendall, L. A., *Helping Children Understand Sex.* Science Research Associates, Chicago.

Krug, O., and H. L. Beck, *A Guide to Better Discipline.* Science Research Associates, Chicago.

Landis, P. H., and J. Haer, *Helping Children Adjust Socially.* Science Research Associates, Chicago.

Leonard, C. W., *Why Children Misbehave.* Science Research Associates, Chicago.

Levine, M., and J. Seligmann, *Helping Boys and Girls Understand Their Sex Roles.* Science Research Associates, Chicago.

Menninger, W. C., *Self-understanding—A First Step to Understanding Children.* Science Research Associates, Chicago.

Metropolitan Life Insurance Company, *The Baby.* New York.

Mohr, G. J., *When Children Face Crises.* Science Research Associates, Chicago.

Montagu, A., *Helping Children Develop Moral Values.* Science Research Associates, Chicago.

National Association for Mental Health, *Eating Problems of Children*. New York.

Neugarten, B. L., *Your Children's Heredity*. Science Research Associates, Chicago.

Olson, W. C., and J. Lewellen, *How Children Grow and Develop*. Science Research Associates, Chicago.

Osborne, E. G., *Democracy Begins in the Home*. Public Affairs Pamphlet No. 192, Public Affairs Committee, New York.

Osborne, E. G., *How to Teach Your Child about Work*. Public Affairs Pamphlet No. 216, Public Affairs Committee, New York.

Redl, F., *Understanding Children's Behavior*. Bureau of Publications, Teachers College, Columbia University, New York.

Ridenour, N., *Building Self-confidence in Children*. Science Research Associates, Chicago.

Ridenour, N., and I. Johnson, *Some Special Problems of Children—Aged 2 to 5 Years*. The National Association for Mental Health, New York.

Ross, H., *Fears of Children*. Science Research Associates, Chicago.

Thurstone, T. G., and K. M. Byrne, *Mental Abilities of Children*. Science Research Associates, Chicago.

Van Riper, C., *Helping Children Talk Better*, Science Research Associates, Chicago.

Weitzman, E., *Guiding Children's Social Growth*. Science Research Associates, Chicago.

Witty, P. A., and H. Bricker, *Your Child and Radio, TV, Comics, and Movies*. Science Research Associates, Chicago.

Wrightstone, J. W., *What Tests Can Tell Us about Children*. Science Research Associates, Chicago.

Bibliography for Tests in Chapter 14

Bayley, N., *The California First-year Mental Scale*. University of California Syllabus Series, No. 243. Institute of Child Welfare, Berkeley, Calif., 1933.

Bayley, N., *The California Infant Scale of Motor Development*. University of California Syllabus Series, No. 259. Institute of Child Welfare, Berkeley, Calif., 1936.

Bühler, C., *The First Year of Life*. The John Day Company, Inc., New York, 1930.

Cunningham, B. V., "An Experiment in Measuring Gross Motor Development in Infants and Young Children," *Journal of Educational Psychology*, Vol. 18, 1927.

Cunningham, K. S., *The Measurement of Early Levels of Intelligence*, Teachers College Contributions to Education, No. 259, New York, 1927.

Kennedy-Fraser, D., *The Terman-Merrill Intelligence Scale in Scotland*. University of London Press, Ltd., London, 1945.

Kuhlman, F., *A Handbook of Mental Tests*. Warwick and York, Inc., Baltimore, 1922.

Linfert, H. E., and H. M. Hierholzer, "A Scale for Measuring the Mental Development of Infants During the First Year of Life," *Studies in Psychology and Psychiatry*, Vol. 1, No. 4, 1928.

McNemar, Q., *The Revision of the Stanford-Binet Scale*. Houghton Mifflin Company, Boston, 1942.

Stutsman, R., "Performance Tests for Children of Pre-school Age," *Genetic Psychology Monographs*, Vol. 1, No. 1, 1926.

Terman, L. M., and M. A. Merrill, *Measuring Intelligence*. Houghton Mifflin Company, Boston, 1937.

List of Visual Aids

The visual aids listed below and on the following pages can be used to supplement the material in this book. For the convenience of users the films have been grouped by chapters, but it is recommended that each film be reviewed before use in order to determine its suitability for a particular group or unit of study.

Motion pictures and filmstrips are included in the following list, the character of each being indicated by the self-explanatory abbreviations "MP" and "FS." Immediately following this identification is the name of the producer. In cases where the distributor is different from the producer, the distributor's name is also given. The abbreviations given for these names are identified in the list of film sources on page 375. Unless otherwise indicated, the motion pictures are 16mm black-and-white sound films and the filmstrips are 35mm black-and-white silent filmstrips. The length of motion pictures is given in minutes (min), that of filmstrips in frames (fr).

Most of the films can be borrowed or rented from state and local film libraries, and users should consult *A Directory of 2660 16mm Film Libraries,* obtainable for 50 cents from the Superintendent of Documents, U.S. Government Printing Office, Washington 25, D.C.

This list is a selective one, and film users should examine the latest annual editions and supplements of *Educational Film Guide* and *Filmstrip Guide,* published by the H. W. Wilson Company, New York. The *Guides,* standard reference books, are available in most college and public libraries.

Introduction—How to Be a Good Baby Sitter

The Baby Sitter (MP YAF 14min). Outlines the training needed for the job and points out the responsibilities of both parents and sitters.

Certified Baby Sitter (FS BDC 40fr). Portrays the relationship of the baby sitter, parent, and child in actual situations; demonstrates methods for the care of children below school age.

Child Care (FS series YAF). Four filmstrips describing problems and techniques of baby sitters. Titles are: *Getting Acquainted* (36fr); *Keeping Children Happy* (38fr); *Keeping Children Safe* (36fr); *Special Daytime Problems* (35fr).

Enter the Baby Sitter (FS BDC 38fr). Demonstrates methods used by boy and girl sitters in an average American home.

Chapter 1—Preparing for the Baby

Before the Baby Comes (MP KB 12 min). Explains the value of prenatal examinations, and the clothes, diet, exercise, and other hints for expectant mothers.

Expectant Father (MP RKO/McGraw 17min). One of the "This Is America" Series, this film portrays classes for expectant fathers conducted by the Visiting Nurse Service of New York City.

Mother and Her Child (MP CNFB 55min color or b&w). Story of a couple, from the time they suspect they are going to have a baby until their son's first birthday. Pictures their monthly visits to the doctor; his advice on diet, exercise, and clothing; and instructions for care of the baby.

Motherhood (MP NMPCo 10min). Deals with prenatal care, including regular visits to the doctor, and the value of baths, rest, exercise, proper clothing, etc., for expectant mothers.

Nine to Get Ready (FS CNFB 54fr color). Tells the story of prenatal care—how to protect and nourish the baby before it is born.

Prenatal Care (MP   Med Film   23min). Portrays three women in normal pregnancy through the nine-month period, and explains recommended exercise, clothing, and diet during this time.

Chapter 2—The Newborn Baby

Care of the Newborn Baby (MP   USOE/UWF   31min). Nurse's functions and duties in teaching parents to care for newborn babies; what the nurse can do in the home, clinic, and hospital; and how to hold, dress, bathe, and feed a baby. (Accompanying filmstrip, 93fr, also available.)

Childbirth: Normal Delivery (MP   Cited   16min   color). Gives a close-up of the actual birth of a baby. Photographed under medical supervision. (Distribution restricted to medical schools, hospitals, and nursing and educational institutions. Lectures or showings must be under medical supervision.)

Heredity and Pre-natal Development (MP   McGraw   21min). Discusses cell growth and heredity, describes fertilization of ovum and traces development of fetus until delivery, considers development of physical functions of newborn, and stresses connection between physical and emotional sensitivity.

Labor and Childbirth (MP   Med Film   17min). Story of a young couple expecting their first child, beginning of labor, trip to the hospital, admission to maternity ward, delivery of the baby, and return to the hospital room with baby and husband.

Postnatal Care (MP   Med Film   12min). Shows a mother in her hospital room, doing exercises, caring for her baby, nursing the baby, etc., and discusses the father's relationship to the new family situation.

Chapter 3—Facts about Children

Dr. Spock (MP MOT/McGraw 27min). Presents the theories and practices of Dr. Spock and his suggestions to parents for dealing with children from infancy to age six.

Infant Care (MP IIAA 9min color). Through animation

shows the things a mother should do during the prenatal period and through infancy to have strong, sturdy children.

Infants Are Individuals (MP EBF 15min). Demonstrates that individuality and personality are apparent in youngsters from their earliest day. Shows how certain behavior patterns disclosed in infancy persist into later life.

Know Your Baby (MP Can Health/Sterling 11min color or b&w). Illustrates methods of care of the new baby. Shows the consideration and understanding necessary until the family adjusts itself to the demands of the newcomer.

Life Begins (MP Yale/EBF 60min). Pictures twenty-four years of clinical practice and research on problems of infancy at the Yale University Clinic of Child Development under the direction of Dr. Arnold L. Gesell.

Life with Baby (MP MOT/McGraw 18min). Shows how children grow mentally and physically. A popular version and condensation of the Gesell Child Development Series.

Life with Junior (MP MOT/McGraw 18min). Follows Junior through a typical day. Shows in some detail the work of the Child Study Association of America.

Techniques of Anthropometric Measurement (MP Calif U 13 min silent). Describes the methods used in securing anthropometric measurements on young children for purposes of research. Devised for the use of students of child development.

Your Children and You (MP BIS 31min). Concerns the care of young children from the first months to the age of four or five. Offers advice on physical and psychological training.

Chapter 4—How a Child Grows

Ages and Stages (MP series). Films produced by the National Film Board of Canada for the Canadian Department of Health and Welfare, distributed in the U.S. by the McGraw-Hill Book Company, Inc. Titles and running times of the individual films are: *He Acts His Age* (15min); *The Terrible Twos and the Trusting Threes* (20min); *The Frustrating Fours and Fascinating Fives* (22min); *From Sociable Six to Noisy Nine* (22min).

Baby's First Year (MP KB 12min). Stresses cleanliness and the value of proper diet and exercise. Covers baby's formula as well as breast-feeding.

Child Development (MP series Yale/EBF). Ten films, each 11min, produced at the Yale University Clinic of Child Development with the collaboration of Dr. Arnold L. Gesell. The titles of the films are: *Baby's Day at Forty-eight Weeks; Baby's Day at Twelve Weeks; Behavior Patterns at One Year; Early Social Behavior; From Creeping to Walking; Growth of Infant Behavior: Early Stages; Growth of Infant Behavior: Later Stages; Learning and Growth; Posture and Locomotion; Thirty-six Weeks Behavior Day.*

The Child Grows Up (MP KB 12min). Shows the activities of the normal child from one to six, and includes habit training, play and equipment for developing mind and body, nursery-school activities, eating, and physical examinations.

How a Baby Grows (MP series Yale/EBF silent). Ten films, each 15min, picturing various aspects of infant behavior. The titles of the films are: *Baby's Bath; Bottle and Cup Feeding; Conquest of the Spoon; Early Play; Growth of Adaptive Behavior; Growth of Motor Behavior; How Behavior Grows; Infants Are Individuals; Self-Discovery in a Mirror; Twins Are Individuals.*

Judy's Diary (MP series Wisc U silent). Pictures the development of a baby from birth to age two. Titles and running times are: *By Experience I Learn* (25min); *Morning Until Night* (30min); *Now I Am Two* (30min).

Principles of Development (MP McGraw 17min). Outlines the fundamentals of child growth and development and considers the variables which make each child different from every other one.

Chapter 5—Feeding and Clothing the Child

Baby Care: Feeding (MP PSC 23min). Discusses feeding of babies by breast and bottle. Illustrates preparation of formulas and sterilization and storage of equipment and food.

Feeding the Infant (MP EBF 15min silent). Demonstrates the feeding of breast-fed and bottle-fed babies, preparation of utensils and formula, and the addition of other foods to the diet.

Feeding Is a Social Affair (MP BDC 10min color). Portrays good family relationships with the father participating in the feeding of the baby, formula preparation by the application of terminal heat, and method of giving bottle to the baby so as to create feelings of emotional security.

Food As Children See It (MP Gen Mills 18min color). Offers ideas for solving feeding problems together with menu planning and food selection and preparation based on the Basic 7.

Chapter 6—Physical Care of the Child

The Baby's Bath (MP Yale/EBF 15min silent). Illustrates methods of bathing a baby. Emphasizes the value of the bath not only for cleanliness but also as an opportunity for exercise, enjoyment, and social contact with the mother. Produced at the Yale University Clinic of Child Development with the collaboration of Dr. Arnold L. Gesell.

Bathing the Infant (MP EBF 15min silent). Shows various types of equipment which may be used in bathing the baby, methods of handling the infant during the bath, and the routine of dressing the baby.

Bathing Time for Baby (MP J&J 13min color). Through animation shows one technique of how to bathe a baby.

Child Care and Development (MP McGraw 17min). Considers the habits of daily physical care that contribute to a happy, healthy child. Good habits of eating, bathing, the wearing of proper clothing, and outdoor exercise are covered.

Chapter 7—Learning Body Control

Development of Locomotion (MP Calif U 10min silent). Depicts developmental sequences in children from six to fifteen months of age. Gives examples of the various methods of locomotion.

Large Muscle Motor Skills for Four Year Olds (MP   Calif U   10min   silent   color). Through individual sequences showing running, balancing, jumping, pedaling, pumping, kicking, throwing, catching and bouncing, hitting and punching, pushing and pulling, climbing, suspending own weight, tumbling, and guiding a wagon, indicates the types and levels of large muscle motor skills that are characteristic of children of this age.

Your Children Walking (MP   BIS/McGraw   20min). Gives instructions, with examples, for teaching a child how to walk and to hold himself properly, and stresses the need for suitable footwear.

Chapter 9—The Child and His Emotions

Answering the Child's Why (MP   EBF   13min). Dramatizes actual situations in which youngsters meet with positive or negative attitudes toward their questions, and suggests the resulting effect on their personalities.

Children's Emotions (MP   McGraw   22min). Discusses the major emotions of childhood—fear, anger, jealousy, curiosity, and joy—and what parents can do in understanding and dealing with these emotions in their children.

Shyness (MP   CNFB/McGraw   23min). Examines abnormal shyness in children, its causes and how, through a greater understanding by parents and teachers, this problem may be handled.

This Is Robert (MP   NYU   80min). Traces the development of an aggressive but appealing child from his early nursery-school days to his first year in a public school.

Chapter 10—Mealtime and Bedtime Problems

Meal Time Can Be a Happy Time (MP   Wisc U   22min). Helps parents to establish pleasant eating habits for children.

Why Won't Tommy Eat? (MP Can Health/Sterling 19min color or b&w). Uncovers both physical and mental causes of the problem of the child who refuses to eat.

Your Children's Meals (MP BIS 14min). Looks at mealtime from the child's and the parent's point of view.

Your Children's Sleep (MP BIS 23min). Stresses the importance of sound, healthy sleep, and advises parents on ways in which they can help secure it for their children.

Chapter 11—The Child in the Family

Baby Meets His Parents (MP EBF 11min). Points out how differences in personality can be accounted for, not only by heredity, but also by the human relationships and environmental factors experienced during the first years of life.

Martha Belongs (MP Wisc U 12min color). Emphasizes the early contacts of a baby with her own family and the need of an infant to have opportunities to develop at her own pace and to have freedom for exercise. Points up natural opportunities for sex education of older children in the family.

Sibling Rivalries and Parents (MP McGraw 11min). Shows the rivalry for attention, love, and esteem among brothers and sisters and how to hold friction to a minimum.

Chapter 13—Discipline, Good and Bad

Fears of Children (MP IFB 30min). Parent-child situation with mother and father disagreeing about disciplinary measures, resultant conflict in their five-year-old son, and magnification of his fears.

Preface to a Life (MP USPHS/UWF 29min). Parental influence on a child's developing personality, illustrated by a series of episodes showing the effects of an overly solicitous mother and an overly demanding father; and, in contrast, the healthy childhood resulting when both parents accept their child as an individual.

Chapter 15—Play and Playthings

The Child at Play (MP TC 18min). Shows the nature of children's spontaneous play by depicting the unrestrained play activity of a three-year-old child.

Children's Play (MP McGraw 27min). Points up the changing form of children's play at each age level. Emphasizes the need for playtime, ample space for play, proper equipment, companions, the health needed to enjoy play, etc.

Early Play (MP Yale/EBF 15min silent). Stresses the importance of determining each youngster's preferences in play and play objects.

Understanding Children's Play (MP NYU 10min). How adults can understand and help children through observation of their use of toys and toy materials.

Your Children's Play (MP BIS/McGraw 20min). Gives examples of play behavior of one- to eight-year-olds, and emphasizes the need for parents to understand the reasons for such behavior patterns.

Chapter 16—The Child's Companions

Children Growing Up with Other People (MP BIS/UWF 30min). Shows how youngsters emerge from their early involuntary dependence into self-reliant members of their respective family, school, and other groups.

Social Development (MP McGraw 16min). Offers an analysis of social behavior at different age levels and the reasons underlying the changes in behavior patterns as the child develops.

Chapter 17—A Place of His Own

Beginning Responsibility: Taking Care of Things (MP Coronet 10min color or b&w). Explains why children should care for things at home and at school.

Chapter 18—The Child and His Clothes

Clothing for Children (MP Coronet 10min color). Covers methods and problems involved in clothing young children. Describes styles and types of dress for various ages.

Chapter 19—Personality Building

Children Learning by Experience (MP BIS/UWF 40min). Develops the themes that all children want to learn, enjoy practicing simple skills, strive to understand the world about them, learn some things at second hand, and learn a great many things through play and imagination.

Chapter 20—Getting Ready for School

We Go to School (MP Coronet 10min color or b&w). Shows children entering school for the first time, what they can expect from school and what the school, in turn, expects from them.

Film Sources

BDC—Baby Development Clinic, 600 South Michigan Ave., Chicago 5.

BIS—British Information Services, 30 Rockefeller Plaza, New York 20.

Calif U—University of California, University Extension, Visual Department, 2272 Union St., Berkeley, Calif.

Can Health—Canadian Department of Health and Welfare, Ottawa, Canada. (Films distributed by Sterling.)

Cited—Cited Films, Inc., 30 Rockefeller Plaza, New York 20.

CNFB—Canadian National Film Board, 1270 Avenue of the Americas, New York 20.

Coronet—Coronet Instructional Films, Coronet Building, Chicago 1.

EBF—Encyclopaedia Britannica Films, Inc., 1150 Wilmette Ave., Wilmette, Ill.

Gen Mills—General Mills Film Library, Inc., 400 Second Ave., South, Minneapolis, Minn.

IFB—International Film Bureau, 57 East Jackson Blvd., Chicago 4.

IIAA—Institute of Inter-American Affairs, 499 Pennsylvania Ave., N.W., Washington 25, D.C.

J&J—Johnson & Johnson, Promotion Department, New Brunswick, N.J.

KB—Knowledge Builders, 625 Madison Ave., New York 22.

McGraw—McGraw-Hill Book Company, Inc., Text-Film Department, 330 West 42nd St., New York 36.

Med Film—Medical Films, Inc., 116 Natoma St., San Francisco 5.

MOT—March of Time, Inc. (Films distributed by McGraw.)

NMPCo—National Motion Pictures Company, West Main St., Mooresville, Ind.

NYU—New York University Film Library, 26 Washington Square, New York 3.

PSC—Pennsylvania State College, Audio-Visual Aids Library, State College, Pa.

RKO—RKO Pathé, Inc., Hollywood, Calif. (Film distributed by McGraw.)

Sterling—Sterling Films, Inc., 205 East 43rd St., New York 3.

TC—Teachers College, Columbia University, Bureau of Publications, 525 West 120th St., New York 27.

USOE—U.S. Office of Education, Washington 25, D.C. (Film distributed by UWF.)

USPHS—U.S. Public Health Service, Washington 25, D.C. (Film distributed by UWF.)

UWF—United World Films, Inc., 1445 Park Ave., New York 29.

Wisc U—University of Wisconsin, Bureau of Visual Instruction, University Extension Division, 1312 West Johnson St., Madison 6, Wis.

YAF—Young America Films, Inc., 18 East 41st St., New York 17.

Yale—Yale University, Clinic of Child Development, New Haven, Conn. (Films distributed by EBF.)

Index

Adenoids, enlarged, 61
Affection, the child's, 161–163
  expressions of, 163
  for the family, 162–163
Allergies, 61, 114–115, 179
Ambidexterity, 123
Amusements, 264–268
Anemia, 61
Anger, 155–156
Appetite, 115, 176–**177**
Arm control, 123

Babbling, 141
Baby sitter, attitude of, xxix–**xxxi**
  need for, xiii–xiv
  qualifications of, xvii–xx
Baby-sitting, with a baby, xxxvii–
    xlii
  benefits of, xiv–xvi
  getting job of, xx–xxiv
  with an older child, xlv–xlvi
  preparation for, xxv–xxix
  problems of, xxxvii–xlviii
  qualifications for, xvii–xx
  with several children, xlvi–
    xlviii
  things to avoid in, xxxi–xxxiii
  things to do while, xxxiii–
    xxxvii
  with a toddler, xlii–xlv
Baby talk, 148, 149
Bassinet, 97
Bath, baby's, 100–106
  child's, 317–318

Bathinette, 100
Bed, for the baby, 97–98
  preparation for, xli, xliii–**xlv,**
    xlv–xlvi, 186–188
  as punishment, 233–234
  safety in, 97, 99
  youth-sized, 98–99
Bedtime fears, 190–191
Bedtime problems, xliv–xlv, **171–**
    173, 184–191
Bed-wetting, 188–190
Behavior problems, overcoming,
    216–219
  parents' attitude toward, 215–
    216
  testing for, 209–210
  types of, 206–208, 210–215,
    284–286
Birth, danger during, 16
  expenses involved in, 9–**11**
  preparation for, 4–7
  probable date of, 13
Birth cry, 30–31
Biting, 175–176
Bladder control, 133–135
Body control, and intelligence,
    240
  learning, 117–135
  pattern of, 121–125
Body proportions, changes in,
    50–51
  of the infant, 29, 50–51
  significance of, 51–52
Bones, infant, 29, 52
  softness of, 52–54

Books for the child, 264–267, 349

Bottle-feeding, 66–68

Bowels, control of, 133–135
 normal functioning of, 115

Breast-feeding, 63–66

Bribery as discipline, 227–228

Brother-sister relationships, 279

Bubbling, xl–xli, 72–74

Bullying, 285–286

Calmness, developing, 334

Cheerfulness, cultivating, 289, 327–328

Chewing, 175–176

Chromosomes, 24–29

Clothes, 306–317
 appropriate, 311–313
 care of, 91–93
 child's preferences in, 313–315
 for the infant, 81–87
 layette, 12–13
 for the older baby, 87–88
 and personality, 315–317
 for the toddler, 89–91

Clumsiness, 118, 132–133

Cod-liver oil (*see* Fish-liver oils)

Colds, 114

Colostrum, 63

Comics, 267

Companions, 275–291
 adult, 276–278
 brothers and sisters as, 279
 neighborhood, 279–281
 substitute, 281–284

Companionship, importance of, 258, 275–276

Comprehension, 142–144

Concentration, developing, 347

Constipation, 66, 111

Corporal punishment, xlviii, 231–232

Cost of having a baby, 9–11

Courage, developing, 329–332

Crawling, 124, 126

Creeping, 124, 126

Crib, 97–98

Crying, xli–xlii, 30–31, 137–139

Curiosity, 163–164

Dawdling, as behavior problem, 206–207
 over food, 183–184

Defects, minor, 60–61

Development (*see* Mental growth; Physical growth)

Diapering a baby, xxxix–xl, 81–87

Diapers, 81–87
 washing, 91–92

Differences in children, 37–39

Digestion, 115

Diphtheria, 113

Discipline, 221–236, 346–347
 as baby sitter's problem, xlvi–xlviii
 educating by, 224–227
 parental attitude toward, 222–224
 punishment as, 230–236
 and relatives in the home, 325
 rewards as, 227–230
 in school, 346–347

Diseases, 58–61, 111–115
 immunization against, 111–115
 psychological effects of, 59–60, 167

Disposition (*see* Personality)
Dressing, the infant, 81–87
  the older baby, 87–88
  of self, 306–312
Drink, learning to, 175–176

Ears, cleaning baby's, 101, 102
  (*See also* Hearing)
Eating habits, importance of,
  171–173
  learning, 174–176, 180–183
Eating utensils, 180–183
Emotional problems, 212–213
Emotionality, causes of, 166–
  168, 340
Emotions of a child, 152–168
  characteristics of, 152–154
  effective use of, 164–166
Entertaining toddler, xlii–xliii
Enthusiasm, developing, 328
Enuresis, 188–190
Environment, effect of, 39–40,
  323–326
  ideal, for child, 293–294
Equipment, for bathing, 100,
  317–318
  brushing teeth, 106
  the child's room, 296–301
  eating, 181–183
  grooming, 319
  the new baby, 11–13
  play, 256–257, 259, 261–272
  sleeping, 97–99
  toilet training, 134–135
Exercise, baby's, 109–111
  during pregnancy, 14
  in play, 260
Eve infections, 61

Eye strain, 56
Eyes, caring for baby's, 101, 102
  (*See also* Vision)

Family adjustments to the baby,
  17–20, 195–196
Family relationships, 193–196,
  276–279
  cooperative, 194–195
  and personality, 323–326
Fastening garments, 310–311
Father, role of, 193–194, 195
Fatigue, 166–167
Fears, bedtime, 190–191
  behavior resulting from, 158
  causes of, 157
  common, 157–158
Feeding, the baby, xl, 63–68,
  74–77
  bottle, 66–68
  breast, 63–66
  the child, xlv, 177–**178**
  forced, 177
  problems in, 176–184
  self, 180–184
  the toddler, xliii
Fish-liver oils, 78–79, 80
Fontanelles, 52
Food, amount of, 176–178
  for the baby, 68–72, 74–77
  likes and dislikes in, 58, 178–180
  ready-to-heat, 77
  vitamins in, 78–80
  for the young child, 80–81
Formula for the baby, 68–69
  preparation of, 69–72
Fresh air, 108–109
Friends (*see* Companions)

Games, "Mother," 262–263
  neighborhood, 263–264
Gamma globulin, 114
Gardening, value of, 302–304
Genes, 24
Gesture habit, 140–141
Gestures, 139–140
Gifts as rewards, 229–230
Grammatical mistakes, 147
Grooming, habits of, 318–319
Growth (see Mental growth;
    Physical growth)
Guidance, need for, 42–43
Gum massage, 106–107

Hair, prenatal, 29–30
Hand control, 123–124
Head, control of, 122
  shampooing of baby's, 101
  size of, at birth, 29
  "soft spots" in bones of, 52
Health, poor, 167
  (See also Diseases)
Health problems, 211–212
Hearing, at birth, 31–32
  defective, 56, 60–61
  of the young child, 56
Height, at birth, 29
  increase in, 48–50
Heredity, carriers of, 24
  and personality, 321–322
Holding a baby, xxxviii, xxxix
Holidays and routine, 202–203
Home, ideal type for a child,
    293–294
Hospital, choice of, 8–9
  return from, 22–23
Humor, cultivating, 328–329

Identical twins, 27–28
Illness (see Diseases)
Imaginary companions, 282
Immunization, 111–115
Individuality, expressing, 336
Infantile paralysis, 114
Infections, of the ear, 56, 61
  of the eye, 61
  (See also Diseases)
Influenza, 114
Interest and ability, 40–41, 120
Isolation as punishment, 235

Jealousy, 20 159–160
  behavior in, 160

Layette, minimum, 12–13
  nonessential items in, 13
Leadership, qualities of, 287–288
  training for, 288–289
Learning, to bathe, 317–318
  body control, 117–135
  to dress, 306–311
  to eat, 174–176, 180–183
  effective use of emotions, 164–
    166
  forced, 121
  to groom, 318–319
  by imitation, 131–132
  obstacles to, 41–42, 117–119
  opportunities for, 117–119
  to play, 258
  preschool, 338–353
  readiness for, 40–41, 120–121,
    130–131
  sociability, 260, 281, 289–291,
    327–336, 344–346
  to talk, 137–150

Left-handedness, 123–124
Leg control, 124–125, 126–127
Lifting a baby, xxxviii, xxxix
Lisping, 148, 149–150
Locking up as punishment, 233
Lockjaw, 115
Loneliness, 281–284

Mannerisms, 212
Manners, 289–291
Mattresses, 98
Maturation, 39–40
Mealtime problems, with appetite, 176–178
with dawdling, 183–184
with food likes and dislikes, 178–180
in learning to eat, 175–176
mother's attitude toward, 172–173
with utensils, 180–183
Measles, 114
Memorizing, 348
Mental growth, 35–42, 240
forcing or retarding, 41–42
and interest, 40–41
and muscle control, 240
and physical growth, 39–40, 47
testing of, 238–254
Miscarriage, 15
"Morning sickness," 15–16
Mother, affection of child for, 162
physical preparation of, 6–7
pregnancy period of, 3–23
psychological preparation of, 4–5
visiting the school, 340–342

Muscle control, problems of, 212
Music, 267–268

Nagging as punishment, 232–233
Nail-biting, 212
Naps, 185–186
Natural childbirth, 14
Negativism, 156
Neighborhood friends, 279–281
Neighborhood games, 263–264
Newborn baby, 24–32
behavior of, 30–31
sensitivities of, 31–32
size of, 29
Nightclothes, xli, 91, 99–100
Nonidentical twins, 27–29
Nostrils, cleaning baby's, 101, 102
Nursery, minimum needs in, 12
nonessential items in, 13
Nursing, 63–66

Obesity, tendency to, 61
Old wives' tales, 16–17
Outdoor play space, 108–109, 257–258, 301–304
Overeating, 177–178
Ovum, 26, 27–29

Pain sense, 31, 56
Pampering the child, 276–278, 325
Panties, training, 89, 135
waterproof, 86–87, 89
Parent-child relationships, 276–278
(*See also* Family relationships)

Parents, attitude toward behavior problems, 215–216
attitude toward discipline, 222–224
and baby sitters, xvi, xxxvi
(*See also* Mother; Father)
Pattern of growth, 39–42, 48
Permanency, value of, 295
Personality, attractive traits in, 326–336
and clothes, 315–317
early formation of, 321–322
and environment, 323–326
and heredity, 321–322
home influences on, 323–326
Pets, 283–284
Physical defects, 60–61
Physical growth, 39–40, 47–58
and body proportions, 50–52
of bones, 52–54
in height, 48–50
and mental growth, 39–40, 47
pattern of, 39–42, 48
of teeth, 54–56
in weight, 48–50, 115
Pictures, 264–265, 267
Play, energy for, 256
equipment for, 256–257, 259, 261–272
knowing how to, 258
"parallel," 286
playmates for, 258, 275
skills used in, 128–130, 343–344
space for, 108–109, 257–258, 301–304
time for, 256
values of, 258–260
varieties of, 260–268

Playpen, for exercising, 109
for use out-of-doors, 108–109
Playroom, the child's, 301
Playthings (*see* Toys)
Poliomyelitis, 114
Posture, and clothing, 313
early development of, 128
poor, 54
Praise as reward, 228–229
Pregnancy period, 3–23
activity during, 14
diet during, 7
length of, 13
"morning sickness" in, 15–16
physical preparation during, 6–7
possible problems during, 14–16
psychological preparation during, 4–5
superstitions about, 16–17
Prenatal care (*see* Pregnancy period)
Prenatal hair, 29–30
Preparation for baby, with the doctor, 5–6
of equipment, 11–13
of the home, 20–22
psychological, 3–5, 17–20
Prepared baby foods, 77
Preschool groups, 339–340, 341
Problem children, 36–37
Problems, of baby-sitting xxxvii–xlviii
bedtime, xliv–xlv, 171–173, 184–191
behavior, 206–219, 284–286
mealtime, 171–184

Pronunciation, errors in, 148–150
learning, 147–148
Punishment, bad forms of, 231–234
cautions in use of, 235–236
and discipline, 221–222
good forms of, 234–235
occasions justifying, 230–231

Quarreling, xlvii, 284–285

"Read Method," 14
Readiness, for learning, 40–41, 120–121, 130–131
for reading, 349
for school, test of, 350–353
Reading, to the child, 265–267
readiness for, 349
Reasoning ability, developing, 348
Records, listening to, 267–268
Relatives in the home, 325
Respect for others, cultivating, 290
Responsibilities of the child, in the home, 302–305
in school, 346
social, 289–291
Rewards, effective, 228–230
purpose of, 227–228
Right-handedness, 123–124
Room, child's, 295–301, 304
Rooming-in plan, 8–9
Routine, baby's, 196–198
breaks in, 200–204, 339
importance of, 196, 339
young child's, 198–200

Safety, in the bath, 106
in bed, 97, 99
of children, xxxiii–xxxv
in exercising, 109
of playthings, 269
Safety belt, 97
Salk vaccine, 114
Scarlet fever, 113–114
Schedule (see Routine)
Schick test, 113
School adjustments, 338–353
Scolding, 232–233
Self-assertiveness, developing, 336
Self-confidence, developing, 334–336
Self-evaluation, 291
Self-feeding, 180–184
Sense of humor, cultivating a, 328–329
Sensory experience, of the newborn baby, 31–32
of the young child, 56–58
Sentence formation, 146
Sex, determination of, 25–26
differences due to, 37–39
Shyness, 158–159
Skills, early childhood, 125–132
learning, 131–132
for school, 342–344, 347–349
Skin eruptions, 61
Skinniness, excessive, 61
Sleep, amount of, 32, 94–95, 185
clothes for, xli, 91, 99–100
daytime, 185–186
habits of, 171–173, 184–191
positions in, 95–96
preparation for, 186–188
safety in, 97, 99

Sleeping bag, 97, 99–100
Slurring in speech, 148, 149–150
Smallpox, 112–113
Smell, sense of, 31, 58
Social adjustments to school, 344–346
Social problems, 214–215
Social responsibilities, 289–291
Spanking, xlviii, 231–232
Speech, learning, 137–150
  "play," 141
  problems, 212
Spermatozoon, 26, 27–29
Spoiling the child, 276–278, 325
Stammering, 149, 150
Standing, 124–125, 127
Stories, 265–267
Strangers, 203–204
Stuttering, 148, 150
Substitute companions, 281–284
Sun bath, 107–108
Superstitions about pregnancy, 16–17
Swallowing, 175–176
Sympathy, developing, 333–334

Talking (see Speech)
Taste, sense of, 31, 58
Taste buds, 58
Teasing, 285–286
Teeth, care of, 106
  cutting, 54–56
Television, 268
Temper tantrums, 155–156
Tests, of school readiness, 350–353
  for young children, 238–254

Tetanus, 115
  toxoid for 113, 115
Thwarted desires, 167–168
Toddler, taking care of, xlii–xlv
Toilet training, 89, 133–135
Tonsils, diseased, 61
Toys, favorite, 269–272
  necessity for, 256–257
  place for, 301
  selection of, 268–269
  types of, 259, 270–271, 272
Training panties, 89, 135
Treats, depriving of, 235
  as rewards, 230
Trunk control, 122
Twins, 27–29

Unselfishness, cultivating, 332–333
Unsocial behavior, forms of, 284–287

Vaccination, 112–113
Vision, at birth, 31–32
  defective, 60
  of the young child, 56
Vitamins, 78–79, 80
Vocabulary, child's, 142–146

Walking, 125
Watching others, 264, 286–287
Weaning, 77–78
Weight, at birth, 29, 63
  increase in, 48–50, 115
  and overeating, 178
Whooping cough, 113